AN ELEMENTARY
OLD ENGLISH GRAMMAR

BY

JOSEPH WRIGHT

Ph D., D.C.L., LL.D , Litt.D.

Fellow of the British Academy ; Professor of Comparative
Philology in the University of Oxford

AND

ELIZABETH MARY WRIGHT

OXFORD
AT THE CLARENDON PRESS
1923

Oxford University Press

*London   Edinburgh   Glasgow   Copenhagen
New York   Toronto   Melbourne   Cape Town
Bombay   Calcutta   Madras   Shanghai*

Humphrey Milford Publisher to the UNIVERSITY

Printed in England

PREFACE

THIS Elementary Old English Grammar is in a great measure an abridgement of our larger work on the subject. In order to render the book more suitable for beginners we have omitted many philological details both in the phonology and the accidence. On the other hand some new details have been embodied, and the whole material has been considerably rearranged. To the student about to embark on the study of Old English we cannot give better advice than that stated in the preface to the larger Grammar, viz. 'From our long experience as teachers of the subject, we should strongly recommend the beginner not to work through the phonology at the outset, but to read Chapter I and paragraphs 45-64 (omitting the notes), and then to learn the paradigms, and at the same time to read some easy texts such as are to be found in any of the Old English Readers. This is undoubtedly the best plan in the end, and will lead to the most satisfactory results. In fact, it is in our opinion a sheer waste of time for a student to attempt to study in detail the phonology of any language before he has acquired a good working knowledge of its vocabulary and inflexions.' If this little book helps to lighten his labours in acquiring an accurate knowledge of Old English, and arouses his interest in the subject, so as to lead him on to the study of larger works, we shall feel ourselves amply rewarded for our labours.

JOSEPH WRIGHT.
ELIZABETH M. WRIGHT.

OXFORD,
 February, 1923.

CONTENTS

PAGES

INTRODUCTION 1–2

Classification of the Germanic languages (§ 1); the periods of Old English (§ 2); the Old English dialects (§ 3).

CHAPTER I

ORTHOGRAPHY AND PRONUNCIATION 3–12

Vowels (§§ 4–5); consonants (§§ 6–7); accentuation (§§ 8–14).

CHAPTER II

THE PRIM. GERMANIC EQUIVALENTS OF THE INDO-GERMANIC VOWEL-SOUNDS 12–21

The Indo-Germanic vowel-system (§§ 15–16); independent changes (§§ 17–19); dependent changes (§§ 20–5); the prim. Germanic vowel-system (§ 26).

CHAPTER III

THE OE. DEVELOPMENT OF THE PRIM. GERMANIC VOWEL-SYSTEM OF ACCENTED SYLLABLES 21–43

Independent changes: (*a*) the short vowels (§§ 29–34); (*b*) the long vowels (§§ 35–40); (*c*) the diphthongs (§§ 41–4). Dependent changes: 1. ǣ (§ 45); 2. the influence of nasals (§§ 46–50); 3. breaking (§§ 51–5); 4. the influence of initial palatals (§ 56); 5. umlaut: (*a*) palatal umlaut (§§ 57–8), (*b*) guttural umlaut (§ 59); 6. the influence of w (§§ 60–5); 7. the influence of labials, &c. (§ 66); 8. monophthongization (§ 67); 9. vowel contraction (§§ 68–9); 10. the lengthening of short vowels (§§ 70–6); 11. the shortening of long vowels (§§ 77–8); 12. the formation of new diphthongs (§ 79).

CHAPTER IV

THE OE. DEVELOPMENT OF THE PRIM. GERMANIC VOWELS OF UNACCENTED SYLLABLES 44–56

The treatment of Indg. final consonants in prim. Germanic (§ 80). Vowels which were originally final or became final in prim. Germanic: 1. the short vowels (§§ 81–4); 2. the long vowels (§§ 85–8); 3. the diphthongs (§§ 89–90). Summary with table (§ 91). The vowels in OE. final syllables (§ 92): *a.* the short vowels (§ 93); *b.* the long vowels (§ 94); *c.* the diphthongs (§ 95). Final vocalic nasals and liquids in prehistoric OE. (§ 96). The vowels in OE. medial syllables (§§ 97–101). Svarabhakti vowels (§ 102).

CHAPTER V

ABLAUT (§§ 103–5) 56–59

CHAPTER VI

THE PRIM. GERMANIC DEVELOPMENT OF THE INDO-GERMANIC CONSONANTS 60–74

Table of the Indo-Germanic consonant-system (§ 107); the first sound-shifting (§§ 108–14); Verner's law (§§ 115–18); the Indg. combinations of explosives + t or s (§ 119); assimilation of consonants (§§ 120–4); the loss of consonants (§§ 125–8); other consonant changes (§§ 129–31); table of prim. Germanic consonants (§ 132).

CHAPTER VII

SPECIAL WEST GERMANIC CHANGES OF THE PRIM. GERMANIC CONSONANTS 75–76

Prim. Germanic z (§ 133); prim. Germanic đ (§ 134); the doubling of consonants (§§ 135–7).

CHAPTER VIII

THE OE. DEVELOPMENT OF THE PRIM. GERMANIC CONSONANT-SYSTEM 77–90

1. The voicing of consonants (§ 139); 2. the unvoicing of consonants (§ 140); 3. the vocalization of consonants (§ 141); 4. assimilation (§ 142); 5. metathesis (§ 143); 6. the loss of consonants (§ 144); 7. the simplification of double consonants (§ 145); 8. the doubling of consonants (§ 146). The semivowels (§§ 147–51); the liquids (§ 152); the nasals (§§ 153–4); the labials (§§ 155–8); the dentals (§§ 159–64); the sibilant s (§ 165); the gutturals (§§ 166–76).

CHAPTER IX

NOUNS 91–117

Classification of nouns (§§ 177–8). Declension of nouns:—
A. The strong declension: 1. the a-declension (§§ 179–210); 2. the ō-declension (§§ 211–28); 3. feminine abstract nouns in -īn

Contents

PAGES

(§§ 229-30); 4. the i-declension (§§ 231-40); 5. the u-declension (§§ 241-5).

B. The weak declension: masculine n-stems (§§ 247-9); feminine n-stems (§§ 250-2); neuter n-stems (§§ 253-4).

C. Minor declensions: 1. Monosyllabic consonant stems (§§ 255-60); 2. stems in -þ (§ 261); 3. stems in -r (§ 262); 4. stems in -nd (§§ 263-5); 5. stems in -os, -es (§§ 266-8).

CHAPTER X

ADJECTIVES 117–132

General remarks on the declension of adjectives (§ 269). The strong declension (§ 270):—a-stems (§§ 271-8); ja-stems (§§ 279-81); wa-stems (§§ 282-4); i-stems (§ 285); u-stems (§ 286). The weak declension (§§ 287-8). The declension of participles (§§ 289-90). The comparison of adjectives (§§ 291-3). Numerals:— Cardinal and ordinal (§§ 294-7); other numerals (§§ 298-302).

CHAPTER XI

PRONOUNS 132–138

1. Personal pronouns (§§ 303-6). 2. Reflexive pronouns (§ 307). 3. Possessive pronouns (§ 308). 4. Demonstrative pronouns (§§ 309-11). 5. Relative pronouns (§ 312). 6. Interrogative pronouns (§§ 313-14). 7. Indefinite pronouns (§ 315).

CHAPTER XII

VERBS 138–174

The classification of verbs (§§ 316-17). The full conjugation of several strong verbs as models (§ 318). The endings of strong verbs (§§ 319-26). General remarks on the strong verbs (§§ 327-31). The classification of the strong verbs (§§ 332-63). The classification of weak verbs (§§ 364-82). Minor groups:—Preterite-presents (§§ 383-90). Verbs in -mi (§§ 391-5).

CHAPTER XIII

ADVERBS (§§ 396-401). PREPOSITIONS (§ 402). CONJUNCTIONS (§ 403) 175–179

INDEX 180–192

ABBREVIATIONS, ETC.

Dor.	= Doric	NE.	= New English
Germ.	= Germanic	NHG.	= New High German
Goth.	= Gothic	Nth.	= Northumbrian
Gr.	= Greek	OE.	= Old English
Indg.	= Indo-Germanic	OHG.	= Old High German
instr.	= instrumental	O Icel.	= Old Icelandic
Ken.	= Kentish	OS.	= Old Saxon
Lat.	= Latin	Prim.	= Primitive
loc.	= locative	Skr.	= Sanskrit
ME.	= Middle English	WS.	= West Saxon
MHG.	= Middle High German		

The asterisk * prefixed to a word denotes a theoretical form, as OE. dæg, *day*, from prim. Germanic *ðaʒaz.

For the sound-values of the letters ƀ, đ, ʒ, χ used in the writing of prehistoric forms, see § 107, note 4.

The paragraphs referring to the *OE. Grammar* are to those of the second edition.

INTRODUCTION

§ 1. OLD ENGLISH is a member of the West Germanic division of the Germanic (Teutonic) branch of the Indo-Germanic family of languages.

The Germanic branch consists of:—

1. **Gothic.** Almost the only source of our knowledge of the Gothic language is the fragments of the biblical translation made in the fourth century by Ulfilas (b. about 311 A.D., d. 383), the Bishop of the West Goths.

2. **Old Norse** (Scandinavian), which is subdivided into two groups: (*a*) East Norse, including Swedish, Gutnish, and Danish; (*b*) West Norse, including Norwegian and Icelandic.

The oldest records of this branch are the runic inscriptions, some of which date as far back as the third or fourth century.

3. **West Germanic,** which is composed of:—

(*a*) High German, the oldest monuments of which belong to about the middle of the eighth century.

(*b*) Low Franconian, called Old Low Franconian or Old Dutch until about 1200.

(*c*) Low German, with records dating back to the ninth century. Up to about 1200 it is generally called Old Saxon.

(*d*) Frisian, the oldest records of which belong to the fourteenth century.

(*e*) English, the oldest records of which belong to about the end of the seventh century.

§ 2. The division of a language into fixed periods must of necessity be more or less arbitrary. What are given as the characteristics of one period have generally had their beginnings in the previous period, and it is impossible to say with perfect accuracy when one period begins and another ends. For practical purposes Old English may be conveniently divided into two periods: early Old English from about 700 to 900; and late Old English from 900 to 1100.

§ 3. The oldest records of OE. exhibit clearly defined dialectal peculiarities which have been dealt with in the phonology, so that the student can easily collect together for himself the chief characteristics of each dialect. In this grammar early West Saxon is taken as the standard of OE., and is treated in greater detail than the other dialects. In using OE. poetry for grammatical purposes the student should remember that it was for the most part originally written in the Anglian dialect, but that it has come down to us chiefly in late West Saxon copies which contain many Anglian forms. OE. is usually divided into four dialects:—

(*a*) Northumbrian, embracing the district between the Firth of Forth and the Humber.

(*b*) Mercian, between the Humber and the Thames.

(*c*) West Saxon, south of the Thames, except Kent and Surrey.

(*d*) Kentish, embracing Kent and Surrey.

Northumbrian and Mercian are often classed together and called Anglian.

Even in the oldest recorded OE. there was of course no such thing as a uniform Northumbrian, Mercian, West Saxon, or Kentish dialect. Within each principal division there must have been some or many sub-dialects, and this is one of the main reasons why we find certain phonological peculiarities in texts ascribed to one or other of the four principal dialects. So-called phonological irregularities sometimes also arose from copyists introducing into manuscripts forms peculiar to their own dialect, or in transcribing manuscripts from one dialect into another they sometimes left dialect forms peculiar to their original; and in transcribing manuscripts from e. g. early WS. into late WS. forms belonging to the older period were often copied.

PHONOLOGY

CHAPTER I

ORTHOGRAPHY AND PRONUNCIATION

§ 4. OE. was written in the British modified form of the Latin alphabet with the addition of þ and ƿ (= w) from the runic alphabet. Vowel length was mostly omitted in writing, but in the case of long vowels it was sometimes represented by doubling the vowel or by using the diacritic sign ´, as huus, hús, *house*. The sign ¯, placed over vowels, is used in this grammar to mark long vowels and diphthongs.

A. The Vowels.

§ 5. The OE. vowel-system was represented by the six elementary letters a, e, i, o, u, y, the ligatures æ, œ, and the digraphs ea, eo, io, and ie, the latter having the value of diphthongs. They all had both a short and a long quantity.

a had the same sound as the a in NHG. ab, gast, as assa, *donkey*; dagas, *days*; hara, *hare*. a before nasals was probably a low-back-wide vowel like the a as pronounced in many Scottish dialects in such words as ant, man, which English people often mistake for o, especially when lengthened. In OE. it was accordingly often written o and may be pronounced like the o in NE. not, as land, lond, *land*; mann, monn, *man*; nama, noma, *name*.

ā had the same sound as the a in NE. father, as ān, *one*; cnāwan, *to know*; twā, *two*.

æ had the same sound as the a in NE. hat, as æt, *at*; fæder, *father*; mægden, *maiden*.

ǣ had the same sound as the ai in NE. air, and the è in French père, as ǣnig, *any*; sǣd, *seed*; sǣ, *sea*.

e had the same sound as the e in NE. end, west, as etan, *to eat*; helpan, *to help*; mete, *meat*.

ē had the same sound as the e in NHG. reh, as hēr, *here*; cwēn, *queen*; tēþ, *teeth*.

i had the same sound as the i in NE. sit, as ic, *I*; sittan, *to sit*; niman, *to take*.

ī had the same sound as the i in NHG. ihn, and nearly the same sound as the ee in NE. feed, as īs, *ice*; bītan, *to bite*; fīf, *five*.

o had the same sound as the o in NE. not, as oxa, *ox*; nosu, *nose*; dohtor, *daughter*.

ō had the same sound as the o in NHG. bote, and the eau in French beau, as ōþer, *other*; sōna, *soon*.

u had the same sound as the u in NE. put, as under, *under*; full, *full*; duru, *door*.

ū had the same sound as the ou in French sou, and nearly the same sound as the oo in NE. food, as ūt, *out*; sūcan, *to suck*; cū, *cow*.

œ had the same sound as the ö in NHG. götter, as œxen, *oxen*; dat. dœhter, *to a daughter*.

ōē had the same sound as the ö in NHG. schön, as bōēc, *books*; dōēma(n), *to judge*.

y had the same sound as the ü in NHG. mütter, as yfel, *evil*; þyncan, *to seem*.

ȳ had the same sound as the ü in NHG. grün, as ȳþ, *wave*; hȳdan, *to hide*.

It is difficult to determine what was the precise pronunciation of the a, e, o in the second element of diphthongs. In these combinations they had the function of consonants and may be pronounced as very short unstressed ă, ĕ, ŏ. The first element of the diphthongs ea, ēa was a very open sound like the æ in OE. fæder, and the a in NE. hat, but the e in the diphthongs eo, ēo was like the e in NE. bed or like the close é in French

§ 5] *Orthography and Pronunciation* 5

été. In the long diphthongs each of the elements was longer than in the short diphthongs.

ea = æ + ă, as **eall**, *all*; **wearm**, *warm*; **hleahtor**, *laughter*; **weaxan**, *to grow*.

ēa = ǣ + a, as **ēage**, *eye*; **hlēapan**, *to leap*; **strēa**, *straw*.

eo = e + ŏ, as **eorþe**, *earth*; **meolcan**, *to milk*; **sweostor**, *sister*.

ēo = ē + o, as **dēop**, *deep*; **sēon**, *to see*; **cnēo**, *knee*.

ie = i + ĕ, as **ieldra**, *older*; **giest**, *guest*; **hierde**, *shepherd*.

īe = ī + e, as **hīeran**, *to hear*; **līehtan**, *to give light*; **nīewe**, *new*.

io = i + ŏ, as **mioluc, miolc**, *milk*; **liornian**, *to learn*.

īo = ī + o, as **frīond**, *friend*; **līode**, *people*.

From what has been said above we arrive at the following OE. vowel-system:—

Short vowels a, æ, e, i, o, u, œ, y
Long vowels ā, ǣ, ē, ī, ō, ū, œ̄, ȳ
Short diphthongs ea, eo, ie, io
Long diphthongs ēa, ēo, īe, īo

NOTE.—1. æ was often written ae, ę in the oldest records. In the oldest period of the language there must have been two short e-sounds, viz. e = Germanic e (§ 31), and e = the i-umlaut of æ (§ 57), the latter probably being more open than the former, but the two sounds seem to have fallen together at a very early date, and are accordingly not distinguished in this grammar. Some scholars distinguish them by writing the former e and the latter ę. And in like manner they also sometimes distinguish the o = Germanic o (§ 23), and the o = Germanic a before nasals (§ 46), by writing the former o and the latter ǫ. In late OE. e, y were often written for æ, i and vice versa. In Ken. ǣ was sometimes written in mistake for ĕ, as **ætan** = **etan**, *to eat*; **hǣr** = **hēr**, *here*. In late Nth. æ, œ, y were sometimes written ai, oi, ui. œ, œ̄ (§ 57), written oe in OE. manuscripts, were best preserved in the Anglian dialects. They were unrounded to e, ē in WS. about the end of the ninth and in Ken. about the end of the tenth century. Long ī was sometimes written ig finally and occasionally also medially, as **hig** = **hī**, *they*; **bigspell** = **bīspell**, *parable*. The ō in words like **gōs**, *goose* (§ 50), and **mōna**, *moon* (§ 49), must originally have been an open ō like the a in NE. all, but it fell together with Germanic long close ō (§ 39) at an early period. The diphthong ĕa was sometimes written æa, æo in the oldest records. ĕo was often written for ĭo in the oldest WS. For ĕo of whatever origin Nth. often has ĕa; and Ken. often has ĭa (ya) for WS. ĕa, ĕo, ĭo. In late WS. the combinations ǣw, ēw, of whatever origin, were often written ēaw, ēow. The combination ēaw was occasionally written ēuw, ēuu, ēu, ēw in Anglian. ie and īe occur chiefly in WS. After ĭe had regularly become ĭ in WS. the ĭe was sometimes wrongly written for old ĭ.

2. A diphthong may be defined as the combination of a sonantal with a consonantal vowel. It is called a falling or a rising diphthong according as the stress is upon the first or second element. The OE. diphthongs were generally falling diphthongs, but the diphthongs which arose from the influence of initial palatal c, g, sc (§ 56) upon a following palatal vowel, were originally rising diphthongs which at a later period became falling diphthongs through the shifting of the stress from the second to the first element of the diphthong.

B. The Consonants.

§ 6. The OE. consonant-system was represented by the following letters: b, c, d, f, g, h, k, l, m, n, p, r, s, t, þ, (ð), *w, x.

v (written u) and z (= ts) were very rarely used except occasionally in late loanwords. c, cc, nc, sc; g, ng; and h (except initially), hh were guttural (back) or palatal (front) according to the sound-law stated in § 166. On the vocalic liquids and nasals in OE. see § 96.

Of the above letters b, d, l, m, n, p, t had the same sound-values as in Modern English. The remaining letters require special attention.

c. Guttural or back c, sometimes written k in the oldest oldest records, was pronounced nearly like the c in NE. could. Palatal or front c (often written ce before a following guttural vowel) was pronounced nearly like the k in NE. kid. In the OE. runic alphabet the two k-sounds had separate characters. Examples of guttural c are: cēlan, *to cool*; cyssan, *to kiss*; cnēo, *knee*; sprecan, *to speak*; bōc, *book*; weorc, *work*; bucca, *he-goat*; drincan, *to drink*; þancian, *to thank*; and of palatal c:

cinn, *chin*; cīese, *cheese*; cēosan, *to choose*; bēc, *books*; crycc, *crutch*; benc, *bench*; þenc(e)an, *to think*; of sc : sceal, *shall*; scēap, *sheep*; scōh, *shoe*; wascan, *to wash*; fisc, *fish*. See §§ 166–7.

f. Initially, finally, and medially before voiceless consonants, also when doubled, f was a voiceless spirant like the f in NE. fit, shaft, as fæder, *father*; ceaf, *chaff*; sceaft, *shaft*; pyffan, *to puff*. Medially between voiced sounds it was a voiced spirant (often written b in the oldest records) nearly like the v in NE. vine, five, as giefan, *to give*; seofon, *seven*; wulfas, *wolves*; hræfn, *raven*; lifde, *he lived*. See §§ 139, 158.

g was used to represent several different sounds : (*a*) a guttural or back and a palatal or front explosive; (*b*) a guttural and a palatal spirant which had separate characters in the OE. runic alphabet. The palatal explosive and the palatal spirant were often written ge before a following guttural vowel with e to indicate the palatal nature of the g.

Before guttural vowels initial g was a guttural explosive and was pronounced like the g in NE. good, but in the oldest OE. it was a guttural spirant like the g often heard in NHG. sagen (cp. § 168), as gāst, *spirit*; god, *God*. Before palatal vowels initial g was a palatal spirant nearly like the j in NHG. jahr and the y in NE. ye, yon, as geaf, *he gave*; giefan, *to give*; geoc, *yoke*.

Medial gg was always a guttural explosive like the g in NE. good, as dogga, *dog*; stagga, *stag*. Medial and final cg was a palatal explosive nearly like the g in NE. give, as lecg(e)an, *to lay*; secg(e)an, *to say*; brycg, *bridge*. The g in medial and final ng was a guttural or a palatal explosive, the former being nearly like the g in NE. longer, as sungon, *they sang*; hungor, *hunger*; lang, *long*; and the latter nearly like the g in NE. finger, as lengra, *longer*; streng, *string*; þing, *thing*.

Medial intervocalic g was a guttural or a palatal spirant, the former being nearly like the g in NHG. sagen, as boga, *bow*; fugol, *bird*; lagu, *law*; and the latter nearly like the g in NHG.

siegen, as **bīeg(e)an**, *to bend*; **fæger**, *fair*; **hyge**, *mind*; and similarly with final g, as **dāg**, *dough*; **plōg**, *plough*; **mearg**, *marrow*; beside **dæg**, *day*; **weg**, *way*; **bodig**, *body*. See § 170.

NOTE.—ʒ is generally used for g in OE. manuscripts, and often also in printed texts and grammars. In this grammar ʒ is only used to represent the prim. Germanic voiced spirant (§§ 112, 115).

h. Initial h (except in the combination **hw**) was an aspirate like the h in NE. hand, as **hūs**, *house*; **hlūd**, *loud*; **hring**, *ring*. Initial **hw** was pronounced χw like the wh in many Scottish dialects, as **hwā?**, *who?*; **hwǣte**, *wheat*. In all other positions h, including hh, was a guttural or a palatal spirant, the former being like the ch in NHG. nacht, noch, as **dohtor**, *daughter*; **eahta**, *eight*; **crohha**, *crock, pot*; **scōh**, *shoe*; **holh**, *hollow*; **furh**, *furrow*; and the latter like the ch in NHG. nicht, ich, as **flyht**, *flight*; **siehþ**, *he sees*; **hliehhan**, *to laugh*. See §§ 173–6. In the oldest records final h was sometimes written ch, as **elch** = **eolh**, *elk*.

k was sometimes used to express the guttural c (see above), as **kynn**, *race, generation*; **knēo**, *knee*.

r was trilled in all positions as in modern Scottish, as **rīdan**, *to ride*; **duru**, *door*; **word**, *word*; **fæder**, *father*.

s. Initially, finally, medially before voiceless consonants, and when doubled, s was a voiceless spirant like the s in NE. sit, as **sunu**, *son*; **standan**, *to stand*; **sweostor**, *sister*; **hūs**, *house*; **dagas**, *days*; **cyssan**, *to kiss*. Medially between voiced sounds, it was a voiced spirant like the s in NE. rise, as **cēosan**, *to choose*; **nosu**, *nose*; **bōsm**, *bosom*; **ōsle**, *ousel*.

þ. Initially, medially when doubled, and finally þ was a voiceless spirant like the th in NE. thin, as **þencan**, *to think*; **þwang**, *thong*; **moþþe**, *moth*; **mūþ**, *mouth*; **mōnaþ**, *month*. Medially between voiced sounds, it was a voiced spirant like the th in NE. then, as **baþian**, *to bathe*; **brōþor**, *brother*; **eorþe**, *earth*; **fæþm**, *fathom*.

NOTE.—Initial þ was written th until about 900 in imitation of Latin. Afterwards it was written ð, and þ (borrowed from the runic alphabet). And the voiced spirant was often written d in imitation of the contemporary Latin pronunciation.

w had the same sound-value as the **w** in NE. wet, as **wæter**, *water*; **wlanc**, *proud*; **wrītan**, *to write*; **twā**, *two*; **sāwol**, *soul*.

NOTE.—w was represented by uu, u in the oldest records, and then from about the beginning of the ninth century it was generally represented by Þ borrowed from the runic alphabet. In late Nth. it was sometimes represented by wu, v, and before ă, ǣ, ĕ by wo, vo, uo, o.

x was pronounced like the **x** in NE. six, as **weaxan**, *to grow*; **āxian**, *to ask*; **siex**, *six*.

§ 7. From what has been said above we arrive at the following OE. consonant-system:—

		Labial.	Inter-dental.	Dental.	Guttural.	Palatal.
Explosives	voiceless	p, pp		t, tt	c, cc	c, cc
	voiced	b, bb		d, dd	g, gg	g, cg
Spirants	voiceless	f, ff	þ, þþ	s, ss	h, hh	h, hh
	voiced	f	þ	s	g	g
Nasals		m, mm		n, nn	n	n
Liquids				l, ll; r, rr		
Semi-vowel w						

To these must be added the aspirate **h**, and **x**. The double consonants were pronounced long as in Modern Italian and Swedish, thus **habban** = hab-ban, *to have*; **swimman** = swim-man, *to swim*. From the above table it will be seen that the OE. alphabet was very defective in its consonants, insomuch as each of the letters c, f, g, h, n, s, and þ was used to represent two or more sounds.

STRESS (ACCENT).

§ 8. In the parent Indg. language the chief accent of a word did not always fall upon the same syllable, but was free or movable as in Greek, cp. e.g. Gr. nom. πατήρ, *father*, voc. πάτερ, acc. πατέρα, gen. πατρός. This free accent was still preserved in prim. Germanic at the time when Verner's law operated (§ 115). At a later period of the prim. Germanic language, the chief accent of a word became confined to the root- or stem-syllable. This confining of the chief accent to the root-syllable was the cause of the great weakening—and eventual loss—which the vowels underwent in unaccented syllables in the prehistoric period of the individual Germanic languages (Ch. IV).

§ 9. The rule for the accentuation of uncompounded words is the same in OE. as in the oldest period of the other Germanic languages, viz. the chief stress fell upon the stem-syllable and always remained there even when inflexional endings and suffixes followed it, as beran, *to bear*; sealfian, *to anoint*; dagas, *days*; hēafodu, *heads*; æþelingas, *noblemen*; macode, *he made*; maþelode, *he spoke*; mistig, *misty*; grēting, *greeting*; heofonlic, *heavenly*; lēofost(a), *dearest*; huntigestre, *huntress*. The position of the secondary stress in trisyllabic and polysyllabic words fluctuated in OE., and in the present state of our knowledge of the subject it is impossible to formulate any hard and fast rules concerning it.

In compound words it is necessary to distinguish between compounds whose second element is a noun or an adjective, and those whose second element is a verb. In the former case the first element had the chief accent in the parent Indg. language; in the latter case the first element had or had not the chief accent according to the position of the verb in the sentence. But already in prim. Germanic the second element of compound verbs nearly always had the chief accent; a change which was mostly brought about by the compound and simple verb existing side by side. This accounts for the difference in the accentuation of such pairs as ándgiet, *intelligence* : ongíetan, *to understand*; ándsaca, *adversary* : onsácan, *to deny*; bígang, *practice* : begángan, *to practise*; órþanc, *device* : aþéncan, *to devise*; úpgenge, *fugitive* : opgángan, *to escape*; wíþersaca, *opponent* : wiþsácan, *to oppose*.

§ 10. As has been stated above, compound words, whose second element is a noun or adjective, had originally the chief accent on the first syllable. This simple rule was preserved in OE., as brȳdguma, *bridegroom*; dēaþstede, *death-place*; æftergield, *additional payment*; fēowergield, *fourfold payment*; æþelcund, *of noble origin*; brynehāt, *burning hot*; wordsnotor, *eloquent*. Nouns like ālíefednes, *permission*; onfángennes, *reception*; ongíetennes, *understanding*; ongínn, *beginning*, are no exception to the rule, because such nouns were formed direct from the corresponding verbs: pp. ālíefed, onfángen, ongíeten, inf. ongínnan.

§ 11. Already in the oldest period of the language many nouns and adjectives were formed from verbs containing an inseparable particle, and accordingly had the chief stress on the second element, as bebód, *command*; behāt, *promise*; belímp, *occurrence*; forhǽfednes, *temperance*; forlórennes, *destruction*; behēfe, *suitable*. In like manner the prefix ge- was already unaccented in the oldest period of the language—probably partly also in prim. Germanic—and therefore words compounded with it had the chief stress on the second element, as gebrōþor, *brethren*; gescéaft, *creation*; gemǽne, *common*; gesúnd, *healthy*.

§ 12. In compound nouns and adjectives the chief secondary stress was upon that syllable of the second element which would have the chief stress if it were used alone, as brýdgùma, *bridegroom*; féowergìeld, *fourfold payment*; géarowỳrdig, *eloquent*. But compounds which were no longer felt as such did not have a strong secondary stress upon the second element, as ēorod from eoh + rād, *troop of cavalry*; hlāford from hlāf + weard, *lord*.

§ 13. In the oldest period of the language, the compound verbs had the chief stress upon the second or first element according as the first element was inseparable or separable, as becúman, *to become*; gebǽran, *to behave*; forgíefan, *to forgive*; opféallan, *to fall off*; tōbérstan, *to burst asunder*; ætníman, *to deprive*; oferwéorpan, *to overthrow*; underníman, *to comprehend*; þurhwúnian, *to abide continuously*; ymbbíndan, *to bind round*. Verbs like ándswarian, *to answer*; fúltumian, *to support*; órettan, *to fight*, are no exception to the rule, because such verbs were formed direct from the nouns: ándswaru, fúltum, óret. Examples of separable verbs are: ǽftersprecan, *to claim*; bístandan, *to support*; éftflōwan, *to flow back*; úprǣran, *to raise up*; íncuman, *to come in*; tódōn, *to put to*; útdrīfan, *to drive out*.

§ 14. In compound adverbs the first element had the chief or secondary stress according as it was the more or the less important element of the compound, as éal(l)mǣst, *almost*; éalneg from ealne + weg, *always*; éalswā, *quite so*; but onwég, *away*; tōgǽdere, *together*; þǣrínne, *therein*.

CHAPTER II

THE PRIMITIVE GERMANIC EQUIVALENTS OF THE INDO-GERMANIC VOWEL-SOUNDS

§ 15. The parent Indo-Germanic language had the following vowel-system:—

    Short vowels a, e, i, o, u, ə

    Long ,,   ā, ē, ī, ō, ū

    Short diphthongs ai, ei, oi, au, eu, ou

    Long ,,   āi, ēi, ōi, āu, ēu, ōu

    Short vocalic l, m, n, r

NOTE.—1. The short vowels i, u, ə, the long vowels ī, ū, and vocalic l, m, n, r occurred originally only in syllables which did not bear the principal accent of the word. See *OE. Grammar*, § 16, note 1.

2. ə, the quality of which cannot be precisely defined, arose from the weakening of an original ā, ē, ō, caused by the loss of accent. It is generally pronounced like the e in NHG. **gabe** and in NE. **litter**.

3. Besides the ordinary long vowels ā, ē, ō with the 'broken' or acute accent the parent Indg. language had also the three long vowels ã, ẽ, õ

(also sometimes written â, ê, ô) with the 'slurred' or circumflex accent. The former were bimoric and the latter trimoric in length. The difference between the two kinds of long vowels was still preserved in final syllables in the oldest historic period of the separate Germanic languages, see § 85.

4. Diphthongs only occurred before consonants and finally. When a diphthong came to stand before a vowel its second element belonged to the following vowel, as ĕit, ĕut, tĕi, tĕu, but tĕ-je, tĕ-we.

5. Strictly speaking the combination a, e, or o + nasal or liquid is also a diphthong, because the history and development of such combinations are precisely parallel with those of the diphthongs ai, ei, oi, and au, eu, ou.

6. The long diphthongs were shortened before consonants in the prehistoric period of all the European languages, and they then had the same further development as the original short diphthongs. In this grammar no further account will be taken of them in stem-syllables. For their treatment in final syllables see § 89.

√7. In philological works the vocalic liquids and nasals are often written l̥, m̥, n̥, r̥ in order to distinguish them from consonantal l, m, n, r. Upon theoretical grounds it used to be assumed that the parent Indg. language also had long vocalic nasals and liquids, but scholars are now generally agreed that the forms which were supposed to contain these sounds admit of an entirely different explanation; see Wright, *Greek Grammar*, § 68.

§ 16. The Indg. vowel-system underwent various changes during the prim. Germanic period. These changes were of two kinds, viz. independent and dependent. Independent changes are those which take place independently of neighbouring sounds, whereas dependent sound-changes are those which depend upon or are due to the influence of neighbouring sounds.

1. INDEPENDENT CHANGES.

§ 17. The short vowels o and ə became a; the long vowel ā became ō; of the diphthongs ei became long ī, oi, ou became ai, au; and the vocalic nasals and liquids developed a u before (rarely after) them, and then became consonantal, whence um, un, ul, ur. Examples are:—

o (= Lat. o, Gr. o) > a in stem-syllables, as Lat. quod, Goth. hva, O.Icel. hvat, OS. hwat, OHG. hwaz, OE. hwæt (§ 29), *what*; Lat. octō, Gr. ὀκτώ, Goth. ahtáu, OS. OHG. ahto, OE.

eahta (§ 51), *eight*; Lat. hostis, *stranger, enemy*, Goth. gasts, OS. OHG. gast, OE. giest (§ 57), *guest*. See § 93.

ǝ > a in all the Indg. languages except in the Aryan branch, where it became i, as Lat. pater, Gr. πατήρ, Goth. fadar, O.Icel. faðer, OS. fadar, OHG. fater, OE. fæder (§ 29), but Skr. pitár-, *father*; Lat. status, Gr. στατός, Skr. sthitás, *standing*, Goth. staþs, O.Icel. staðr, OS. stad, OHG. stat, OE. stede (§ 57), prim. Germanic *stađiz, *place*.

ā (= Lat. ā, Gr. Doric ā, Attic, Ionic η) > ō, as Lat. māter, Gr. Dor. μάτηρ, O.Icel. mōðer, OS. mōdar, OE. mōdor, *mother*; Lat. frāter, Goth. brōþar, O.Icel. brōðer, OS. brōthar, OE. brōþor, *brother*.

ei (Lat. ī (older ei), Gr. ει) > ī, as Gr. στείχω, *I go*, Goth. steigan (ei = ī), O.Icel. stīga, OS. OHG. OE. stīgan, *to ascend*; Gr. λείπω, *I leave*, Goth. leiƕan, OS. OHG. līhan, *to lend*.

oi (= O.Lat. oi, later ū, Gr. οι, Goth. ái, O.Icel. OHG. ei, OS. ē, OE. ā) > ai, as Gr. οἶδε, Goth. wáit, O.Icel. veit, OHG. weiz, OS. wēt, OE. wāt, *he knows*; Gr. πέ-ποιθε, *he trusts*, Goth. báiþ, O.Icel. beið, OHG. beit, OS. bēd, OE. bād, *he waited for*; Gr. οἰνή, *the one on dice*, O.Lat. oinus, later ūnus, Goth. áins, O.Icel. einn, OHG. ein, OS. ēn, OE. ān, *one*.

ou (= O.Lat. ou, later ū, Gr. ου, Skr. ō, Goth. áu, O.Icel. au, OS. ō, OHG. ou, (ō), OE. ēa) > au, as Indg. *roudhos, Lat. rūfus, Goth. ráuþs, O.Icel. rauðr, OS. rōd, OHG. rōt, OE. rēad, *red*; Indg. *bhe-bhoudhe, Skr. bu-bódha, *has waked*, Goth. ana-báuþ, *he ordered*, O.Icel. bauð, OS. bōd, OHG. bōt, OE. bēad, *he offered*.

m (= Lat. em, Gr. α) > um, as Gr. βάσις, *gait, step*, Goth. ga-qumþs, *assembly*, OHG. kumft, *a coming*; Gr. ἑ-κατόν, Lat. centum (with n from m by assimilation to the dental, and similarly in the Germanic languages), Goth. OS. OE. hund, OHG. hunt, Indg. *kmtóm, *hundred*; acc. sing. Lat. pedem, Gr. πόδα, Goth. fōtu (§ 80), *foot*.

n (= Lat. en, Gr. α) > un, as acc. pl. Gr. πόδας, Goth.

fōtuns, *feet*; Gr. ἀθρέω from *Ϝαθρέω, *I gaze at*, O.Icel. undr, OS. wundar, OHG. wuntar, OE. wundor, *wonder*; Lat. commentus (pp.) *invented*, Gr. αὐτό-ματος, *acting of one's own will*, Goth. ga-munds, OHG. gi-munt, OE. ge-mynd (§ 57), *remembrance*.

l (= Lat. ol, (ul), Gr. αλ, (λα)) > ul, (lu), as Gr. πίμ-πλαμεν, *we fill*, Goth. fulls, O.Icel. fullr, OS. OE. full, Indg. *plnos, *full*; Goth. wulfs, O.Icel. ulfr, OHG. wolf, OE. OS. wulf, Indg. *wlqʷos, *wolf*.

r (= Lat. or, (ur), Gr. αρ, ρα, Skr. r̥) > ur, (ru), as Skr. vavr̥timá, *we have turned*, O.Icel. urðom, OS. wurdun, OHG. wurtum, OE. wurdon, *we became*; Gr. θαρσύς, θρασύς, *bold*, θαρσέω, *I am of good courage*, OHG. gi-turrum, OE. durron, *we dare*; Lat. porca, *the ridge between two furrows*, OHG. furuh, OE. furh, *furrow*.

§ 18. The remaining Indg. vowel-sounds, viz. the short vowels, a, e, i, u, the long vowels ē, ī, ō, ū, and the diphthongs ai, au, eu did not undergo any independent changes during the prim. Germanic period. Examples are:—

a (= Lat. a, Gr. α): Lat. ager, Gr. ἀγρός, Goth. akrs, O.Icel. akr, OS. akkar, OHG. ackar, OE. æcer (§ 29), *field*, *acre*; Gr. ἅλς, Lat. gen. salis, Goth. O.Icel. OS. salt, OHG. salz, OE. sealt (§ 51), *salt*.

e (= Lat. e, Gr. ε): Lat. edō, Gr. ἔδω, *I eat*, O.Icel. eta, OE. OS. etan, OHG. eʒʒan, *to eat*; Lat. ferō, Gr. φέρω, *I bear*, O.Icel. bera, OS. OHG. OE. beran, *to bear*.

i (= Lat. i, Gr. ι): Lat. piscis, Goth. fisks, O.Icel. fiskr, OS. fisk, OHG. OE. fisc, *fish*; Skr. vidmá, Gr. Hom. Ϝίδμεν Goth. witum, O.Icel. vitom, OS. witun, OHG. wiʒʒum, OE. witon, *we know*, cp. Lat. vidēre, *to see*.

u (= Lat. u, Gr. υ): Gr. gen. κυνός, Goth. hunds, O.Icel. hundr, OHG. hunt, OS. OE. hund, *dog, hound*; Gr. θύρᾱ, OS. duri, OHG. turi, OE. duru, *door*.

✓ ē : Indg. ē (= Lat. ē, Gr. η) was a long open sound and is generally written ǣ (= Goth. ē, O.Icel. OS. OHG. ā, OE.

(WS.) ǣ) in works on Germanic philology in order to distinguish it from the long close ē which arose in prim. Germanic, see § 25. It should be noted that the two sounds were kept apart in all the old Germanic languages except Gothic. Examples of Indg. ē are: Lat. ēdimus, Goth. ētum, O.Icel. ātom, OS. ātun, OHG. āʒum, OE. ǣton, *we ate*; Lat. mēnsis, Gr. μήν, *month*, Goth. mēna, O.Icel. māne, OS. OHG. māno, OE. mōna (§ 49), *moon*.

ī (= Lat. ī, Gr. ῑ): Lat. su-īnus (adj.), *belonging to a pig*, Goth. swein, O.Icel. svīn, OS. OHG. OE. swīn, *pig, swine*; Lat. sīmus, OS. sīn, OHG. sīm, OE. sī-en, *we may be*.

ō (= Lat. ō, Gr. ω), Gr. πλωτός, *swimming*, Goth. flōdus, O.Icel. flōð, OS. OE. flōd, *flood, tide*; Gr. Doric πώς, Goth. fōtus, O.Icel. fōtr, OS. OE. fōt, *foot*.

ū (= Lat. ū, Gr. ῡ): Gr. μῦς, Lat. O.Icel. OHG. OE. mūs, *mouse*; Lat. pūteō, *I smell bad*, Gr. πύθω, *I make to rot*, Goth. fūls, O.Icel. fūll, OHG. OE. fūl, *foul*.

ai (= O.Lat. ai, later ae, Gr. αι, Goth. ái, O.Icel. OHG. ei, OS. ē, OE. ā): aedēs, *sanctuary*, originally, *fire-place, hearth*, Gr. αἴθω, *I burn*; OHG. eit, OE. ād, *funeral pile, ignis, rogus*; Lat. caedō, *I hew, cut down*, Goth. skáidan, OHG. sceidan, OS. skēdan, OE. scādan, *to divide, sever*.

au (= Lat. au, Gr. αυ, Goth. áu, O.Icel. au, OS. ō, OHG. ou, (ō), OE. ēa): Lat. auris, Goth. áusō, OS. OHG. ōra, OE. ēare, *ear*; Lat. augeō, Gr. αὐξάνω, *I increase*, Goth. áukan, O.Icel. auka, OS. ōkian, OHG. ouhhōn, OE. ēacian, *to add, increase*.

eu (= O.Lat. ou, later ū, Gr. ευ, Goth. iu, O.Icel. jō, (jū), OS. OHG. eo, later io, OE. ēo): Gr. γεύω, *I give a taste of*, Goth. kiusan, O.Icel. kjōsa, OS. OHG. kiosan, OE. cēosan, *to test, choose*; O.Lat. doucō, later dūcō, *I lead*, Goth. tiuhan, OS. tiohan, OHG. ziohan, OE. tēon (§ 68), *to lead, draw*. Prim. Germanic eu was still preserved in old Germanic proper names found in ancient authors, as Teutomērus, Reudigni; in the oldest Norse runic inscriptions, as -leuƀaR, *dear*; and in the oldest OE. glosses, as **steupfædær**, later **stēopfæder**, *stepfather*.

§ 19. From the independent changes which have been stated in § 17 it will be seen that the following vowel-sounds fell together:—a, o, ǝ; original u and the u which arose from Indg. vocalic l, m, n, r; ā and ō; ī and ei; ai and oi; au and ou; and that the Indg. vowel-system was reduced to the short vowels a, e, i, u, long vowels ǣ, ī, ō, ū, and the short diphthongs ai, au, eu. In the following paragraphs will be stated the dependent changes which these simple vowels and diphthongs underwent during the prim. Germanic period.

2. Dependent Changes.

§ 20. A guttural nasal (ŋ) disappeared before χ with lengthening of a preceding a, i, u to the nasalized vowels ą̄, į̄, ų̄, which became denasalized in the prehistoric period of Gothic and the West Germanic languages, but remained in the oldest Old Norse. The normal equivalents of these nasalized vowels are:—ā, ī, ū in Goth. OS. and OHG.; ō, ī, ū in OE.; and ą̄ (written ā), ē, ō in O.Icel. Examples are:—

a + ŋχ > ą̄χ, as Goth. OS. OHG. **fāhan**, O.Icel. **fā**, OE. **fōn** (§ 68), from **faŋχanan*, *to catch*, cp. Lat. **pangere**, *to fasten*; pret. Goth. **þāhta** (inf. **þagkjan**), O.Icel. **þátta**, OS. **thāhta**, OHG. **dāhta**, OE. **þōhte**, from **þaŋχtō-*, *I thought*, cp. O.Lat. **tongēre**, *to know*.

i (= Indg. i, e) + ŋχ > į̄χ, as Goth. **þeihan**, OS. **thīhan**, OHG. **dīhan**, OE. **þēon** (cp. § 68), from **þiŋχanan* older **þeŋχanan*, *to thrive*, cp. Lithuanian **tenkù**, *I have enough*; and similarly OHG. **sīhan**, OE. **sēon**, *to strain*; OHG. **fīhala**, O.Icel. **fēl**, OE. **fēol**, *file*. The result of this sound-law was the reason why verbs of the type **þiŋχanan* passed from the third to the first class of strong verbs (§ 334) in the prehistoric period of all the Germanic languages, cp. the isolated pp. OS. **gi-thungan**, OE. **ge-þungen**, *full-grown*.

u + ŋx > ū, as pret. Goth. þūhta, OS. thūhta, OHG. dūhta, O.Icel. þōtte, OE. þūhte, *it seemed*, beside inf. Goth. þugkjan, OS. thunkian, OHG. dunken, O.Icel. þykkja, OE. þyncan (§ 57), *to seem*; Goth. ūhtwō, OS. OHG. OE. ūhta, O.Icel. ōtta, from *uŋxtwõ, *daybreak, dawn*, cp. Gr. ἀκτίς, *ray, beam*.

§ 21. e became i under the following circumstances:—

1. Before a nasal + consonant, as Goth. OS. OE. bindan, O.Icel. binda, OHG. bintan, *to bind*, cp. Lat. of-fendimentum, *chin-cloth*, of-fendix, *knot, band*; Goth. winds, O.Icel. vindr, OS. OE. wind, OHG. wint, Lat. ventus, *wind*; and similarly in early Lat. loanwords, as OE. minte, OHG. minza, Lat. menta, mentha, *mint*; OE. gimm, OHG. gimma, Lat. gemma, *gem*. This explains why OE. bindan, *to bind*, and helpan, *to help*, belong to the same ablaut-series. See § 104.

2. When followed by an i, ī, or j in the next syllable, as Goth. OS. OHG. ist, OE. is, from *isti, older *esti = Lat. est, Gr. ἔστι, *is*; Goth. midjis, O.Icel. miðr, OS. middi, OHG. mitti, OE. midd, Lat. medius, Indg. *medhjos, *middle*; OS. birid, OHG. birit, *he bears*, from an original form *bhéreti, through the intermediate stages *ƀéređi, *ƀériđi, *ƀíriđi.

This sound-law accounts for the difference in the stem-vowels of such pairs as OE. feld (OHG. feld), *field* : gefilde (OHG. gifildi), *a plain*; heord (OHG. herta), *herd* : hierde (OHG. hirti), *shepherd*; inf. helpan : hilpst (OHG. hilfis), *thou helpest*; hilpþ (OHG. hilfit), *he helps*, and similarly in the second and third person singular of the present indicative of many other strong verbs; pp. legen, seten : inf. licgan, *to lie down*, sittan, *to sit*.

3. In unaccented syllables, except in the combination -er when not followed by an i in the next syllable, as OE. fēt, older fœ̄t, from *fōtiz, older *fōtes, *feet*, cp. Gr. πόδες. Indg. e remained in unaccented syllables in the combination -er when not followed by an i in the next syllable, as acc. OS. fader, OHG. fater, OE. fæder, Gr. πατέρα, *father*; OE. hwæþer, Gr. πότερος, *which of two*.

§§ 22–3.] *Indo-Germanic Vowel-Sounds* 19

§ 22. i, followed. originally by an ă, ŏ, or ē in the next syllable, became e when not protected by a nasal + consonant or an intervening i or j, as O.Icel. verr, OS. OHG. OE. wer, Lat. vir, from an original form *wiros, *man*; OHG. OE. nest, Lat. nīdus, from an original form *nizdos, *nest*. In historic times, however, this law has a great number of exceptions owing to the separate languages having levelled out in various directions, as OE. spec beside spic, *bacon*; OHG. lebēn beside OE. libban, *to live*; OHG. quec beside OE. cwic, *quick, alive*.

§ 23. u, followed originally by an ă, ŏ, ē, or the combination -eno- (cp. §§ 93. 2, 290) in the next syllable, became o when not protected by a nasal + consonant or an intervening i or j, as OS. dohter, OHG. tohter, OE. dohtor, Gr. θυγάτηρ, *daughter*; O.Icel. ok, OHG. joh, OE. geoc (§ 56, note 4), Gr. ζυγόν, *yoke*; OHG. OE. gold, *gold*, beside OHG. guldīn, OE. gylden, *golden*; pp. of strong verbs, as O.Icel. boðenn, OS. gibodan, OHG. gibotan, OE. boden (§ 335), *offered*, O.Icel. holpenn, OS. giholpan, OHG. giholfan, OE. holpen (§ 341), *helped*, O.Icel. borenn, OS. OHG. giboran, OE. boren (§ 344), *borne*, beside O.Icel. bundenn, OS. gibundan, OHG. gibuntan, OE. bunden (§ 340), *bound*. Every prim. Germanic o was of this origin. Cp. § 17.

This sound-law accounts for the difference in the stem-vowels of such pairs as OS. OE. god, OHG. got, *god* : OE. gyden, OHG. gutin, *goddess*; OE. coss, *kiss* : cyssan, *to kiss*; fox : fyxen, *she-fox*; pret. bohte, worhte : inf. bycgan, *to buy*, wyrcan, *to work*, see § 57. It was best preserved in OHG. In O.Icel. OS. and OE. we often find u where we should regularly expect o. The u in these cases was partly due to levelling out in various directions and partly to the influence of neighbouring consonants, especially an f, w, m, or n (see §§ 48, 66), as O.Icel. fullr, OS. OE. full, beside OHG. fol, *full*; O.Icel. ull, OE. wull(e), beside OHG. wolla, *wool*; O.Icel. numenn, OS. ginuman, OE. numen, beside O.Icel. nomenn,

OHG. ginoman, *taken*; O.Icel. hunang, OE. hunig, beside OS. honeg, OHG. honang, *honey*.

§ 24. The diphthong eu became iu when the next syllable originally contained an i, ī, or j (cp. § 21. 2), but remained eu when the next syllable originally contained an ă, ŏ, ē (cp. § 18). The iu remained in Goth. OS. and OHG., but became jū (ȳ by i-umlaut) in O.Icel. and īo (īe by i-umlaut) in OE., as Goth. liuhtjan, OS. liuhtian, OHG. liuhten, OE. līehtan, *to give light*: OS. OHG. lioht, OE. lēoht, *a light*; OS. kiusid, OHG. kiusit, O.Icel. kȳs(s), OE. cīesþ, *he chooses*, beside inf. OS. OHG. kiosan, O.Icel. kjōsa, OE. cēosan, *to choose*; OS. liudi, OHG. liuti, OE. līode, *people*. See § 18.

§ 25. Besides ǣ (= Indg. ē, § 18) prim. Germanic also had a long close ē which arose from various sources. The two sounds fell together in Gothic, but were kept apart in all the other languages. Apart from the ē in the preterite of a small number of the seventh class of strong verbs (§§ 356-8), and in a few Latin loanwords, it only occurs in a few words. Its chief sources seem to be:—(*a*) From the Indg. long diphthong ēi which regularly stood in ablaut relation to ĭ, as Goth. O.Icel. OS. OE. hēr, OHG. hēr, later hear, hiar, hier, *here*: Goth. hi-drē, OE. hi-der, *hither*; OE. cēn, OHG. kēn, later kean, kian, kien, *torch*: OE. cīnan, *to crack*; OHG. zēri, &c., *beautiful*: OS. OE. tīr, O.Icel. tīrr, *renown, glory, splendour*; OS. mēda, OE. mēd, OHG. mēta, &c., Indg. *mēizdhā : Goth. mizdō, OE. meord, Gr. μισθός, *pay, reward*. (*b*) Latin loanwords, as OE. bēte, OHG. bieẓẓa, Lat. bēta, *beetroot*; Goth. mēs, OE. mēse, OHG. meas, mias, vulgar Latin mēsa, *table*. (*c*) The pret. of a small number of the seventh class of strong verbs (§§ 356-8), as O.Icel. OS. OE. hēt, OHG. hiaẓ, beside Goth. haíháit, *he called*; O.Icel. OS. OE. lēt, OHG. liaẓ, beside Goth. laílōt, *he let*. For a comprehensive article on the subject, see Feist, Paul-Braune's *Beiträge zur Geschichte der deutschen Sprache und Literatur*, vol. xxxii, pp. 447 ff.

The Primitive Germanic Vowel-system.

§ 26. In the previous paragraphs have been stated the vowel-changes which the Indg. vowel-system underwent during the prim. Germanic period. By summing up these changes we are now in a position to arrive at the vowel-system which existed at the end of the prim. Germanic period, i.e. just before the parent Germanic language became differentiated into the various separate languages:—

> Short vowels   a, e, i, o, u
> Long oral vowels   ǣ, ē, ī, ō, ū
> Long nasal vowels ą̄,   į̄,   ų̄
> Diphthongs   ai, au, eu, iu

For the equivalents of the long nasal vowels ą̄, į̄, ų̄ in the separate languages see § 20. We shall now proceed to trace the development of the other prim. Germanic simple vowels and diphthongs in OE. And in so doing we shall first deal with the vowels and diphthongs of accented syllables, and then with those of unaccented syllables.

CHAPTER III

THE OE. DEVELOPMENT OF THE PRIMITIVE GERMANIC VOWEL-SYSTEM OF ACCENTED SYLLABLES

§ 27. In dealing with the development of the prim. Germanic vowels in OE. we shall adopt the same method as we did in dealing with the development of the Indg. vowels in prim. Germanic, i.e. we shall first deal with the independent changes, and then with the dependent changes.

1. Independent Changes.

§ 28. Prim. Germanic a became æ, but the short vowels e, i, o, u underwent no independent changes. The long nasal vowel ą became ō, and į, ų had the same development in OE. as prim. Germanic oral ī, ū (§ 18). The long vowels ǣ, ē, ī, ō, ū underwent no independent changes. The diphthongs ai, au, eu, iu became ā, ēa, ēo, īo.

a. *The Short Vowels.*

§ 29. Germanic a became æ. Examples in closed syllables are: dæg, Goth. dags, O. Icel. dagr, OS. dag, OHG. tag, *day*; and similarly bæþ, *bath*; bræs, *brass*; glæd, *glad*; hwæt, *what*; pæþ, *path*; sægde, *he said*; in the pret. sing. of strong verbs belonging to classes IV (§ 344) and V (§ 346), as bær, *he bore*; stæl, *he stole*; sæt, *he sat*; wæs, *he was*; and in open syllables when followed by a palatal vowel or a vocalic nasal or liquid in the next syllable, as æcer, *field, acre*; fæder, *father*; hlædel, *ladle*; nægel, nægl, *nail*; fæþm, *embrace, fathom*; wægn, *wagon*; sing. gen. dæges, dat. dæge.

NOTE.—1. a often occurs where we should expect æ. In such cases the a is due to levelling and new formations, as sing. gen. paþes, dat. paþe, beside pæþes, pæþe, due to the plural forms paþas, paþa, paþum (§ 182); fem. gen. dat. acc. singular sace, swaþe, beside sæce, swæþe, due to the nom. sing. sacu, *strife, quarrel*; swaþu, *track*; and plural saca, swaþa, &c. (§ 213); masc. gen. sing. glades, beside nom. glæd, *glad*, due to forms like dat. sing. and pl. gladum (§ 271); imperative of strong verbs belonging to class VI (§ 352), as far, sac, due to the influence of the inf. faran, *to go, travel*; sacan, *to quarrel*.

2. æ became e in Ken. and s. Mercian, as deg, feder, wes = WS. dæg, fæder, wæs. And then æ (ae) was sometimes written by ignorant scribes for old e, as ætan, aetan = etan, *to eat*.

§ 30. But Germanic a remained or else æ became a again in open syllables when <u>originally</u> followed by a guttural vowel (ă, ŏ, ŭ) in the next syllable, as pl. nom. acc. dagas, gen. daga, dat. dagum, beside sing. nom. acc. dæg, *day*, gen. dæges, dat. dæge; neut. nom. acc. pl. baþu, *baths*, beside sing. bæþ; caru,

§§ 31-4] *Short Vowels of Accented Syllables* 23

care; hafoc, *hawk*; hara, *hare*; macaþ, *he makes*; macode, *he made*; inf. macian from *makōjan (§ 94. 3); and similarly in other weak verbs belonging to class II (§ 381); in closed syllables before double consonants (except hh, ll, rr), sc, and st, when the next syllable originally contained a guttural vowel, as assa, *donkey*; habban, *to have*; mattoc, *mattock*; flasce, *flask*; brastlian, *to crackle*; before the w which was regularly preserved in OE., as gen. dat. sing. clawe beside nom. clēa, *claw* (§ 144); þawian, *to thaw*.

§ 31. e: OE. OS. OHG. beran, O. Icel. bera, *to bear* (§ 18); and similarly feld, *field*; feþer, *feather*; nefa, *nephew*; setl, *seat*; snegl, *snail*; weder, *weather*; in the present of strong verbs belonging to classes III (§ 341), IV (§ 344), and V (§ 346), as helpan, *to help*; meltan, *to melt*; stelan, *to steal*; teran, *to tear*; etan, *to eat*; wefan, *to weave*.

§ 32. i: OE. OHG. fisc, Goth. fisks, O.Icel. fiskr, OS. fisk, *fish* (§ 18); and similarly blind, *blind*; cild, *child*; hring, *ring*; lim, *limb*; scip, *ship*; twig, *twig*; in the second and third pers. sing. pres. indic. of strong verbs belonging to classes III (§ 341), IV (§ 344), and V (§ 346), as hilp(e)st, hilp(e)þ, bir(e)st, bir(e)þ, it(e)st, iteþ, it(t), beside inf. helpan, *to help*; beran, *to bear*; etan, *to eat*; in the pret. pl. and pp. of strong verbs belonging to class I (§ 332), as biton, biten beside inf. bītan, *to bite*; in the inf. and pres. of strong verbs belonging to class III (§ 340), as bindan, *to bind*; singan, *to sing*.

NOTE.—i appears as e in the Lat. loanwords peru (Lat. pirum), *pear*; segn (Lat. signum), *sign*.

§ 33. o: OE. folc, O.Icel. OS. OHG. folk, *folk* (§ 23); and similarly bodig, *body*; bord, *board*; col, *coal*; dogga, *dog*; frogga, *frog*; morgen, *morning*; nosu, *nose*; open, *open*; word, *word*; in the pp. of strong verbs belonging to classes II (§ 335), III (§ 341), and IV (§ 344), as coren, *chosen*; holpen, *helped*; stolen, *stolen*.

§ 34. u: OE. OS. hund, Goth. hunds, O.Icel. hundr, OHG.

hunt, *dog, hound* (§ 18); and similarly **duru**, *door*; **hungor**, *hunger*; **sunu**, *son*; **tunge**, *tongue*; in the pret. pl. of strong verbs belonging to classes II (§ 335), and III (§§ 340-3), as **flugon**, *we flew*; **bundon**, *we bound*; and in the pp. of strong verbs belonging to class III (§ 340), as **bunden**, *bound*; **suncen**, *sunk*.

NOTE.—But u became o in the prefix **or-** (= Goth. **us-**, OHG. **ur-**, *out*), as **orsorg**, *without anxiety*; **orwēne**, *despairing*; and in the Lat. loan-words **box** (Lat. **buxus**), *boxtree*; **copor** (Lat. **cuprum**), *copper*.

b. *The Long Vowels.*

§ 35. Prim. Germanic ą̄ (§ 20) became ō, as **brōhte**, Goth. OS. OHG. **brāhta**, *I brought*; and similarly **fōn**, *to grasp, seize*; **hōn**, *to hang*; **tōh**, *tough*; **þōhte**, *I thought*.

§ 36. ǣ: WS. **dǣd**, Goth. **ga-dēþs**, O.Icel. **dāð**, OS. **dād**, OHG. **tāt**, *deed* (§ 18); and similarly **blǣdre**, *bladder*; **ǣfen**, *evening*; **mǣl**, *meal-time*; **nǣdl**, *needle*; **þǣr**, *there*; in the pret. pl. of strong verbs belonging to class V (§ 346), as **ǣton**, *they ate*; **sǣton**, *they sat*.

NOTE.—1. ǣ became ē in Anglian and Ken., as **dēd**, **sēton** = WS. **dǣd**, **sǣton**. ę̄, ae were often written for this ē in late Ken.

2. The ā in early Lat. loanwords had the same development in OE. as Germanic ǣ, as **nǣp** (Lat. **nāpus**), *turnip*; **strǣt** (Lat. **strāta**), *street*.

§ 37. ē: OE. Goth. O.Icel. OS. **hēr**, OHG. **hēr**, **hear**, **hiar**, *here* (§ 25); and similarly **cēn**, *torch*; **mēd**, *pay, reward*; in the pret. of strong verbs belonging to class VII (§§ 356-8), as **hēt**, **lēt**, **hēng**, beside inf. **hātan**, *to call*; **lǣtan**, *to let*; **hōn**, *to hang*.

NOTE.—Lat. ē became ī in early loanwords, as **cīpe** (Lat. **cēpa**), *onion*; **pīn** (Lat. **poena**, late Lat. **pēna**), *torture*; but ē remained in later loan-words, as **bēte** (Lat. **bēta**), *beetroot*; **crēda** (Lat. **crēdō**, *I believe*), *creed*.

§ 38. ī: OE. OS. **bītan**, Goth. **beitan**, O.Icel. **bīta**, *to bite* (§ 18); and similarly **drīfan**, *to drive*; **hwīt**, *white*; **līf**, *life*; **rīdan**, *to ride*; **smītan**, *to smite*; **tīd**, **tīma**, *time*.

§§ 39–44] *Long Vowels of Accented Syllables* 25

§ 39. ō : OE. OS. fōt, Goth. fōtus, O.Icel. fōtr, *foot* (§ 18); and similarly blōd, *blood*; brōþor, *brother*; dōn, *to do*; gōd, *good*; mōdor, *mother*; stōl, *stool*; in the pret. of strong verbs belonging to class VI (§ 352), as fōr, *he went, travelled*; swōr, *he swore*.

§ 40. ū : OE. O.Icel. OS. OHG. hūs, *house* (§ 18); and similarly brūn, *brown*; hlūd, *loud*; mūs, *mouse*; rūst, *rust*; sūcan, *to suck*; þūhte, *it seemed* (§ 20); þūsend, *thousand*.

c. *The Diphthongs.*

§ 41. Prim. Germanic ai became ā (§§ 17–18), as hāl, Goth. háils, O.Icel. heill, OS. hēl, OHG. heil, *whole, sound*; and similarly āc, *oak*; bān, *bone*; gāt, *goat*; hlāford, *lord*; sāwol, *soul*; stān, *stone*; twā, *two*; in the pret. sing. of strong verbs belonging to class I (§ 332), as bāt, *he bit*; rād, *he rode*.

§ 42. Prim. Germanic au became ēa (§§ 17–18), as ēage, Goth. áugō, O.Icel. auga, OS. ōga, OHG. ouga, *eye*; and similarly bēacen, *beacon*; dēaþ, *death*; dēaf, *deaf*; ēare, *ear*; hēafod, *head*; hlēapan, *to leap*; lēaf, *leaf*; in the pret. sing. of strong verbs belonging to class II (§ 335), as cēas, *he chose*; frēas, *it froze*.

NOTE.—ēo beside ēa occurs in Nth., especially in s.Nth., as dēof, hēofod, ēore, beside dēaf, hēafod, ēare.

§ 43. Prim. Germanic eu became ēo (§ 18), as dēop, Goth. diups, O.Icel. djūpr, OS. diop, OHG. tiof, *deep*; and similarly dēor, *deer*; flēos, *fleece*; sēoc, *sick*; þēof, *thief*; in the present of strong verbs belonging to class II (§ 335), as cēosan, *to choose*; crēopan, *to creep*; scēotan, *to shoot*.

NOTE.—1. īo was often written for ēo in early WS. and Mercian.

2. In Nth., especially in n.Nth., the ēo generally became ēa, and thus fell together with ēa from Germanic au (§ 42); and in Ken. it became īo (also written īa) and thus fell together with īo from Germanic iu (§ 24), as Nth. dēar, Ken. dīor, dīar = WS. and Mercian dēor, *deer*.

§ 44. Prim. Germanic iu became īo (§ 24). In WS. īo

generally became īe (later ī, ȳ) by i-umlaut, see § 57. But when no umlaut took place early WS. had īo beside ēo. Although these two diphthongs were of different origins ēo began to be written for īo, and vice versa, at an early period, and in the end completely supplanted it. It is difficult to account for the forms without umlaut, unless we may suppose that they are not pure WS. (see § 24). Examples are: cīesþ, Goth. kiusiþ, *he chooses*; līehtan, Goth. liuhtjan, *to give light*. dīere, beside dīore, dēore, *dear*; geþīedan beside geþīodan, geþēodan, *to join, associate*; stīeran beside stīoran, stēoran, *to steer*; līode, lēode, *people*.

2. DEPENDENT CHANGES.

1. ǣ.

§ 45. Prim. Germanic ǣ became ā before a liquid, labial, or guttural followed by a guttural vowel, but there are numerous exceptions to this rule which were due to the analogy of forms where ǣ was regular. Regular forms were: slāpol, *sleepy*; sǣl, *opportunity*; tǣl, *calumny*; swǣr, *heavy*; mǣg, *kinsman*, beside forms like dat. pl. sālum, tālum, swārum, māgum, from which were formed a new singular sāl, tāl, swār, māg; inf. slāpan, *to sleep*, beside the second and third pers. singular slǣp(e)st, slǣp(e)þ, from which was formed a new inf. slǣpan; pret. pl. lāgon, *they lay*; þāgon, *they received*; wāgon, *they carried*, beside the new formations lǣgon, þǣgon, wǣgon, due to the analogy of preterites like ǣton, *they ate*; sǣton, *they sat*; and in the pret. pl. of some verbs the new formation with ǣ became generalized, as stǣlon, *they stole*; bǣron, *they bore*; wǣron, *they were*; sprǣcon, *they spoke*. See also §§ 49, 64.

2. *The Influence of Nasals.*

§ 46. Prim. Germanic a became rounded in OE. to a sound intermediate between the o in NE. on and the a in NHG. mann. In the oldest period of the language it was nearly always written a, in the ninth century it was mostly written o, and in late WS. and Ken. mostly a, which indicates that it had become a again, but it remained in some parts of Mercian, and has been preserved in many of the Midland dialects down to the present day. Examples are : mann, monn, Goth. manna, *man* ; nama, noma, Goth. namō, *name*; standan, stondan, *to stand*; lang, long, *long*; in the pret. sing. of many strong verbs belonging to class III (§ 340), as dranc, dronc, *he drank*; fand, fond, *he found*; sang, song, *he sang*. In this grammar the sound will generally be written a.

NOTE.—The a became full o in unstressed adverbial and pronominal forms, as hwonne, *when*; on, *on*; þonne, *then*; masc. acc. sing. hwone, *whom*; þone, *the*.

§ 47. e became i before Germanic m, as niman, OHG. neman, *to take* ; rima, *rim*.

NOTE.—e became i before nasal + consonant in early Lat. loanwords, but remained in later loanwords, as gimm (Lat. gemma), *gem*; minte (Lat. mentha), *mint*, but templ (Lat. templum), *temple*.

§ 48. o became u before nasals, as pp. cumen, OHG. quoman, *come* ; numen, OHG. ginoman, *taken*; hunig, OHG. honag, *honey* ; and also in early Lat. loanwords, as munuc (Lat. monachus), *monk*; pund (Lat. pondō), *pound*. See also §§ 23, 66.

§ 49. Before nasals prim. Germanic ǣ became ō through the intermediate stage ā, as mōna, Goth. mēna, OS. OHG. māno, *moon* ; and similarly c(w)ōmon, *they came* ; nōmon, *they took* ; mōnaþ, *month* ; sōna, *soon*.

§ 50. Nasals disappeared before the voiceless spirants f, þ, s, and the preceding vowels a (o), i, u became ō, ī, ū through the intermediate stage of long nasalized vowels, as ōþer, Goth. anþar, *second, other* ; sōfte, OHG. samfto, *gently, softly* ; fīf, Goth. fimf, *five* ; sīþ, Goth. sinþs, *way* ; cūþ, Goth. kunþs, *known* ; ūs, Goth. uns, *us* ; and similarly gōs, *goose*; tōþ, *tooth*; fīfel, *sea-monster* ; mūþ, *mouth* ; sūþ, *south*.

NOTE.—n remained when it came to stand before a voiceless spirant at a later period, as **pinsian** from Lat. **pensāre**, *to weigh, consider*; **winster** beside **winester**, OHG. **winister**, *left* (*hand*).

3. BREAKING (FRACTURE).

§ 51. Breaking is due to the influence of an **l**, **r**, or **h** + consonant, or simple **h**, upon a preceding palatal vowel, whereby a guttural glide was developed between the vowel and the consonant, which then combined with the vowel to form a diphthong. In this manner the Germanic vowels **a** (= OE. **æ**), **e**, **i**; **ǣ**, **ī** eventually became **ea**, **eo**, **io**; **ēa**, **īo**. For the monophthonization of these diphthongs at a later period, see § 67.

æ was broken to **ea** (= **æa**) before **l**, **r**, or **h** + consonant (also **x** = **hs**), and simple **h**, as **healdan**, Goth. **haldan**, *to hold*; **bearn**, Goth. **barn**, *child*; **eahta**, Goth. **ahtáu**, *eight*; **weaxan**, OHG. **wahsan**, *to grow*; **seah**, OHG. **sah**, *he saw*; and similarly **ceald**, *cold*; **eall**, *all*; **sealt**, *salt*; **weall**, *wall*; **dearr**, *I dare*; **heard**, *hard*; **wearm**, *warm*; **hleahtor**, *laughter*; **meaht** (later **miht**), *power, might*; **neaht** (later **niht**), *night*, see § 67; **fleax**, *flax*; **sleah**, *slay thou*.

NOTE.—1. Forms without breaking often occur in the oldest WS. and Ken.

2. Forms like **ærn** (Goth. **razn**), *house*; pret. sing. **arn** (Goth. **rann**), *he ran*; **gærs** (Goth. **gras**), *grass*, are due to a late metathesis of the **r**.

3. Breaking took place in Anglian before **r** + consonant (other than **c**, **g**, **h**), but not before **l** + consonant.

4. **eo** was often written for **ea** in Nth., especially in s.Nth., as **eorm**, **heord** = WS. **earm**, **heard**.

5. **a** remained unbroken in late Lat. loanwords, as **alter** (Lat. **altāre**), *altar*; **fals** (Lat. **falsus**), *false*; **martyr** (Lat. **martyr**), *martyr*; **palm** (Lat. **palma**), *palm-tree*.

§ 52. **e** was broken to **eo** before **lc**, **lh**, before **r** and **h** + consonant (also **x** = **hs**), and before simple **h**, as **meolcan**, OHG. **melcan**, *to milk*; **seolh**, OHG. **selah**, *seal*; **weorþan**, OHG. **werdan**, *to become*; **feohtan**, OHG. **fehtan**, *to fight*; **seox**, OHG. **sehs**, *six*; **seoh**, *see thou*; and similarly **āseolcan**, *to* *become languid*; **eolh**, *elk*; **eorþe**, *earth*; **beorcan**, *to bark*; **steorra**, *star*; **weorc**, *work*. But already at an early period eo became **ie** (later **i, y**) under certain conditions before **ht** and **hs**, as **cnieht, cniht**, *boy*; **siex, six**, *six*, see § 67.

NOTE.—1. Breaking is older than the metathesis of **r** in forms like **berstan** (OHG. **brestan**), *to burst*; **fersc**, *fresh*; **þerscan**, *to thrash*.

2. Breaking did not take place in Anglian before **lc, lh**.

3. **ea** was often written for **eo** in Nth., especially in n.Nth., as **hearte**, *heart*, **stearra**, *star* = WS. and Mercian **heorte, steorra**. The eo became **io** in Ken., as **hiorte, stiorra**.

4. Nth. kept **eo** and **io** apart, but in Mercian they fell together in **eo** in the ninth century. In Ken. **io** was used for **eo** and vice versa. They were kept apart in early WS., but fell together in **eo** in late WS.

§ 53. **i** was broken to **io** (older **iu**) before **r** and **h + consonant**, and simple **h**, but in WS. and Mercian the **io** eventually became **eo** and thus fell together with the **eo** from **e**, see note 4 above, as **liornian, leornian** from **lirnōjan*, *to learn*; **miox, meox** from **mihst*, *manure*, cp. Goth. **maíhstus**, *dunghill*; **tiohhian, teohhian** from **tihhōjan*, *to arrange, think, consider*.

§ 54. Prim. Germanic **ǣ** was broken to **ēa** (= **ǣa**) before **h**, as **nēah**, Goth. **nēƕ**, OHG. **nāh**, *near* (§ 18); **nēar** from **nēahur*, older **nǣhur*, *nearer* (§ 68).

NOTE.—The non-WS. **ē** from older **ǣ** (§ 18) was broken to **ēo**, also written **īo** in Mercian, and **īo, īa** in Ken.

§ 55. **ī** was broken to **īo** (older **īu**) before **h** and **ht**, but already in early WS. and Mercian the **īo** mostly became **ēo** (= Anglian **ī**), as **līoh, lēoh** (OHG. **līh**), *lend thou*; **wīoh, wēoh**, *idol*, cp. OHG. **wīh**, *holy*; **līon, lēon** (OHG. **līhan**), *to lend* (§ 68); **līoht, lēoht** (Goth. **leihts**), adj. *light*.

4. THE INFLUENCE OF INITIAL PALATALS.

§ 56. Between initial palatal **c** (§ 166), **g** (= Germanic **ʒ**, § 168), **g** (= Germanic **j**, § 150), **sc**, and the following palatal vowel, a glide was developed in prim. OE., which combined with the vowel to form a rising diphthong, and then at a later period the rising diphthong became a falling diphthong through the shifting of the stress from the second to the first element of the diphthong (see § 5, note 2). In this manner prim. OE. æ, e, ǣ became ea, ie, ēa in WS. :—

æ became ea (older eǽ), as ceaf, *chaff*; ceaster (Lat. castra), *city, fortress*; geaf (Goth. gaf), *he gave*; geat (O.Icel. gat), *gate, opening*; sceal (Goth. skal), *I shall*; sceatt (Goth. skatts), *money, property*.

e became ie (older ié), as cieres, cires (Lat. acc. cerasum), *cherry-tree*; giefan (OHG. geban), *to give*; forgietan (OS. forgetan), *to forget*; giest, *yeast*, cp. OHG. jesan, *to ferment*; scieran (OHG. sceran), *to shear*; scield, *shield*.

ǣ became ēa (older eá through the intermediate stage eǽ), as cēace, *jaw*; forgēaton, *they forgot*; gēafon, *they gave*; gēar (OHG. jār), *year*; scēap (OHG. scāf), *sheep*; scēaron, *they sheared*.

NOTE.—1. ĕa became ĕ (§ 67) and ie became i (§ 67) in late WS.

2. Forms like ceald, *cold*; cealf, *calf*; geard, *yard*; scealt, *thou shalt*; ceorfan, *to carve*; georn, *eager*, are due to breaking, which was older than the influence of initial palatals upon a following æ, e.

3. The combinations scă-, scŏ- were often written sceă-, sceŏ- with e to denote the palatal pronunciation of the sc-, as sceacan, *to shake*, sceādan, *to divide*, sceolde, *I should*, sceōh, *shoe*, beside scacan, scādan, scolde, scōh.

4. In forms like gioc, geoc (OHG. joh), *yoke*; giong, geong (OHG. jung), *young*; geōmor (OHG. jāmar), *sad*, the io, eo, eō may have been rising diphthongs, but it is difficult to determine how far they were diphthongs at all, and how far the i, e were merely inserted to indicate the palatal nature of the g = Germanic j (§ 150).

5. For WS. ea Anglian has æ beside ea, and Ken. e, as cæster (ceaster), gæt (geat), scæl (sceal), Ken. cester, get, scel. e also occurs occasionally in Mercian.

6. For WS. ie, ēa Anglian and Ken. have e, ē, as gefa(n), sceld, gēfon, gēr, scēf.

5. Umlaut (Mutation).

a. Palatal Umlaut.

§ 57. Palatal umlaut, generally called i-umlaut, is the modification (palatalization or fronting) of an accented vowel through the influence of an ĭ or j which originally stood in the following syllable. This process took place in prehistoric OE.—probably in the sixth century—and the ĭ or j had for the most part disappeared in the oldest OE. records. The i, which remained, mostly became e at an early period (§ 84 note), so that for the proper understanding of the forms which underwent i-umlaut it is necessary to compare them with the corresponding forms of some other Germanic language, especially with the Gothic. The result of i-umlaut is generally the fronting of guttural (back) vowels, as a to e, u to y. It rarely consists in the raising of front vowels, as in æ to e, ĕa to ĭe. The simple vowels and diphthongs which underwent i-umlaut in OE. are: a(o), æ, o, u; ā, ō, ū; ea, io; ēa, īo :—

a(o) > e (but æ in the oldest period of the language), as ende, Goth. andeis, stem andja-, *end*; lengra, OHG. lengiro. *longer*; lengþ(u) from *langiþu, *length*; sendan, Goth. sandjan, *to send*; pl. menn, prim. Germanic *manniz : sing. mann, *man*. bærnan, Goth. brannjan, *to burn*; ærnan, Goth. rannjan, *to run, gallop*, with metathesis of r and preservation of the older stage of umlaut.

æ > e, as bedd, Goth. badi, *bed*; bet(e)ra, Goth. batiza, *better*; hebban, Goth. hafjan, *to raise*; hell, Goth. halja, *hell*; here, Goth. harjis, *army*; settan, Goth. satjan, *to set*.

o > e (older œ). All native words containing this umlaut are new formations due to levelling or analogy, because prim. Germanic u did not become o in OE. when followed by an i or j in the next syllable (§ 23). Examples are: dat. sing. dehter, *to a daughter*, from *dohtri with o levelled out from the other cases (e. g. nom. dohtor), the regular form would be *dyhter from *duhtri; **efes** (OHG. **obasa**) beside **yfes**, *eaves*, cp. Goth. **ubizwa**, *porch*; pl. nom. acc. **exen**, beside nom. sing. **oxa**, *ox*; **mergen** (Goth. **maúrgins**), beside **morgen**, *morning*.

u > y, as **bycgan**, Goth. **bugjan**, *to buy*; **cyning**, OHG. **kuning**, *king*; **cynn**, Goth. **kuni**, *race, generation*; **gyden**, OHG. **gutin**, *goddess*; **gylden**, OHG. **guldīn**, *golden*; **yfel**, Goth. **ubils**, *evil*; and similarly in early Lat. loanwords, as **cylen** (Lat. culīna), *kiln*; **cycene** (late Lat. coquina, cucīna), *kitchen*; **mynster** (Lat. monasterium), *minster* (see § 48).

ā > ǣ (Ken. ē), as **ǣnig**, *any* : **ān**, *one*; **hǣþ**, Goth. **háiþi**, *heath*; **hǣlan**, Goth. **háiljan**, *to heal*; **hwǣte**, Goth. **hváiteis**, *wheat*; **sǣ**, Goth. **sáiws**, prim. Germanic *saiwiz, *sea*.

ō > ē (older ǿ), as **fēt**, OS. **fōti**, prim. Germanic *fōtiz, *feet*; **dēman**, Goth. **dōmjan**, *to judge*; dat. sing. **brēþer** from *brōþri : nom. **brōþor**, *brother*; **sēcan**, Goth. **sōkjan**, *to seek*; **cwēn** from *kwōni-, older *kwǣniz, Goth. **qēns**, *queen, wife* (§ 49); **ēhtan** from *ōhtjan, OS. **āhtian**, *to persecute*; **fēhþ**, OS. **fāhid**, *he seizes* (§ 20); **ēst** from *ōsti-, older *anstiz, Goth. **ansts**, *favour*; **tēþ**, prim. Germanic *tanþiz, *teeth* (§ 50).

ū > ȳ, as **brȳcst** from *brūkis, *thou enjoyest*; **mȳs** from prim. Germanic *mūsiz, *mice*, **rȳman**, OS. **rūmian**, *to make room*; **cȳþan** from *kūþjan, older *kunþjan, Goth. **gaswi-kunþjan**, *to make known* (§ 50).

ea > ie (later i, y), as **fiellan** from *fealljan, Goth. *falljan, *to fell*; **fielþ** from *fealliþ, *he falls*; **ieldra**, Goth. **alþiza**, *older*; **ierfe**, Goth. **arbi**, *inheritance*; **wierman**, Goth. **warmjan**, *to warm*; **hliehhan**, Goth. **hlahjan**, *to laugh*; **sliehþ**, Goth. **slahit**, *he slays* (§ 51); **cietel**, Lat. **cattilus**, *kettle*; **giest**, Goth. **gasts**, prim. Germanic *gastiz, *guest*; **scieppan**, Goth. **skapjan**, *to create* (§ 56).

io > ie (later i, y), in WS., as **hierde** from *hiordi, OHG. **hirti**, *shepherd*; **ierre**, OHG. **irri**, *angry*; **smierwan**, OHG. **smirwen**, *to anoint*; **fieht**, OHG. **fihtit**, *he fights*; **siehþ**, OHG. **sihit**, *he sees*, see § 51.

ēa > īe (later ī, ȳ), as **gelīefan**, Goth. **galáubjan**, *to believe*;

hīeran, Goth. háusjan, *to hear*; hīehst(a), Goth. háuhists, *highest*; nīed, Goth. náuþs, prim. Germanic *nauđiz, *need*, see §§ 17–18.

io > īe (later ī, ȳ), cīesþ from *kīosiþ, Goth. kiusiþ, *he chooses*; tīehþ, from *tīohiþ, *he leads, draws*; līehtan, Goth. liuhtjan, *to give light*, see § 24; gelīehtan from *-līohtjan, *to lighten, make easier*; līehþ, OHG. līhit, *he lends*, see § 55.

NOTE.—1. The i-umlaut of a before l + consonant and of ea before h + consonant is æ (also e) in Anglian and æ (later e) in Ken., as Anglian ældra, Ken. ældra later eldra, = WS. ieldra, *older*; Angl. mæht, Ken. mæht later meht, = WS. mieht, *power, might*; Angl. hlæhha(n) = WS. hliehhan, *to laugh*. The i-umlaut of ea before r + consonant is e in the non-WS. dialects, as erfe = WS. ierfe, *inheritance*.

2. i for y (= the i-umlaut of u) occurs occasionally in early WS., as cining, *king*, scildig, *guilty*, disig, *foolish*, beside cyning, scyldig, dysig. In late WS. and Anglian y was often unrounded to i, especially before and after c, g, h, and then y often came to be written for original i. ȳ became ē in the ninth century in Ken.; ǣ also became ē in this dialect, and then the old traditional spelling with ȳ was sometimes wrongly used, as cyrran for cerran = WS. cierran, *to turn*; yfter for efter = WS. æfter, *after*; mȳgþ for mēgþ = WS. mǣgþ, *family, kindred*; lȳssa for lēssa = WS. lǣssa, *less*. In late Ken. ǣ was also often written for ē.

3. ie only occurs in WS. and is therefore a special characteristic of this dialect. The ĭe became ў in the ninth century in some parts of the WS. area and in the other parts it became ĭ (see § 67). In the ninth century ie was often written i and conversely old i was often written ie, which shows that the two sounds had fallen together in i. Corresponding to WS. ie preceded by an initial palatal c-, g-, sc- (§ 56) the other dialects have e, as cele, *cold*, gest, *guest*, sceppan, *to create* = WS. ciele, giest, scieppan.

4. The i-umlaut of ēa (= WS. īe) is ē in the non-WS. dialects, as gelēfan, hēran, nēd = WS. gelīefan, hīeran, nīed.

5 The i-umlaut of ĭo did not take place in the non-WS. dialects, so that we have io in Nth. and Ken., and io (eo) in Mercian, as Nth. Ken. hiorde, *shepherd*, iorre, *angry*, Mercian heorde, iorre = WS. hierde, ierre. Nth. Ken. īo (also written īa in the latter dialect), Mercian īo beside ēo (later mostly ēo), as Nth. Ken. dīore, *dear*, līode, *people*, but in Mercian īo beside ēo.

§ 58. a became æ when followed by an umlauted vowel in the

next syllable, as æces (æx) from *akysi, older *akusi-, *axe*; and similarly æþele from *aþali (OS. aðali), *noble*; gædeling (OS. gaduling), *companion*; hærfest from *χaruƀist, *harvest*; mægden from *maʒadīn (OHG. magatīn), *maiden*. The æ in the above examples is sometimes called the secondary umlaut of a.

NOTE.—1. The a in the stem-syllable of the present participle and gerund of strong verbs belonging to class VI (§ 352) is due to the a of the infinitive, as farende for *færende from *farandi, *travelling*; farenne for *færenne from *farannjai.

2. The regular forms of the second and third pers. singular of the pres. indicative of strong verbs belonging to class VI (§ 352) would have e, as in OHG. feris, *thou goest*; ferit, *he goes*, but in OE. the a of the other forms of the present was extended to the second and third pers. singular, and then a became æ by i-umlaut, as færest, færeþ.

b. Guttural Umlaut.

§ 59. Guttural umlaut is the modification of an accented vowel (a, e, i) through the influence of a primitive OE. guttural vowel (u, ŏ, a) in the next syllable whereby a guttural glide was developed after the vowels a, e, i, which then combined with them to form the diphthongs ea, eo, io. This sound-change took place about the end of the seventh century. As a rule umlaut only took place before a single consonant. When the vowel which caused umlaut was u, it is called u-umlaut, and when ŏ or a, it is called o/a-umlaut. In WS. it was limited to the u-umlaut of e, and to the u-, o/a-umlaut of i, and generally only took place before labials and liquids :—

e > eo, as eofor (OHG. ebur), *boar*; heofun, heofon, *heaven*; heolster from older helustr, *hiding-place*; meolu, *meal*; heorut, heorot, *hart*; teoru, *tar*. The regular forms due to u-umlaut were often obliterated by levelling, as melu, with mel- from the gen. melwes, dat. melwe; pl. nom. speru, *spears*, dat. sperum, due to the forms of the singular, as spere, gen. speres, gen. pl. spera; and similarly with many other forms. When the e was preceded by w, umlaut took place before consonants which generally prevented it from taking place, as **hweogol**, *wheel*; **sweotol**, *plain, clear*; **sweostor**, *sister*.

i > io, which then became eo in the ninth century:—

1. u-umlaut of i, as **cliopude, -ode**, beside inf. **clipian**, *to call*; **cliopung**, *calling*; **mioluc, miolc** (later **milc**), *milk*; **sioluc**, *silk*; **siolufr, siolfor**, *silver*; pret. **tiolude, -ode**, beside inf. **tilian**, *to aim at*. The regular forms due to u-umlaut were mostly obliterated in WS. by levelling and new formations, as pl. **clifu**, *cliffs*, **scipu**, *ships* (Anglian **cliofu, sciopu**), due to levelling out the stem-forms of those cases which had no u in the ending. Pret. plural **drifun, -on**, *they drove*, **gripun, -on**, *they seized*, due to preterites like **bitun, -on**, *they bit*, **stigun, -on**, *they ascended*. Pret. **tilode** beside **tiolode**, formed direct from the inf. **tilian**. And conversely forms like inf. **cliopian** (**cleopian**), **tiolian** (**teolian**), were formed from the pret. **cliopode, tiolode**.

2. o/a-umlaut of i, as **liofas(t)**, *thou livest*; **liofaþ**, *he lives*, beside pret. **lifdes(t), lifde**; **hiora, heora**, older **hira**, *their, of them*.

NOTE.—1. u- and o/a-umlaut of a to ea only took place in Mercian, as **ealu**, *ale*; **beadu**, *battle*; **featu**, *vats*; **heafuc**, *hawk*; **steaþul**, *foundation*; pret. **gleadude, -ode**, *he rejoiced*, from which a new inf. **gleadian** for **gladian** was formed. **fearan**, *to go, travel*; gen. pl. **feata**, *of vats*. The ea then became æ before c and g, as **mægun**, *they can*; **dræca**, *dragon*; **dægas**, *days* = WS. **magun, -on, draca, dagas**.

2. e became eo, and i became io by u-, o/a-umlaut in Ken. before all single consonants, and in Anglian (but Nth. generally ea) before all single consonants except gutturals (c, g). For examples before labials and liquids see above. Examples before other consonants are:—

e > eo (but Nth. generally ea), as **eosol**, *donkey*; **meodu**, *mead (drink)*; **meotod**, *creator* = WS. **esol, medu, metod**; Ken. **breogo**, *prince*; **reogol** (Lat. *regula*), *rule* = WS. and Anglian **brego, regol**. **beoran**, *to bear*; **eotan**, *to eat*; **weofan**, *to weave* = WS. **beran, etan, wefan**; Ken. **weogas**, *ways*; **spreocan**, *to speak* = WS. and Anglian **wegas, sprecan**; Nth. **beara(n), eata(n)** = WS. **beran, etan**.

i > io (but in Mercian the io became eo in the ninth century), as **liomu, leðmu**, *limbs*; **siodu** (WS. **sidu**), *custom*; **sionu** (WS. **sinu**), *sinew*; Ken. **siocol**, *sickle*; **stiogol**, *stile* = WS. and Anglian **sicol, stigol**. **behionan**, *on this side of*; **glioda**, *kite, vulture*; **niomaþ**, *they take*;

piosan (WS. pisan), *peas*; wiotan, *to know*; Ken. stiocaþ = WS. and Anglian sticaþ, *he pricks*.

3. WS. ealu, *ale*, and forms like eafora, *son*; heafuc, -oc, *hawk*, &c., are all originally from the Mercian dialect. And forms like liomu, *limbs*; nioþor, *lower*; behionan, *on this side of*; wiotan, *to know*, &c., which occasionally occur in WS. prose are not pure WS.

6. THE INFLUENCE OF w.

§ 60. Final ew became eu, and then eu became ēo at the same time as Germanic eu became ēo (§ 43), as sing. nom. cnēo, Germanic stem-form *knewa-, *knee*; trēo, *tree*; þēo, *slave, servant*. See § 149. Antevocalic ew became eow, as sing. gen. cneowes, treowes, þeowes. Forms like cnēow, trēow, þēow had the w from the inflected forms. And conversely forms like cnēowes, trēowes, þēowes had ēo from the uninflected forms.

§ 61. a became e by i-umlaut, and then at a later period the e became eo before w, as eowestre (cp. Goth. awistr), *sheepfold*; meowle (Goth. mawilō), *girl*; streowede beside strewede (Goth. strawida), *he strewed*.

§ 62. Prim. Germanic aww (= Goth. aggw) became auw in West Germanic which regularly became ēaw in OE. (§ 42), as dēaw (Goth. *daggwa-), *dew*; glēaw, *wise*, cp. Goth. glaggwō, *diligently*; hēawan (Goth. *haggwan), *to hew*.

Prim. Germanic eww (= Goth. iggw) became euw in West Germanic, and then euw became ēow in OE. (§ 43), as trēow (OS. treuwa), *trust, faith*, cp. Goth. triggwa, *covenant*.

Prim. Germanic ewwj became īowj through the intermediate stages iwwj, iuwj (cp. § 24), and then iōwj became īew(e) in WS. (§ 57) and īow(e), ēow(e) in the other dialects, as WS. getrīewe, non-WS. getrīowe, getrēowe (OHG. gitriuwi), prim. Germanic *-trewwjaz, cp. Goth. triggws, *true, faithful*. And similarly West Germanic iwwj from prim. Germanic ewj (§ 135), as WS. nīewe, nīwe, non-WS. nīowe, nēowe, prim. Germanic stem-form *newja-, *new*.

§ 63. The initial combination weo-, of whatever origin, became wu- (rarely wo-) in late WS., as swurd, *sword*, swuster, *sister*, wurþan beside worþan, *to throw*, wurþan, *to become*, beside older sweord, sweostor, weorþan, weorþan; but worc, *work*, worold, *world*, beside wurc, wurold, older weorc, weorold.

y, of whatever origin, became u in late WS. in the initial combination wyr + consonant, as wurm from older wyrm, *worm*; wursa from older wyrsa, still older wiersa (§ 67), *worse*. And then wyr + consonant sometimes came to be written for older wur + consonant, as cwyrn, older cwiorn, cweorn, *hand-mill*; swyrd, *sword*; swyster, *sister*, see above.

The initial combination wio-, of whatever origin, generally became wu- in WS., as c(w)ucu from older cwiocu, cwicu, *alive*; betwux (betux), *betwixt*; wucu (Goth. wikō), *week*; wuduwe (Goth. widuwō), *widow*; wuht (OHG. wiht), *creature, thing*.

NOTE.—1. The initial combination weo- became wo- in late Nth., but remained in Mercian and Ken., as Nth. sword, *sword*; worþa, *to become*; worold, *world*; wosa from older weosa = WS. wesan, *to be*.

2. The initial combination wio- generally became wu- in Anglian, but remained in Ken., as Anglian wudu, Ken. wiodu, *wood*; wuta, *to know*. But before gutturals we have wi- in Anglian, as betwix, cwic(u), wicu, wiht. The wio- became wu- at an early period in Anglian, and then u became y by i-umlaut, as wyrsa, *worse*; wyrrest(a), *worst*; wyrþe, *worthy*.

3. ĕ was often rounded to œ̆ after w in Nth., as wœg, *way*, twœlf, *twelve*, cuœpa, *to say* = WS. weg, twelf, cweþan; huœr, *where*, wœpen, *weapon*, wœron, *they were* = WS. hwǣr, wǣpen, wǣron.

§ 64. Prim. Germanic ǣ (§ 18) became ā before w, as blāwan (OHG. blāen), *to blow*; cnāwan (OHG. knāen), *to know*; sāwan (OHG. sāen), *to sow*; sāwon (OS. sāwun), *they saw*.

§ 65. Unaccented ā = Germanic ai (§§ 17–18) became ō when originally followed by w, as ō (Goth. áiw), *ever*, beside accented ā; and similarly in the compounds ōwþer, *one of two*, nōwþer, *neither of two*, ōwiht, *anything*, nōwiht, *nothing*, beside āwþer, &c.

7. The Influence of Labials, &c.

§ 66. In a certain number of words we have **u** in OE. where we should regularly expect **o** (see § 23). This occurs especially before and after labials, as bucc (OHG. boc), *buck*; bucca, *he-goat*; fugol (OHG. fogal), *bird, fowl*; full (OHG. fol), *full*; furþor, *further*; furþum, *even*; lufian, *to love*; lufu, *love*; murcnian, *to murmur, grumble*; murnan, *to mourn*; spura beside spora, *spur*; spurnan beside spornan, *to kick*; ufan (OHG. obana), *above*; ufor, *higher*; wulf (OHG. wolf), *wolf*; wulle (OHG. wolla), *wool*; cnucian beside cnocian, *to knock*; scurf, *scurf*; turf, *turf*.

8. Monophthongization (Smoothing).

§ 67. Under certain conditions the diphthongs ĕo, ĭo, and ĕa were smoothed to monophthongs during the OE. period, and the diphthong ĭe was always smoothed to ĭ (y̆):—

The diphthongs eo, io before h + dental and x (= hs), when not followed by a guttural vowel, became ie at an earlier period— before the time of Alfred—and then later the ie became i (rarely y), as cneoht, cnieht, cniht, *boy*; reoht, rieht, riht (ryht), *right*; seox, siex, six, *six*; Pihtisc, *Pictish*; Wioht, Wieht, Wiht (Wyht), *Wight*; gewihte (gewyhte), *weight*; stiht(i)an, *to arrange*; but regularly cneohtas, *boys*; Peohtas, *Picts*; feohtan, *to fight*. Then levelling out often took place in both directions, whence cnihtas, Pihtas beside the regular forms cneohtas, Peohtas; and cneoht, gefeoht, *fight*, beside the regular forms cniht, gefiht.

ea became e in late WS. through the intermediate stage æ before h + consonant (also x = hs) and simple h, as ehta, *eight*, wexan, *to grow*, seh, *he saw* = early WS. eahta, weaxan, seah (§ 51), and after initial palatal c-, g-, sc-, as celf, *calf*, gef, *he gave*, scelt, *thou shalt* = early WS. cealf, geaf, scealt (§ 56).

ēa became ē in late WS. through the intermediate stage ǣ before c, g, h, and also after initial palatal c-, g-, sc-, when not followed by a guttural vowel in the next syllable, as bēcen, *beacon*, bēg, *ring, bracelet*, hēh, *high* = early WS. bēacen, bēag, hēah; cēp, *cheap*, gēt, *he poured out*, scēt, *he shot* = early WS. cēap, gēat, scēat; cēce, *jaw*, gēr, *year*, scēp, *sheep* = early WS. cēace, gēar, scēap; but regularly pl. gen. and dat. gēara, gēarum (§ 56).

ĭe, of whatever origin, became ĭ, ў in early WS., although the ĭe was often retained in writing, and in the ninth century ĭe was sometimes written for old ĭ, which shows that the two sounds had fallen together, see § 57, note 3. Before certain consonants, especially before c, g, h, old ў (§ 57) also became ī at an early period in some parts of the WS. area, although the ў beside ĭ was preserved in writing even in late WS., and then ў also came to be written for ĭ from older ĭe :—

ie > i, y, as ildu, *old age*; irfe, yrfe, *inheritance*; miht, *power, might*; niht, *night*; hlihhan, *to laugh*; cile, cyle, *cold*; scippan, *to create*; hirde, hyrde, *shepherd* (§ 57).

ie > ī, ў, as hīran, hȳran, *to hear*; nīd, nȳd, *need* (§ 57); līhtan, lȳhtan, *to give light* (§ 24).

NOTE.—1. In Anglian the diphthongs ĕa, ĕo, ĭo were smoothed to the monophthongs ǣ (later æ (e), ē), ĕ, ĭ before c, g, h; liquid + c, g, or h; hh, ht, and x (= older hs) :—

ea became æ, which remained in the oldest glosses, and then later became e before r + c, g, or h, as sæh, *he saw*, hlæhha(n), *to laugh*, fæht, *he fought*, mæht, *power, might*, wæxan, *to grow* = WS. seah, hliehhan (§ 57), feaht, weaxan (§ 51); ærc, *ark*, mærg, *marrow*, færh, *boar, pig* = later erc, merg, ferh = WS. earc, mearg, fearh (§ 51). æ beside ea occurs after initial palatal c-, g-, sc-, as cæster, ceaster, *city, fortress*; gæt, geat, *gate*; scæl, sceal, *shall* (§ 56).

eo became e, as seh, *see thou*, werc, *work*, dwerg, *dwarf*, ferh, *life*, selh, *seal*, fehta(n), *to fight*, sex, *six* = early WS. seoh, weorc, dweorg, feorh, seolh, feohtan, seox (§ 52).

io became i, as milc from miolc, older mioluc, *milk* (§ 59. 1); birce, *birch-tree*, gebirhta(n), *to make bright*, rihta(n), *to set straight*, getihhia(n), *to arrange, think, consider*, mixen, *dunghill* = WS. bierce, gebierhtan, riehtan (§ 57), getiohhian (§ 53), mioxen, meoxen (cp. § 53).

ēa became ǣ later ē before c, g, h, as bǣcen, *beacon*, lǣc, *leek*, ǣge, *eye*, bǣg, *ring, bracelet*, hēh, *high*, tēh, *he drew*, later bēcen, lēc, ēge, bēg, hēh, tēh = WS. bēacen, &c. (§ 42).

The i-umlaut of ēa also became ē in the non-WS. dialects, as gelēfan, *to believe*, hēran, *to hear*, nēd, *need* = early WS. gelīefan, hīeran, nīed.

ēo (Nth. ēa, § 43, note 2) became ē before c, g, h and ht, as rēca(n), *to smoke*, sēc, *sick*, flēga(n), *to fly*, lēga(n), *to lie*, þēh, *thigh*, tēh, *draw thou*, lēht, *a light* = WS. rēocan, sēoc, &c.

īo became ī before c, h, ht, as līh, *lend thou* = WS. līoh, lēoh (§ 55); gelīhta(n) = WS. līehtan, *to lighten, make easier* (§ 57); cīcen, older *kīoken from *kiukīn, *chicken*; līhta(n) = WS. līehtan, *to give light* (§ 24).

2. Early Mercian ē, of whatever origin, became ī before ht, hs in late Mercian, as līht older lēht = WS. lēoht, *a light*; līht = WS. lēoht, adj. *light*; nīhsta = WS. nīehst(a), *nearest*.

3. Late Ken. has ĕ for WS. ĭe, as eldra, *older*, felþ, *he falls*, erfe, *inheritance*, slehþ, *he slays* = WS. ieldra, fielþ, ierfe, sliehþ (§ 57); hēran = WS. hīeran, *to hear*.

4. eo, io became i in late Ken., as riht older reoht; Wiht older Wioht, *Wight*.

5. For the monophthongization of eo, io in the initial combinations weo-, wio-, see § 63.

9. VOWEL CONTRACTION.

§ 68. Vowel contraction chiefly took place in OE. when an intervocalic h, w, or j had disappeared.

A long vowel or diphthong absorbed a following short vowel, and when the diphthong was short it became lengthened thereby, as rā beside rāha, *roe*; pl. tān from *tāhan, *toes*; tā older *tāhæ, *toe*; gǣst from *ʒǣ-is older *ʒā-is, *thou goest*; gǣþ from *ʒǣ-iþ, *he goes*; gen. sǣs from *sǣ-es older *sāwis beside nom. sǣ, *sea* (§ 57); dēst from *dō-is, *thou doest*; dēþ from *dō-iþ, *he does*; gen. drȳs from *drȳæs beside nom. drȳ, *magician*; fōn from *fōhan, *to seize*; fō from *fōhu, *I seize*; pl. scōs from *scōhas, beside sing. scōh, *shoe*; dat. pl. þrūm from *þrūhum beside nom. sing. þrūh, *trough*. ēa from *eahu, *water*; ēar from *eahur, *ear of corn*; slēan from *sleahan, *to slay*; slēa from *sleahu, *I slay* (§ 51); sēon from *seohan, *to see*; sēo from *seohu, *I see*; gen. fēos from *feohæs beside nom. feoh, *cattle*; **swēor** from **sweohur*, *father-in-law*. **nēar** from **nēahur*, *nearer*; gen. **hēas** from **hēahæs*: nom. **hēah**, *high*. **tēon** from **tēohan*, *to draw, lead*; **tēo** from **tēohu*, *I draw, lead*; **rēon** from **rēo(w)un**, *they rowed*; **līon, lēon** from **līohan* older **līhan*, *to lend*; **lēo** from **līohu*, *I lend*.

§ 69. **a + u** (from older **wu** or vocalized **w**) became **ēa**, as **clēa** from **cla(w)u*, *claw*; neut. pl. **fēa** from **fa(w)u*, *few*; **strēa** from **straw-*, *straw*.

e + u (from **w**) became **ēo**, as **cnēo** from **cnew(a)-*, *knee*; **trēo** from **trew(a)-*, *tree*.

i or **ij + guttural vowel** became **īo (ēo)**, as **bīo, bēo** (OHG. **bīa**, Germanic stem-form **bijōn-*), *bee*; **fīond, fēond** (Goth. **fijands**), *enemy*; **frīond, frēond** (Goth. **frijōnds**), *friend*; nom. acc. neut. **þrīo, þrēo** from **þri(j)u* = Goth. **þrija**, *three*; **hīo, hēo** from **hi + u*, *she*.

NOTE.—Special Anglian contractions are:—

æ + æ > ǣ, as **slǣ** from **slæhæ* older **sleahæ*, *I may slay*.

e + æ > ē, as **gesē** from **-sehæ* older **-seohæ*, *I may see*.

ē + i > ē, as **nēst(a)** from **nēhist(a)* = WS. **nīehst(a)**, *nearest*.

ĭ + i > ī, as **sīs(t)** from **sihis* = WS. **siehst**, *thou seest*; **sīþ** from **sihiþ* = WS. **siehþ**, *he sees*; **tīþ** from **tihiþ* = WS. **tiehþ**, *he draws, leads*.

Nth. **a + a > ā**, as **slā** from **slaha(n)*, *to slay*; **þwā** from **þwaha(n)*, *to wash*.

10. THE LENGTHENING OF SHORT VOWELS.

§ 70. From our knowledge of ME. phonology it is clear that short vowels must have been lengthened some time during the OE. period before certain consonant combinations, especially before a liquid or nasal + another voiced consonant. But it is impossible to ascertain the date at which these lengthenings took place, and whether they took place in all the dialects at the same time.

§ 71. Final short vowels were lengthened in monosyllables, as **hwā** (Goth. **ƕas**), *who*; **swā** (Goth. **swa**), *so*; **hē**, *he*; **mē**, *me*; **wē**, *we*.

§ 72. Short vowels were lengthened through the loss of **g**

before a following consonant, as **mæden**, *maiden*, **sæde**, *he said*,
wæn, *wagon*, beside older **mægden**, **sægde**, **wægn**; **brēdan**, *to
brandish*, **rēn**, *rain*, beside older **bregdan**, **regn**; **brīdel**, *bridle*,
frīnan, *to ask*, **sīþe**, *scythe*, beside older **brigdel**, **frignan**, **sigþe**;
brōden beside older **brogden**, *brandished*, *woven*.

§ 73. By the loss of a nasal before a following voiceless
spirant, as **ōþer** (Goth. anþar), *other* ; **gōs** (OHG. gans), *goose* ;
sōfte (OHG. samfto), *softly* ; **fīf** (Goth. fimf), *five* ; **swīþ** (Goth.
swinþs), *strong* ; **cūþ** (Goth. kunþs), *known* ; **fūs** (OHG. funs),
ready, eager for. See § 50.

§ 74. By the loss of h after l, r, before a following vowel, as
gen. **hōles** beside nom. **holh**, *hollow* ; pl. gen. **sūla**, dat. **sūlum**,
beside nom. sing. **sulh**, *plough*; gen. sing. **fūre**, pl. gen. **fūra**,
dat. **fūrum**, beside nom. sing. **furh**, *furrow*. See § 76.

§ 75. Short diphthongs were lengthened by the loss of intervocalic h, as **slēan** from *sleahan (Goth. slahan), *to slay* ; **sēon**
from *seohan (OHG. sehan), *to see*. See § 68.

§ 76. By the loss of antevocalic h after l and r, as gen.
sēales, **wēales**, **fēares**, **mēares**, beside nom. **sealh**, *seal*, **wealh**,
foreigner, **fearh**, *boar*, *pig*, **mearh**, *horse* ; gen. **sēoles**, **fēores**,
beside nom. **seolh**, *seal*, **feorh**, *life*; **fēolan** from *feolhan
(Goth. filhan), *to hide*. See § 74.

11. THE SHORTENING OF LONG VOWELS.

§ 77. Long vowels were shortened during the OE. period
before two consonants in polysyllabic forms, before combinations
of three consonants, and before double consonants, as **enlefan**
from older *ǣnlefan, *eleven* ; **samcucu** (from *sāmi-, older
sǣmi- = OHG. sāmi-), *half-dead*; **bledsian**, **bletsian** from
*blōdisōjan, *to bless*. Pl. **bremblas** beside sing. **brēm(b)el**,
bramble. **bliss**, *joy*, **hlammæsse**, *Lammas*, **wimman**, *woman*,
beside older **blīþs**, **hlāfmæsse**, **wīfman**; **blæddre**, *bladder*,
deoppra, *deeper*, beside older **blǣdre**, **dēopra**, see § 146.

§ 78. In the first or second elements of compounds which
were no longer felt as such, as **siþþan**, **sioþþan** from **sīþ + þan**,

since; ēorod from eoh + rād, *troop of cavalry*. Adjectives ending in -lic (= OHG. -līh), as dēadlic, *deadly*.

12. THE FORMATION OF NEW DIPHTHONGS.

§ 79. OE. had far more words containing a diphthong than any other Germanic language. Besides those which were regularly developed from the prim. Germanic diphthongs (§§ 41-4), it also had a large number of words with new diphthongs due to sound-laws which operated at various periods of the language, such as breaking (§ 51), the influence of initial palatal consonants (§ 56), umlaut (§ 59), and vowel contraction (§§ 68-9). The OE. diphthongs which arose from the prim. Germanic diphthongs and those which were due to the above sound-laws were what are called impure diphthongs, i. e. the second element was an a, e, or o, but a number of pure diphthongs and triphthongs also arose, medially before consonants and finally, whose second element was an i or u (generally written w). The i-diphthongs mostly arose from the vocalization of palatal g after a palatal vowel with which it combined to form a diphthong, as late WS. dæi, dæig (Ken. dei), *day*, wei, weig (Ken. wei), *way* beside older dæg (Ken. deg), weg; Nth. Ken. meiden, beside older megden (WS. mægden), *girl*; late WS. Ken. þein, Nth. þeign beside older þegn, *servant*; Ken. grēi (WS. græg), *grey*; Nth. cēiga (WS. cīegan), *to call*. Regular forms with u-diphthongs and triphthongs are: gen. sāwle, sāule (Goth. sáiwalōs) beside nom. sāwol, *soul*; slǣwþ, Ken. slēuþ, *sloth*; WS. cnǣwþ from cnǣweþ, older *cnāwiþ, *he knows*; and similarly flēwþ, *it flows*; meowle (Goth. mawilō), *girl*; masc. nom. acc. pl. neowle beside nom. sing. neowol, *low, deep down*. New u-diphthongs and triphthongs often also arose from the levelling out of w into the uninflected from the inflected forms (§ 149), as snāw beside sna, *snow*, with w-from snāwes, &c.; and similarly stōw, stōu, *place*; mǣw, mēu, mēaw, *seagull*; dēaw, *dew*; strēaw, *straw*; cnēow, *knee*; þēow, *servant*; WS. hīew, hīw beside non-WS. hīow, hēow, *shape, colour*.

CHAPTER IV

THE OE. DEVELOPMENT OF THE PRIMITIVE GERMANIC VOWELS OF UNACCENTED SYLLABLES

§ 80. In the Germanic languages as in all the other languages which had predominantly stress accent, the Indg. vowels underwent far more changes in unaccented than in accented syllables. In final syllables there was a great tendency in all these languages for short vowels to disappear, for long vowels to become shortened, and then partly to disappear, and for diphthongs, whether originally short or long, to become monophthongs, and then to become shortened. These changes took place partly in prim. Germanic, and partly in the prehistoric and historic periods of the separate languages.

Before beginning, however, with the history of the Indg. vowels in final syllables, it is necessary to state what became of the Indg. consonants in final syllables, because the vowels which were originally final, and those which became final in prim. Germanic through the loss of final consonants, generally had the same fate:—

1. Indg. final -m became -n in prim. Germanic. This -n remained after a short accented vowel, and when protected by a particle, as Goth. ƕan, OS. hwan = Lat. quom, *when*; OE. þan, þon, Goth. þan = Lat. tum, *then*; masc. acc. sing. OE. þon-e, late OE. þæn-, þan-e, Goth. þan-a, *the, that* = Skr. tám, Gr. τόν, Lat. tum in is-tum, but in all other forms it, as also Indg. final -n, disappeared in prim. Germanic with nasalization of the preceding vowel. And then during the prim. Germanic period, the short nasalized vowels became oral again, but the long nasalized vowels remained, and only became oral again in the separate languages. The oldest Norse runic inscriptions preserved the short vowels which became final through the loss of a final nasal, but in Goth. O.Icel. and the

West Germanic languages they underwent the same treatment as short vowels which were originally final, as acc. sing. staina = OE. stān, Goth. stáin, O.Icel. OHG. stein, OS. stēn, *stone*; acc. sing. OE. Goth. OS. wulf, O.Icel. ūlf, OHG. wolf = Lat. lupum, Gr. λύκον, *wolf*, see § 84. Acc. sing. of ō-stems, as OE. giefe, Goth. giba, OS. OHG. geba, *gift*, prim. Germanic *ǥeƀō (with nasalized -ō), older -ōn, -ōm = Indg. -ām; gen. pl. OE. O.Icel. daga, OS. dago, OHG. tago, *of days*, prim. Germanic *đaʒõ, (with nasalized -õ), older -õn, -õm = Indg. -õm; and similarly in the gen. pl. of all nouns, adjectives, and pronouns.

2. The Indg. final explosives (t, d) disappeared in prim. Germanic, except after a short accented vowel in monosyllables, and then the vowels which became final underwent the same treatment as original final vowels, as OE. wile, Goth. OS. OHG. wili from *welit, *he will* = O.Lat. velit; OE. O.Icel. OS. OHG. bere, Goth. baírái = Skr. bhárēt, *he may bear*; OE. bǣron, Goth. bērun from an original form *bhērnt, *they bore* (§ 17); but OE. hwæt, O.Icel. hvat, OS. hwat = Lat. quod, *what*; OE. æt, Goth. O.Icel. OS. at = Lat. ad, *at*.

3. Prim. Germanic final -z, which arose from Indg. -s by Verner's law (§ 115), disappeared in the West Germanic languages, but became -r in O.Icel., and -s again in Goth., as OE. dæg, OS. dag, OHG. tag, O.Icel. dagr, Goth. dags, from prim. Germanic *đaȝaz, *day*. Prim. Germanic final -nz disappeared in prim. ON. and West Germanic, as acc. pl. O.Icel. daga, OHG. taga = Goth. dagans, *days*; O.Icel. geste, OS. OHG. gesti = Goth. gastins, *guests*.

4. Indg. final -r remained in prim. Germanic and also in the separate languages, as OE. fæder, Goth. fadar, O.Icel. faðer, OS. fadar, OHG. fater = Lat. pater, Gr. πατήρ, *father*.

NOTE.—The treatment of the Indg. final consonants in prim. Germanic may be stated in general terms thus:—With the exception of -s and -r all Indg. final consonants disappeared in prim. Germanic. In the case of the explosives it cannot be determined whether they had or had not undergone the first sound-shifting (§ 108).

1. The Short Vowels.

§ 81. Indg. final -a, -o (= prim. Germanic a, § 17), and -e disappeared in prim. Germanic, as OE. wāt, Goth. wáit, O.Icel. veit, OS. wēt = Gr. οἶδα, *I know*; OE. æf, *of*, Goth. O.Icel. OS. af = Gr. ἄπο, *of, from, away from*; gen. sing. OE. dæges, older dægæs, Goth. dagis, *of a day*, from early prim. Germanic *đaȝasa, *đaȝesa, Indg. -oso, -eso, cp. O. Bulgarian česo = Goth. ƕis, *whose*; voc. sing. OE. Goth. wulf = Lat. lupe, Gr. λύκε, *wolf*; imperative OE. O.Icel. ber, Goth. baír = Gr. φέρε, *bear thou*; OE. fīf, Goth. fimf = Gr. πέντε, *five*.

§ 82. Indg. final -i, and prim. Germanic -u from older -un, -um = Indg. vocalic -m (§ 17) disappeared during the prim. Germanic period in words of more than two syllables, as OE. bir(e)þ, Goth. baíriþ, Indg. *bhéreti, *he bears*; OE. beraþ, Goth. baírand = Gr. Dor. φέροντι, *they bear*; acc. sing. OE. Goth. guman, from *ȝumanu(n) = Lat. hominem, *man*.

§ 83. Indg. final -i and -u remained in prim. Germanic in dissyllabic words, but in the West Germanic languages they disappeared after long, but remained after short stem-syllables, as voc. sing. OE. giest, Goth. gast, from *ȝasti : nom. *ȝastiz, *guest*; OE. dat. sing. dehter, fēt, from *dohtri, *fōti : nom. sing. dohtor, *daughter*, fōt, *foot*; but OE. mere (masc.), older meri, OHG. meri (neut.) = Lat. mare from *mari, *sea*. Voc. sing. OE. hand, OHG. hant, beside Goth. handu : nom. handus, *hand*; but OS. OHG. fihu, Goth. faíhu = Lat. pecu, *cattle*.

§ 84. Prim. Germanic short vowels in final syllables followed by -z or -n (§ 80) underwent in OE. the same treatment as the original final short vowels, as nom. sing. dæg, *day*, giest, *guest*, stede, *place*, hand, hond, *hand*, sunu, *son* = prim. Germanic *đaȝaz, *ȝastiz, *stađiz, *ȝanduz, *sunuz; acc. sing. OE. dæg, giest, stede, hand, hond, sunu = prim. Germanic *đaȝa(n), *ȝasti(n), *stađi(n), *ȝandu(n), *sunu(n); acc. sing. OE. fōt, Goth. fōtu, prim. Germanic *fōtu(n), cp. Gr. πόδα, *foot* (§ 17).

Gen. sing. of consonantal stems, Indg. -es = prim. Germanic -iz (§ 21), as bēc from *bōkiz, *of a book*; nom. pl. of masc. and fem. consonantal stems, as fēt from *fōtiz, cp. Gr. πόδες, *feet*; **hanan** from *χananiz, *cocks*, cp. Gr. ποιμένες, *shepherds*.

NOTE.—The final -i, which remained in the oldest period of the language, regularly became -e in the seventh century. And final -u became -o at an early period, and then in late OE. -a, whence forms like nom. acc. sing. **sunu, suno, suna,** *son*.

2. THE LONG VOWELS.

§ **85.** The Indg. final long vowels, and those which became final in prim. Germanic through the loss of a final dental consonant (§ 80. 2), were shortened in the prehistoric period of all the languages, when they originally had the 'broken' (acute) accent, but remained unshortened in Gothic when they originally had the 'slurred' (circumflex) accent, see § 15, note 3. In this manner prim. Germanic -ō (= Indg. -ā and -ō), -ǣ (= Indg. ē), and -ī became -a, -a, -i in Goth., and -u, -e, -i in prim. OE., and then the -u and -i underwent the same treatment in OE. as original final -u and -i (§ 83); and Indg. -õ with the 'slurred' (circumflex) accent became -ō in Goth. and -a in OE. The regular operation of this law was often disturbed by analogical formations which will be dealt with in the accidence :—

1. Prim. Germanic -ō (= Indg. -ā and -ō), as Goth. **bōta**, OE. **bōt**, *remedy, advantage*, cp. Gr. χώρα, *land*; Goth. **giba**, OE. **giefu**, *gift*; neut. nom. acc. pl. Goth. **waúrda**, OE. **word**, *words*; Goth. **juka**, OE. **geocu** = O.Lat. **jugā**, *yokes*; Goth. **baíra**, OE. (Anglian) **beru** = Lat. **ferō**, *I bear*; Goth. **hilpa**, OE. (Anglian) **helpu** for *help with the -u restored after the analogy of the verbs with a short stem-syllable.

The -u from older -ō also disappeared in trisyllabic forms after a long medial syllable, as **leornung** from *lirnungu, *learning*; **ǣfnung**, *evening* (§ 218); masc. and neut. dat. sing. **blindum** = Goth. **blindamma**, *blind*. It also disappeared when the stem and medial syllable were short, but remained when the stem-syllable was long and the medial syllable short, as byden from *budinu, *tub*; pl. receed from *rakidu, *halls*; neut. pl. yfel from *ubilu, *evil*; but fem. nom. sing. hāligu, *holy*; hēafodu, *heads*.

2. Prim. Germanic -ǣ (= Indg. ē), as pret. sing. Goth. nasida, OE. nerede, prim. Germanic *nazidǣ(t), *he saved*.

3. Prim. Germanic -ī, as Goth. bandi, OE. bend, *band*, cp. Skr. dēvī́, *goddess*; imperative OE. sēc from *sōkī, *seek thou*; nere from *nazī, *save thou* (= Indg. -eje); Goth. wili, OE. wili, later wile, from older *wilī, *he will* = O.Lat. velīt, later velit.

Prim. Germanic -ī (= Indg. -ei, § 17), the ending of the dat. (originally loc.) sing. of i-stems, as OE. stede, older stedi (OHG. steti), from *stadī, *to a place*; but cwēne for *cwēn (§ 236).

4. Prim. Germanic -ō̃ from Indg. -ō̃d, as Goth. unwēniggō, OE. unwēnunga, *unexpectedly*, cp. O.Lat. meritōd, *deservedly, justly*; OE. ednīwunga, *anew*; fǣrunga, *quickly*.

§ 86. Indg. -ā̃s, -õ̃s with the 'slurred' (circumflex) accent = prim. Germanic -ō̃z, became -ōs in Goth. and -e in OE., as gen. sing. of the ō-stems, Goth. gibōs, OE. giefe, from *ʒebṍz, *of a gift*, cp. Gr. θεᾶς, *of a goddess*; nom. pl. Goth. gibōs, OE. (Anglian) giefe, *gifts*; nom. pl. of a-stems, Goth. dagōs, *days* (for OE. dagas, see § 180, note).

§ 87. The ending of the nom. pl. of i-stems, prim. Germanic -īz from -ij(i)z (= Indg. -ejes, cp. Lat. hostēs from *hostejes, *enemies*), became -eis (= īs) in Goth. and -i (later -e) in OE., as masc. Goth. stadeis, OE. stede, *places*; fem. Goth. ansteis, OE. ēste, *favours*.

§ 88. In dealing with long vowels originally followed by a nasal (§ 80. 1) it is necessary to distinguish between long vowels which originally had the 'broken' (acute) accent, and those which originally had the 'slurred' (circumflex accent):—

1. Early prim. Germanic -ōm (-ōn) (= Indg. -ām and -ōm), later nasalized -ō̃ (§ 80. 1), became -a in Goth. and -e in OE., as acc. sing. of ō-stems, Goth. giba, OE. giefe, from *ʒebō̃m,

-ōn, *gift*, cp. Gr. χώρᾱν, *land*; pret. sing. Goth. nasida, OE. nerede, from early prim. Germanic *naziđōm, -ōn, *I saved*.

2. The ending of the gen. plural of all classes of nouns and adjectives and of such pronouns as had a gen. plural, early prim. Germanic -ŏ̃m, -ŏ̃n (= Indg. -ŏ̃m) became -ō in Goth. and -a in OE., as Goth. gibō, OE. giefa from an original form *ghebhŏ̃m, *of gifts*, cp. Gr. ποδῶν, *of feet*; adj. Goth. fem. blindáizō, OE. blindra, *of blind*; gen. pl. Goth. fem. þizō for *þáizō, OE. þāra, *of the, that*.

3. In Indg. the nom. sing. of n-stems ended partly in -ōn, -ēn and partly in -ŏ̃, -ĕ̃. The various Indg. languages generalized one or other of the two formations, e.g. Gr. generalized the former, and Skr. and Lat. the latter, as nom. sing. ἡγεμών, *leader*; ποιμήν, *shepherd*, beside Skr. rā́jā, *king*; Lat. sermō, *discourse*. The two types of nominative endings existed side by side in prim. Germanic, but in the prehistoric period of the separate languages -ōn (= Goth. -a, OE. -e) became restricted to the feminine and neuter in OE., but to the masculine in Goth., whereas -ŏ̃ (= Goth. -ō, OE. -a) became restricted to the masculine in OE. and to the feminine and neuter in Goth., as fem. OE. tunge, beside Goth. tuggō, *tongue*; neut. OE. ēage, beside Goth. áugō, *eye*; masc. OE. hana, beside Goth. hana, *cock*.

3. THE DIPHTHONGS.

§ 89. The Indg. long diphthongs -āi (-ā̃i), -ōi (-ŏ̃i); -ōu were shortened to -ai; au in prim. Germanic, and then underwent the same further development as prim. Germanic -ai; -au from Indg. -ai, -oi; -au, -ou. The -ai, -au remained in Goth., but became -ǣ, -ō in prim. West Germanic. Then -ǣ, -ō became -e (older -æ), -a in OE.

1. Prim. Germanic -ai, as dat. sing. Goth. gibái, OE. giefe, Indg. *ghebhā̃i, *to a gift*, cp. Gr. θεᾷ, *to a goddess*; dat. sing. dǣge from *đaɣai, older -oi or -ŏ̃i, cp. Gr. loc. οἴκοι, *at home*, dat. θεῷ (Indg. -ŏ̃i), *to a god*; nom. pl. masc. Goth. blindái,

OE. blinde, *blind*, cp. Gr. σοφοί, *wise*; Goth. baírái, OE. bere, *he may bear*, Indg. optative *bhéroĭt.

2. Prim. Germanic -au, as Goth. ahtáu, OE. eahta, Indg. *októu, *eight*; Goth. aíþþáu, OE. eþþa, *or*.

Prim. Germanic -au (= Indg. -ēu), the ending of the dat. (originally loc.) sing. of u-stems, as Goth. sunáu, OE. suna, *to a son*.

§ 90. -eĭs, -oĭs, the Indg. ending of the gen. sing. of i-stems, and -eŭs, -oŭs, the Indg. ending of the gen. sing. of u-stems, became -áis, -áus in Goth. and -e, -a in OE., as Goth. anstáis, OE. ēste, *of a favour*; Goth. sunáus, OE. suna, *of a son*.

SUMMARY.

§ 91. Now that we have traced the history of the Indg. vowels of final syllables in prim. Germanic, Gothic, and Old English, the result may be briefly summarized in the table on p. 51. The sign —, followed by a blank, denotes that the vowel regularly disappeared. From the table it will be seen that all the Indg. endings -i, -is, -im, -es, -ī, -ĭt, -ei became —, -i(e) in OE.; that -u, -us, -um, -m̥, -ā, -ō became —, -u; that -ŏ, -ŏd, -ŏm, -ēu, -ōu, -oŭs became -a; and that -ēt, -ām, -ōm, -ōn, -ãs, -õs, -ai, -oi, -ãi, -õi, -oĭs became -e.

THE VOWELS IN OE. FINAL SYLLABLES.

§ 92. Up to this point we have only dealt with the vowels which were originally final or which became final through the loss of final consonants in prim. Germanic. We shall now deal with the vowels which originally stood in medial syllables, but which came to stand in final syllables through the operation of the sound-laws formulated in the previous paragraphs.

a. *The Short Vowels.*

§ 93. 1. Indg. o remained longer in prim. Germanic in unaccented than in accented syllables (§ 17). During the prim. Germanic period it became a except before m. Before m

§ 91] *Vowels of Unaccented Syllables* 51

Indg.	P.G.	Goth.	OE.	Goth.	OE.
-a, -e, -o	—	—	—	wáit, baír,ƕis	wāt, ber, hwæs
-i	—, -i	—	—, -i(e)	baíriþ, gast, staþ	bir(e)þ, giest, stede
-u	-u	-u	—, -u	handu, sunu	hand, sunu
-os	-az	-s	—	dags, gen. gumins	dæg, gen. guman
-is	-iz	-s	—, -i(e)	gasts, staþs	giest, stede
-us	-uz	-us	—, -u	handus, sunus	hand, sunu
-om	-a(n)	—	—	dag	dæg
-im	-i(n)	—	—, -i(e)	anst, staþ	ēst, stede
-m̥, -um	—, u(n)	—, -u	—, -u	hanan, handu, sunu	hanan, hand, sunu
-es	-iz	-s	—, -i(e)	pl. hanans, baúrgs	hanan, byrg, hnyte
-ā, -ō	-ō	-a	—, -u	waúrda, giba	word, giefu
-ēt	-ǣ	-a	-e	nasida	nerede
-ī, īt	-ī	-i	—, -i(e)	bandi, wili	bend, wile
-ām, -ōm	-ō(n)	-a	-e	giba, nasida	giefe, nerede
-ōn	-ō(n)	-a	-e	guma	tunge, ēage
-ō̃, -ō̃d	-ō̃	-ō	-a	tuggō, unwēniggō	guma, unwēnunga
-ō̃m	-ō̃(n)	-ō	-a	gibō	giefa
-ā̃s, -ō̃s	-ō̃z	-ōs	-e	gibōs, dagōs	giefe
-oi	-ai	-ai	-e	blindái, baírái	blinde, bere, dæge
-ei	-ī		—, -i(e)		stede
-ēu	-au	-áu	-a	sunáu	suna
-ōu	-au	-áu	-a	ahtau	eahta
-ā̃i, ō̃i	-ai	-ái	-e	gibái	giefe, dæge
-oĩs	-aiz	-áis	-e	anstáis	ēste
-oũs	-auz	-áus	-a	sunáus	suna

it became a in Goth., but u in OE., as masc. and neut. dat. sing.
blindum = Goth. blindamma, *blind*; dat. pl. dagum = Goth.
dagam, from *daʒomiz, *to days*. Prim. Germanic a remained
before n, but became e (older æ) in other cases, and then later
the e became i before g, as inf. beran, *to bear*, from *ƀeranan,
older -onom; but gen. sing. dæges older dægæs, from prim.
Germanic *daʒas(a), *of a day*; huneg (OHG. honag), later
hunig, *honey*; maneg (Goth. manags), later manig, *many*.

2. Indg. e remained when not originally followed by a
palatal vowel in the next syllable, as pp. bunden, from -enaz,
bound; hwæþer = Gr. πότερος, *which of two*.

3. Prim. Germanic i remained before palatal consonants,
as englisc, *English*; ūsic, *us*; but in other cases it became e
in the seventh century, as pp. ge-nered = Goth. nasiþs, from
*naziđaz, *saved*; Anglian birest, *thou bearest*, bireþ, *he bears* =
Goth. baíris, baíriþ, WS. Ken. birst, birþ with syncope of
the e.

4. Prim. Germanic u remained before m, but became o at an
early period in other cases, as dat. pl. sunum = Goth. sunum,
to sons; but bǣron older bǣrun = Goth. bērun, *they bore*.

b. *The Long Vowels.*

§ 94. All long vowels underwent shortening in prehistoric
OE.:—

1. ǣ became e, as pret. neredes(t) (older -dæs) from *nazi-
đǣs = Goth. nasidēs, *thou didst save*.

2. ī became i, later e (except before palatal consonants), as
gylden (OHG. guldīn), *golden*; bǣren (OHG. bārīn), *they
might bear*; mihtig (OHG. mahtīg), *mighty*; gōdlic, *goodly*,
beside the stressed form gelīc, *like*.

3. ō became u, which remained before m, but became later
o, a in other cases, as heardost, from -ōst-, *hardest*; sealfaþ =
Goth. salbōþ, *he anoints*; pp. sealfud, -od, -ad = Goth. salbōþs,
anointed; mōnaþ = Goth. mēnōþs, *month*; but always u before

m, as dat. pl. giefum, *to gifts*, tungum, *to tongues* = Goth. gibōm, tuggōm. -ōj- became -i- through the intermediate stages -ēj-, -ej-, -ij-, as sealfian from *salbōjan, *to anoint*; -ōþ from older -anþ, -onþ (§ 50) = Indg. -onti, as beraþ = Gr. Dor. φέροντι, *they bear*.

4. ū became u (later o, a), as fracuþ, -oþ, from *frakunþaz, *wicked* = Goth. frakunþs, *despised*; duguþ from *ðuȝunþ = OHG. tugunt, *valour, strength*.

c. The Diphthongs.

§ 95. The only diphthong concerned is prim. Germanic ai, which remained in Goth., but became e in OE., as binden, Goth. bindáina, *they may bind*.

§ 96. When a nasal or a liquid, preceded by a mute consonant, came to stand finally after the loss of a short vowel (§ 84), it became vocalic, and remained as such in Goth., but in prehistoric OE. a new vowel was generated before it. The vowel thus generated was generally e when the preceding vowel was palatal, but o (u), later also e, when the preceding vowel was guttural, as nom. efen from *ebnaz = Goth. ibns, *even*; nom. acc. æcer from *akr, older *akraz, *akran = Goth. akrs, akr, *field*; nom. acc. fugul, -ol, from *fugl, older *foglaz, *foglan (§ 66) = Goth. fugls, fugl, *bird, fowl*; nom. acc. māþum from *maiþm, older *maiþmaz, *maiþman = Goth. máiþms, máiþm, *gift*; hlūtor = Goth. hlūtrs, *pure, clean*; neut. nom. acc. pl. prim. Germanic *tuŋglō, *stars*, which regularly became *tungl in prim. OE. through the intermediate stage *tunglu (§ 85. 1), and then later tungol; and similarly neut. plurals like morþor, *murders*; wæpen, *weapons*. In OE. the vowel was often levelled out into the inflected forms, and conversely the consonantal l, m, n, r, especially l, m, n, of the inflected forms, were often levelled out into the uninflected form, and then became vocalic again, as gen. æceres beside the regular form æcres; efn, māþm beside the regular forms efen, māþum.

The Vowels in OE. Medial Syllables.

§ 97. Original short medial vowels regularly remained in trisyllabic forms:—

1. After short open stem-syllables, as æþele, *noble*; gen. sing. heofones, wæteres, beside nom. heofon, *heaven*, wæter, *water*; neredest from *naziđēs, *thou didst save*; pp. gen. sing. generedes, nom. pl. ge-nerede beside nom. sing. ge-nered from *-naziđaz.

2. In closed syllables irrespectively as to whether the stem-syllable was long or short, as gen. sing. cyninges, fǣtelses, beside nom. cyning, *king*, fǣtels, *tub*; pres. participle nimende, *taking*; ieldest(a), *oldest*.

3. After consonant combinations, when preceded by a closed stem-syllable, or a stem-syllable containing a long vowel or long diphthong, as pret. hyngrede, timbrede, frēfrede, dīeglede, pp. gen. sing. gehyngredes, getimbredes, gefrēfredes, gedīegledes, beside inf. hyngran, *to hunger*, timbran, *to build*, frēfran, *to comfort*, dīeglan, *to conceal*.

§ 98. Medial short vowels regularly disappeared in open syllables when the stem-syllable was long, as gen. sing. engles, hālges, hēafdes, beside nom. engel, *angel*, hālig, *holy*, hēafod, *head*; gen. dat. sing. mōnþe, sāwle, beside nom. mōnaþ, *month*, sāwol, *soul*; ieldra = Goth. alþiza, *older*; dǣldest = Goth. dáilidēs, *thou didst divide*; hīerdest = Goth. háusidēs, *thou didst hear*; pp. gen. sing. gedǣldes, gehīerdes, nom. pl. gedǣlde, gehīerde, beside nom. sing. gedǣled, gehīered.

§ 99. Original long vowels in medial syllables underwent the same shortening as those which came to stand in final syllables after the operation of the sound-laws formulated in §§ 80–90, as sealfude, later -ode, -ade = Goth. salbōda, *I anointed*; superlative weak decl. earmosta = Goth. armōsta, *poorest*. See § 101, note 3.

§ 100. Short medial guttural vowels, followed by a guttural vowel in the next syllable, often became e by dissimilation, as **hafela**, *head*, beside **hafola**; **gaderian** from *γaðurōjan, *to gather*; pl. nom. **heofenas**, gen. **heofena**, dat. **heofenum**, beside sing. gen. **heofones**, dat. **heofone**, nom. **heofon**, *heaven*; pret. pl. **sealfedon** (OHG. **salbōtun**), *they anointed*, beside sing. **sealfode** (OHG. **salbōta**), *he anointed*.

§ 101. Syncope of one or more vowels generally took place in forms which were originally polysyllabic. In polysyllabic just as in trisyllabic forms, syncope only took place in open syllables. The question as to which of the two medial vowels was syncopated depended upon the vowel in the final syllable. When the vowel in the final syllable regularly disappeared, the vowel in the first medial syllable was syncopated, as pp. masc. and neut. dat. sing. **bundnum** = Goth. **bundanamma**, *bound*; masc. and neut. dat. sing. **hālgum**, *holy*. When the vowel in the final syllable regularly remained, the vowel in the second medial syllable was syncopated, as pp. masc. acc. sing. **generedne** = Goth. **nasidana**, from *-naziðanō(n); masc. acc. sing. **hāligne**, *holy*, **ōþerne**, *other*; but fem. dat. sing. **gaderunge**, *to an assembly*, with retention of u through being in a closed syllable.

NOTE.—1. There are many exceptions to the above sound-laws, which are due to analogical formations. Thus forms like masc. and neut. gen. sing. **micles**, dat. **miclum**, *great*; **yfles**, **yflum**, beside **yfeles**, **yfelum**, *evil*; gen. pl. **glædra**, *glad*, were made on analogy with forms having a long stem-syllable. And forms like gen. sing. **dēofoles** (nom. **dēofol**, *devil*), **hāliges**, *holy*, beside older **dēofles**, **hālges**, were made on analogy with forms having a short stem-syllable.

2. In late OE. syncope often took place after short stems, and sometimes in closed syllables, as **betra**, *better*, **fægnian**, *to rejoice*, **gadrian**, *to gather*, beside older **betera**, **fægenian**, **gaderian**; **betsta** beside older **betesta**, *best*.

3. Original long medial vowels, which were shortened at an early period, were syncopated in trisyllabic forms, but remained when the shortening took place at a later period, as dat. sing. **mōnþe** beside nom. **mōnaþ** (Goth. **mēnōþs**), *month*; but **lōcodest** from *lōkōdǣs, *thou didst look*.

SVARABHAKTI VOWELS.

§ 102. In OE., especially in the later period, a svarabhakti vowel was often developed between r or l+c, g, or h; and between r, l, d, or t+w. In the former case the quality of the vowel thus developed regulated itself after the quality of the stem-vowel. In the latter case it fluctuated between u(o) and e, rarely a. Examples are:—nom. sing. burug, buruh beside burg, burh, *city*; dat. sing. and nom. pl. byrig beside byrg; fyligan beside fylgan, *to follow*; styric beside styrc, *calf*; woruhte, worohte beside worhte, *he worked*. Gen. gearuwes, -owes, -ewes beside gearwes: nom. gearu, *ready*; geoluwes, -owes beside geolwes: nom. geolu, *yellow*; gen. dat. beaduwe, -owe, beside beadwe: nom. beadu, *battle*; frætuwe, -ewe beside frætwe, *trappings*.

CHAPTER V

ABLAUT (VOWEL GRADATION)

§ 103. By ablaut is meant the gradation of vowels both in stem and suffix, which was chiefly caused by the primitive Indo-Germanic system of accentuation. See § 8.

The vowels vary within certain series of related vowels, called ablaut-series. In OE., to which this chapter will be chiefly confined, there are six such series, which appear most clearly in the stem-forms of strong verbs. Four stem-forms are to be distinguished in an OE. strong verb which has vowel gradation as the characteristic mark of its different stems:—(1) The present stem, to which belong all the forms of the present, (2) the stem of the first or third person singular of the preterite indicative, (3) the stem of the preterite plural, to which belong the second pers. pret. singular and the whole of the pret. subjunctive, (4) the stem of the past participle.

§ 103]   *Ablaut (Vowel Gradation)*

By arranging the vowels according to these four stems we arrive at the following system:—

	i.	ii.	iii.	iv.
I.	ī	ā	i	i
II.	ēo	ēa	u	o
III.	i, e	a (æ)	u	u, o
IV.	e	æ	ǣ	o
V.	e	æ	ǣ	e
VI.	a	ō	ō	æ (a)

Three grades of ablaut are to be distinguished—strong, weak, and lengthened. The strong grade occurs in i and ii of I to VI; the weak grade in iii of I to III, and in iv of I to VI; and the lengthened grade in iii of IV to VI. i and ii are sometimes further distinguished as strong grade 1 (sg. 1) and strong grade 2 (sg. 2); and similarly iv of V and VI and iv of I to IV are distinguished as weak grade 1 (wg. 1) and weak grade 2 (wg. 2). The preterite-present verbs have weak grade in iii of IV, whereas the ordinary strong verbs have lengthened grade.

NOTE.—1. The six series given above represent the simple vowels and diphthongs when uninfluenced by neighbouring sounds. For the changes caused by umlaut and the influence of consonants, see the phonology, especially §§ 46–64, and the various classes of strong verbs, §§ 332–54.

2. On the difference in Series III between i and e, see § 21; between a and æ, §§ 29–30; and between u and o, § 23.

3. It should be noted that the u, o in Series II are not of the same origin as the u, o in Series III and the o in Series IV. In Series II the u, o arose from Indg. u (cp. §§ 18, 23), whereas the u, o in Series III and the o in Series IV arose from Indg. vocalic l, m, n, r (cp. §§ 17, 23).

4. Strong verbs belonging to Series II have īe from īo, older iu (§ 24) in the second and third pers. singular; and strong verbs belonging to Series III–V with e in the infinitive have i in the second and third pers. singular of the pres. indicative (§ 21).

5. Although the series of vowels is seen most clearly in the stem-forms of strong verbs, the learner must not assume that ablaut occurs in strong verbs only. Every *syllable* of every word of whatever part of speech contains some form of ablaut. See *OE. Grammar*, § 225.

§ **104.** In this paragraph will be given the prim. Germanic and Gothic equivalents of the above six ablaut-series, with one or two illustrations from OE. For further examples see the various classes of strong verbs, §§ 332–54.

I.

Prim. Germ.	ī	ai	i	i
Gothic	ei	ái	i	i
OE.	bītan, *to bite*	bāt	biton	biten
	līþan, *to go*	lāþ	lidon	liden

NOTE.—Cp. the parallel Greek series λείπω, *I leave*: pf. λέ-λοιπα: aorist ἔ-λιπον.

II.

Prim. Germ.	eu	au	u	o
Gothic	iu	áu	u	u
OE.	bēodan, *to offer*	bēad	budon	boden
	cēosan, *to choose*	cēas	curon	coren

NOTE.—Cp. the parallel Greek series ἐλεύ(θ)σομαι (fut.), *I shall come*: pf. εἰλήλουθα: aor. ἤλυθον.

III.

Prim. Germ.	e, i,	a	u	u, o
Gothic	i,	a	u	u
OE.	helpan, *to help*	healp	hulpon	holpen
	weorþan, *to become*	wearþ	wurdon	worden
	bindan, *to bind*	band	bundon	bunden

NOTE.—1. To this series belong all strong verbs having a medial nasal or liquid + consonant, and a few others in which the vowel is followed by two consonants other than a nasal or liquid + consonant.

2. On the forms healp, wearþ, see § 51, and on weorþan see § 52.

3. Cp. the parallel Greek series δέρκομαι, *I look*: pf. δέ-δορκα: aor. ἔ-δρακον; πένθος, *grief, sorrow*: pf. πέ-πονθα, *I have suffered*: aor. ἔ-παθον.

IV.

Prim. Germ.	e	a	ǣ	o
Gothic	i	a	ē	u
OE.	beran, *to bear*	bær	bǣron	boren
	stelan, *to steal*	stæl	stǣlon	stolen

NOTE.—1. To this series belong all strong verbs whose stems end in a single liquid or nasal.

2. Cp. the parallel Greek series μένω, *I stay*: μονή, *a staying*: μί-μνω, *I stay*; δέρω, *I skin*: δορά, *skin, hide*: pf. part. mid. δε-δαρ-μένος.

V.

Prim. Germ.	e	a	ǣ	e
Gothic	i	a	ē	i
OE.	metan, *to measure*	mæt	mǣton	meten
	cweþan, *to say*	cwæþ	cwǣdon	cweden

NOTE.—1. To this series belong all strong verbs whose stems end in a single consonant other than a liquid or a nasal.

2. Cp. the parallel Greek series τρέπω, *I turn*: pf. τέ-τροφα: aor. ἔ-τραπον.

VI.

Prim. Germ.	a	ō	ō	a
Gothic	a	ō	ō	a
OE.	faran, *to go*	fōr	fōron	færen, faren

§ 105. Class VII of strong verbs embracing the old reduplicated verbs (§§ 353–63) has been omitted from the ablaut-series, because the exact relation in which the vowel of the present stands to that of the preterite has not yet been satisfactorily explained. The old phases of ablaut have been preserved in the present and preterite of a few Gothic verbs, as lētan, *to leave, let*, laílōt, laílōtum, lētans; saian, *to sow*, saí-sō, saí-sō-um, saians.

CHAPTER VI

THE PRIMITIVE GERMANIC DEVELOPMENT OF THE INDO-GERMANIC CONSONANTS

§ 106. In dealing with the consonants we shall first take the changes which took place in prim. Germanic (Ch. VI) and then those which took place in West Germanic (Ch. VII), and lastly those which took place in OE. (Ch. VIII).

In that part of the subject dealing with the changes which the Indg. explosives underwent in prim. Germanic, it will often be necessary to make use of examples from Latin and Greek. It is therefore important to be familiar with the Latin and Greek equivalents of the Indg. explosives. These equivalents will be found in the tables given in § 230 of the *OE. Grammar* or in § 127 of the *Gothic Grammar*.

§ 107. The Indo-Germanic parent language had the following system of consonants :—

		Labial.	Dental.	Palatal.	Velar.
Explosives	tenues	p	t	k	q, q^w
	mediae	b	d	g	ǥ, ǥ^w
	tenues aspiratae	ph	th	kh	qh, q^{w}h
	mediae aspiratae	bh	dh	gh	ǥh, ǥ^{w}h
Spirants	voiceless		s		
	voiced		z		
Nasals		m	n	ń	ŋ
Liquids			l, r		
Semivowels		w(u̯)		j(i̯)	

NOTE.—1. Explosives are consonants which are formed with complete closure of the mouth passage, and may be pronounced with or without voice, i. e. with or without the vocal chords being set in action; in the former case they are said to be voiced (e. g. the mediae), and in the latter voiceless (e. g. the tenues). The aspiratae are pronounced like the simple tenues and mediae followed by an h, e.g. like the th in English **pothook**, ph in **haphazard**, or dh in **madhouse**. The tenues and the tenues aspiratae both became voiceless spirants in prim. Germanic (§§ 109, 111).

The palatal explosives are formed by the front or middle of the tongue and the roof of the mouth (hard palate), like **g, k(c)** in English **get, good, kid, could**; whereas the velars are formed by the root of the tongue and the soft palate (velum). The latter do not occur in English. In the parent Indg. language there were two kinds of velars, viz. pure velars and velars with lip-rounding. The latter are here indicated by ʷ (see § 114). The pure velars and the palatals fell together in prim. Germanic and likewise also in Latin and Greek (§ 114). The palatal and velar nasals only occurred before their corresponding explosives, as ńk, ńg; ᴎq, ᴎgʷ, &c.

2. Spirants are consonants formed by the mouth passage being narrowed at one spot in such a manner that the outgoing breath gives rise to a frictional sound at the narrowed part.

z only occurred before voiced explosives, e.g. *nizdos = Lat. nīdus, English **nest**.

3. The semivowels, nasals, and liquids had the functions both of vowels and consonants. When a vowel disappeared through loss of accent in the combinations vowel + semivowel, liquid, or nasal, the semivowel, liquid, or nasal became vocalic or remained consonantal according as it was followed by a consonant or a vowel in the next syllable. Cp. also § 15, note 1.

4. In the writing down of prim. Germanic forms the signs **þ** (= **th** in Engl. **thin**), **đ** (= **th** in Engl. **then**), **ƀ** (= a bilabial spirant like the **v** in Engl. **vine**), ʒ (= **g** often heard in German **sagen**), χ (= German **ch** and the **ch** in Scotch **loch**) are used.

THE FIRST SOUND-SHIFTING.

§ 108. The first sound-shifting, popularly called Grimm's Law, is rightly regarded as one of the most characteristic features of the Germanic languages. With the exception of Armenian, in which the Indg. mediae became tenues, there is no similar sound-shifting in any of the other branches of the parent Indg. language. The first sound-shifting is so called in order to distinguish it from the special sound-shifting which only took place in Old High German. It relates to the changes which the Indg. explosives underwent in the period of the Germanic primitive community, i.e. before the Germanic parent language became differentiated into the separate Germanic languages. The approximate date at which these changes took place cannot be ascertained, but they must have taken place some hundreds of years before the beginning of the Christian era, as is proved by the forms of Germanic words—chiefly proper names—found in ancient classical writers. Nor is it possible to state the precise chronological order in which the changes took place. The most commonly accepted theory is that the changes took place in the following order:—1. The tenues became tenues aspiratae and thus fell together with the original tenues aspiratae. 2. The new and the original tenues aspiratae became voiceless spirants. 3. The mediae aspiratae became voiced spirants. 4. And lastly the mediae became tenues. But only so much is certain: that at the time the mediae became tenues, the tenues must have been on the way to becoming voiceless spirants, otherwise the two sets of sounds would have fallen together.

§ 109. The Indg. tenues p, t, k, q, qʷ became in prim. Germanic the voiceless spirants f, þ, χ, χ, χw.

p > f. Lat. pēs, Gr. πούς, OE. OS. fōt, Goth. fōtus, O.Icel. fōtr, *foot*; Lat. piscis, OE. fisc, Goth. fisks, O.Icel. fiskr, OS. OHG. fisk, *fish*; Lat. nepōs, OE. nefa, O.Icel. nefe, OHG. nefo, *nephew*.

t > þ. Lat. trēs, Gr. τρεῖς, OE. þrī, Goth. þrija (neut.), O.Icel. þrīr, OS. thria, *three*; Lat. frāter, OE. brōþor, Goth. brōþar, O.Icel. brōðer, OS. brōđar, *brother*; Lat. vertō, *I turn*, OE. weorþan, Goth. waírþan, O.Icel. verða, OS. werđan, *to become*.

k > χ. Lat. canis, Gr. κύων, OE. OS. hund, Goth. hunds, O.Icel. hundr, *dog, hound*; Lat. cor (gen. cordis), Gr. καρδία, OE. heorte, Goth. haírtō, O.Icel. hjarta, OS. herta, *heart*; Lat. pecu, OE. feoh, Goth. faíhu, O.Icel. fē, OS. OHG. fihu, *cattle*; Lat. dūcō, *I lead*, OE. tēon from *tēohan (§ 68), Goth. tiuhan, OS. tiohan, *to draw, lead*.

q > χ. Lat. canō, *I sing*, OE. Goth. hana, O.Icel. hane, OS. OHG. hano, *cock*, lit. *singer*; Lat. vincō (pf. vīcī), *I conquer*, Goth. weihan, OHG. wīhan, *to fight*.

qʷ > χw. Lat. quis, Gr. τίς, OE. hwā, Goth. hʋas, OS. hwē, OHG. hwer, *who?*; Lat. linquō, Gr. λείπω, *I leave*, OE.

līon, lēon from *līohan older *līxwan, Goth. leiƕan, *to lend*. See § 114.

NOTE.—1. The Indg. tenues remained unshifted in the combination s + tenuis, as Lat. spuere, OE. OS. OHG. spīwan, Goth. speiwan, *to vomit, spit*. Gr. στείχω, *I go*, OE. OS. OHG. stīgan, Goth. steigan, O.Icel. stīga, *to ascend*; Lat. hostis, *stranger, enemy*, OE. giest, Goth. gasts, O.Icel. gestr, OS. OHG. gast, *guest*. Gr. σκιά, *shadow*, OE. OS. OHG. scīnan, Goth. skeinan, O.Icel. skīna, *to shine*; Lat. piscis, OE. fisc, Goth. fisks, O.Icel. fiskr, OS. OHG. fisk, *fish*. Gr. θυο-σκόος, *sacrificing priest*, OE. scēawian, OS. scauwōn, OHG. scouwōn, *to look, view*.

2. t also remained unshifted in the Indg. combinations pt, kt, qt, as Lat. neptis, OE. OHG. nift, *niece, grand-daughter*. Lat. octō, Gr. ὀκτώ, OE. eahta, Goth. ahtáu, OS. OHG. ahto, *eight*. Gen. sing. Lat. noctis, Gr. νυκτός, nom. OE. neaht, niht, Goth. nahts, OS. OHG. naht, *night*.

§ 110. The Indg. mediae b, d, g, g, gʷ became the tenues p, t, k, k, kw.

b > p. Gr. βαίτη, *a shepherd's goatskin coat*, OE. pād, Goth. páida, OS. pēda, *coat, cloak*; Lithuanian dubùs, OE. dēop, Goth. diups, O.Icel. djūpr, OS. diop, *deep*; O. Bulgarian slabŭ, *slack, weak*, OE. slǣpan, Goth. slēpan, OS. slāpan, *to sleep*, originally *to be slack*. b was a rare sound in Indo-Germanic.

d > t. Lat. decem, Gr. δέκα, OE. tīen, Goth. taíhun, O.Icel. tīo, OS. tehan, *ten*; Lat. vidēre, *to see*, OE. Goth. OS. witan, O.Icel. vita, *to know*; gen. Lat. pedis, Gr. ποδός, nom. OE. OS. fōt, Goth. fōtus, O.Icel. fōtr, *foot*.

g > k. Lat. genu, Gr. γόνυ, OE. cnēo, Goth. kniu, O.Icel. knē, OS. OHG. knio, *knee*; Lat. ager, Gr. ἀγρός, OE. æcer, Goth. akrs, O.Icel. akr, *field, acre*; Lat. ego, Gr. ἐγώ, OE. ic, Goth. OS. ik, O.Icel. ek, *I*.

g > k. Lat. gelu, *frost*, OE. ceald, Goth. kalds, O.Icel. kaldr, OS. kald, OHG. kalt, *cold*; Lat. jugum, Gr. ζυγόν, OE. geoc, Goth. juk, *yoke*.

gʷ > kw. Gr. Boeotian βανά, OE. cwene, Goth. qinō, OS. OHG. quena, *woman, wife*; Lat. vīvos from *gwīwos, OE. cwicu, Goth. qius, O.Icel. kvikr, OS. quik, OHG. quec, *quick, alive*; Lat. **veniō** from **gwemjō, *I come*, OE. OS. **cuman**, Goth. **qiman**, OHG. **queman**, *to come*. See § 114.

§ 111. The Indg. tenues aspiratae became voiceless spirants in prim. Germanic, and thus fell together with and underwent all further changes in common with the voiceless spirants which arose from the Indg. tenues (§ 110), the latter having passed through the intermediate stage of tenues aspiratae before they became spirants (§ 108). The tenues aspiratae were, however, of so rare occurrence in the Indg. language that two or three examples must suffice for the purposes of this book:—

ph > f. Gr. σφάλλω, *I make to fall*, OE. **feallan**, O.Icel. **falla**, OS. OHG. **fallan**, *to fall*; Skr. **phénas**, OE. **fām**, OHG. **feim**, *froth, foam*.

th > þ. Gr. ἀ-σκηθής, *unhurt*, OE. **sceþþan**, Goth. **skaþjan**, *to injure*; OE. (Anglian) **earþ, arþ**, *thou art*, cp. Skr. **véttha**, Gr. οἶσθα, *thou knowest*.

qʷh > χw. Gr. φάλλη, OE. **hwæl**, O.Icel. **hvalr**, OHG. **hwal**, *whale*.

§ 112. The Indg. mediae aspiratae **bh, dh, gh, ǵh, gʷh** became first of all the voiced spirants **ƀ, đ, ʒ, ǵ, ʒw**. Then during the prim. Germanic period **ƀ, đ** initially, and **ƀ, đ, ʒ, ʒw** medially after their corresponding nasals, became the voiced explosives **b, d, g, gw**:—

b. OE. OS. OHG. **beran**, Goth. **bairan**, O.Icel. **bera**, *to bear*, Skr. **bhárāmi**, Lat. **ferō**, Gr. φέρω, *I bear*; OE. **brōþor**, Goth. **brōþar**, O.Icel. **brōðer**, OS. **brōðar**, OHG. **bruoder**, Skr. **bhrátar-**, Lat. **frāter**, *brother*.

OE. **camb**, OHG. **kamb**, *comb*, Skr. **jámbhas**, Gr. γόμφος, *bolt, nail*; OE. **ymbe**, OS. OHG. **umbi**, Gr. ἀμφί, *around*.

d. OE. **duru**, Goth. **daúr**, OS. **duri**, O.Icel. pl. **dyrr**, Gr. θύρα, *door*; OE. **dohtor**, Goth. **daúhtar**, O.Icel. **dōtter**, OS. **dohter**, Gr. θυγάτηρ, *daughter*.

OE. Goth. OS. **bindan**, O.Icel. **binda**, *to bind*, Skr. **bándhanam**, *a binding*, cp. Lat. **of-fendimentum**, *chin-cloth*, root *bhendh-, *bind*.

g. OE. enge, OS. OHG. engi, *narrow*, cp. Lat. angō, Gr. ἄγχω, *I press tight*; OE. OS. OHG. lang, Goth. laggs, O.Icel. langr, Lat. longus, *long*.

gw. Goth. siggwiþ, *he sings*, cp. Gr. ὀμφή, *divine voice*, Indg. *soṇgʷhá.

§ 113. ƀ, đ, ȝ, ȝw remained in other positions, and their further development belongs to the history of the separate languages. In OE. ƀ (written f) remained between voiced sounds, but became f finally (§ 140). đ became d. ȝ (generally written g) remained in the oldest period of the language (§ 168). For ȝw see § 114. In Goth. ƀ, đ (written b, d) remained medially after vowels, but became explosives (b, d) after voiced consonants. They became f, þ finally after vowels and before final -s. Geminated ƀƀ, đđ, ȝȝ, of whatever origin, became bb, dd, gg in the prehistoric period of all the languages.

Examples are:—nifol, *dark*, cp. Gr. νεφέλη, *mist, cloud*; lēof, Goth. liufs, Indg. *leubhos, *dear*, cp. Skr. lúbhyāmi, *I feel a strong desire*.

ūder, Gr. οὖθαρ, *udder*; rēad, Goth. ráuþs, Indg. *roudhos, cp. Gr. ἐ-ρυθρός, *red*; midd, Goth. midjis, Skr. mádhyas, *middle*.

gēotan, Goth. giutan, *to pour*, cp. Gr. χέ(ϝ)ω, *I pour*; gōs, Gr. χήν, *goose*; wegan, Goth. ga-wigan, *to move, carry*, Lat. vehō from *weghō, *I carry*.

giest, Goth. gasts, *guest*, Lat. hostis, *stranger, enemy*, prim. form *ghostis; stīgan, Goth. steigan, *to ascend*, Gr. στείχω from *steighō, *I go*.

§ 114. We have already seen (§ 107, note 2) that the parent Indg. language had two series of velars: (1) pure velars which never had labialization. These velars fell together with the palatals in the Germanic, Latin, and Greek languages, but were kept apart in Sanskrit. (2) Velars with labialization. These velars appear in the Germanic languages partly with and partly without labialization; in the latter case they fell together with prim. Germanic χ, k, ȝ from Indg. k, g, gh (§§ 109, 110, 112).

The w in prim. Germanic χw, kw, ʒw from Indg. q̑ʷ, g̑ʷ, g̑ʷh, and in prim. Germanic ʒw from Indg. qʷ by Verner's law (§ 115) regularly remained before Indg. ĕ, ĭ, ə, a, ā (= prim. Germanic ō), and also in the combinations vowel + ʒw + liquid or n, but regularly disappeared before Indg. ŭ, ō, o (= prim. Germanic a), and also in the initial combinations kw- or ʒw- + liquid, in the medial combinations -ʒwj-, -ŋʒwr-, -χwt-, and when final. These sound-laws became greatly obscured during the prim. Germanic period through form-transference and levelling out in various directions:—

1. Prim. Germanic χw from Indg. q̑ʷ. Regular forms were: OE. hwīl, Goth. ƕeila, *time*; Goth. saiƕit, *he sees*, Indg. *séqʷeti; Goth. ƕis, Indg. *qʷeso, *whose*; and with regular loss of w OE. heals, Goth. hals, *neck*, Indg. *qʷolsos; OS. OHG. gi-siht, *sight, look*; OE. seah, OS. OHG. sah, *he saw*. After the analogy of forms like Goth. ƕis were formed Goth. ƕas, OE. hwă for *has, *hă, Indg. *qʷos, *who*. From forms like Goth. saiƕit, the ƕ was levelled out into all forms of the verb; and conversely from forms like OE. sēon from *seohan, older *sehan = OS. OHG. sehan, *to see*, Indg. *séqʷonom, the h (= χ) was levelled out into all forms of the present.

2. Prim. Germanic kw from Indg. g̑ʷ. Regular forms were: OE. cwicu, Goth. qius, Lat. vīvus from *gwīwos, *quick, alive*; Goth. qima, OHG. quimu beside OE. cume, *I come*; pret. pl. Goth. qēmun, OE. cwōmon from *cwǣmun, *they came*; OE. cū, OS. kō, Indg. acc. *gʷōm, *cow*. After the analogy of forms like Goth. qima, OHG. quimu, Indg. *gʷémō, the q, qu were levelled out into all forms of these verbs, as pret. qam, quam for *kam, Indg. *gʷómǎ. From forms like Goth. sigqiþ, *he sinks*, the q (= kw) was levelled out into all forms, and conversely from forms like OE. sincan, Indg. *seŋgʷonom, the c was levelled out into all forms.

3. Prim. Germanic ʒw from Indg. g̑ʷh and the ʒw from Indg. qʷ by Verner's law (§ 115) became gw in the medial combination -ŋʒw- before palatal vowels, as Goth. siggwiþ, *he*

sings; But in all other cases either the ȝ or the w regularly disappeared according to the sound-laws stated above.

4. Prim. Germanic ȝw from Indg. ǥʷh. Regular forms were: Goth. **mawi**, *maiden*, beside **magus**, OE. **magu**, *boy, son*; OE. **snīweþ**, OHG. **snīwit**, *it snows*, OHG. pp. **versnigan**; Goth. **siggwiþ**, *he sings*, beside OE. inf. **singan**; Goth. **hneiwiþ**, *he bows, declines*, beside OE. inf. **hnīgan**. And then through levelling out in different directions the **w**, **gw**, or **g** became generalized in the verbs, as OE. **snīwan**, **singeþ**, **hnīgeþ** for *snīgan, *singweþ, *hnīweþ; Goth. **siggwan**, **hneiwan** for *siggan, *hneigan.

5. Prim. Germanic medial -ȝw- from Indg. -qʷ- by Verner's law. Regular forms were: Goth. **siuns**, OE. **sīen** (**sīon**, **sēon**), from *se(ȝ)wnís, *a seeing, face*: Goth. **saíƕiþ**, *he sees*; OE. **hwēol**, **hweowol** from *χwe(ȝ)wlo-, *wheel*; OE. gen. **holwes**, **horwes** beside nom. **holh**, *hollow*, **horh**, *dirt*; pret. pl. subj. **sāwen** (OS. **sāwin**) beside pret. pl. indic. **sǣgon** (Anglian **sēgon**), *we saw*; pp. **sewen** from *se(ȝ)wenós, *seen*.

Analogical formations were: WS. **sāwon** with **w** from the pret. subj. **sāwe**, pl. **sāwen**, and the pp. **sewen**; Anglian pp. **segen** with **g** from **sēgon**; and similarly pp. **sigen** beside the regular form **siwen**, *strained*; and **ligen** for *liwen, *lent*.

NOTE.—In several words the Indg. velars, when preceded or followed by a **w** or another labial in the same word, appear in the Germanic languages as labials by assimilation. The most important examples are: OE. OS. **wulf**, Goth. **wulfs**, OHG. **wolf** = Gr. λύκος for *Fλύκος, prim. form *wlqʷos, *wolf*; OE. **fēower** (but **fyþer-fēte**, *four-footed*), Goth. **fidwōr**, OS. OHG. **fior**, prim. form *qʷetwōres, Lat. **quattuor**, *four*; OE. OS. **fīf**, Goth. **fimf**, OHG. **fimf**, **finf**, prim. form *péroqʷe, cp. Skr. **páńca**, *five*; OE. **weorpan**, Goth. **waírpan**, O.Icel. **verpa**, OS. **werpan**, OHG. **werfan**, *to throw*, cp. O.Bulgarian **vrĭgą**, *I throw*; OE. **swāpan**, OHG. **sweifan**, *to swing*, cp. Lithuanian **swaikstù**, *I become dizzy*.

VERNER'S LAW.

§ 115. One of the most important sound-changes which took place in prim. Germanic is known by the name of Verner's law, and was due to the influence of the Indg. system of accentuation,

In Indg. the principal accent of a word could fall on any syllable just as in Sanskrit, and this system of accentuation was preserved in prim. Germanic at the time Verner's law operated; it was not until a later period of the prim. Germanic language that the principal accent became confined to the root-syllable of a word (see § 8).

After the completion of the first sound-shifting, and while the principal accent of a word was not yet confined to the root-syllable, a uniform interchange took place between the voiceless and voiced spirants, which may be stated thus:—

The medial spirants f, þ, χ, χw, s and the final spirant -s regularly became ƀ, ɖ, ʒ, ʒw, z when the vowel next preceding them did not, according to the original Indg. system of accentuation, bear the principal accent of the word. The ƀ, ɖ, ʒ, ʒw which thus arose from Indg. p, t, k, q, qʷ underwent in the Germanic languages all further changes in common with the ƀ, ɖ, ʒ, ʒw from Indg. bh, dh, gh, ɡh, ɡʷh.

From the above it will be seen that the interchanging pairs of consonants due to Verner's law were in prim. Germanic f—ƀ, þ—ɖ, χ—ʒ, χw—ʒw, and s—z. They underwent various changes partly in prim. Germanic, partly in West Germanic, and partly in the separate languages. Already in prim. Germanic ʒw became differentiated into w and ʒ (§ 114); ɳ disappeared before χ (§ 20), and ɳʒ became ɳg (§ 112), whence the interchange of χ—ɳg; ƀ, ɖ became b, d after their corresponding nasals (§ 112). In West Germanic χw became χ (see § 114); z became r medially and disappeared finally (§ 133); ɖ became d (§ 134). In OE. the two sounds f—ƀ fell together in ƀ (written f) medially, and in f finally (§§ 139–40), so that the original interchange between f—ƀ became entirely obliterated; χ disappeared between vowels (§ 144), when preserved it was written h; and þ, s became voiced between vowels, although the þ, s were preserved in writing (§ 139). So that in OE. we have the following interchanging pairs of consonants:—

            þ—d   s—r

h or loss of h (= prim. Germ. χ)—g
h or loss of h (= prim. Germ. χw)—g, w (= prim. Germ. ʒw)
h or loss of h (= prim. Germ. ŋχ)—ng.

The s, f, h in the combinations sp, st, sk, ss, ft, fs, hs, and ht were not subject to this law.

§ 116. Verner's law manifests itself most clearly in the various parts of strong verbs, where the infinitive, present participle, present tense, and preterite (properly perfect) singular had the principal accent on the root-syllable, but the indicative pret. plural, the pret. subjunctive (properly optative), and past participle had the principal accent on the ending, as prim. Germanic *wérþō > OE. weorþe, *I become* = Skr. vártā-mi, *I turn*; pret. indic. 3. sing. *wárþ(e) > OE. wearþ, *he became* = Skr. va-várta, *he has turned*; pret. 1. pers. pl. *wurđumé > OE. *wurdum (wurdon is the 3. pers. pl. used for all persons) = Skr. va-vṛtimá, *we have turned*; past participle *wurđaná-, -ená- > OE. worden = Skr. va-vṛtāná-; pres. participle berende, *bearing*, cp. Gk. gen. φέροντος.

þ—d. cweþan, *to say*, līþan, *to go*, snīþan, *to cut*; pret. sing. cwæþ, lāþ, snāþ; pret. pl. cwǣdon, lidon, snidon; pp. cweden, liden, sniden.

s—r. cēosan, *to choose*, drēosan, *to fall*, forlēosan, *to lose*; pret. sing. cēas, drēas, forlēas; pret. pl. curon, druron, forluron; pp. coren, droren, forloren.

h—g. flēon (OHG. fliohan), *to flee*, slēan (Goth. slahan), *to strike, slay*, tēon (Goth. tiuhan), *to draw, lead*; pret. sing. flēah, slōh, tēah; pret. pl. flugon, slōgon, tugon; pp. flogen, slægen, togen.

h—g, w. sēon (Goth. saiƕan), *to see*; pret. sing. seah; pret. pl. WS. sāwon, Anglian sēgon; pp. WS. sewen, Anglian segen; sīon, sēon (Goth. *seiƕan), *to strain*; pret. sing. sāh; pret. pl. sigon; pp. siwen, sigen. See § 114. 5.

h—ng. fōn (Goth. fāhan, prim. Germ. *faŋχanan), to *seize*,

hōn (Goth. hāhan, prim. Germ. *χaŋχanan), *to hang*; pret. pl. fēngon, hēngon; pp. fangen, hangen.

§ 117. Causative verbs had originally suffix accentuation, and therefore also exhibit the change of consonants given above, as **weorþan**, *to become*: **ā-wierdan**, *to destroy, injure*, cp. Skr. vártāmi, *I turn*; vartáyāmi, *I cause to turn*; **līþan**, *to go*: **lǣdan**, *to lead*; **ā-rīsan**, *to arise*: **rǣran**, *to raise*; **genesan**, *to recover*: **nerian**, *to save*.

§ 118. Examples of the operation of Verner's law in nounforms, &c., are:— **seofon**, Goth. sibun: Gr. ἑπτά, *seven*. **fæder**: Gr. πατήρ, *father*; **mōdor**: Skr. mātár-, *mother*; **dēad**, *dead*: **dēaþ**, *death*. OE. **tīen** (Goth. taíhun), Gk. δέκα, *ten*, beside -tig (Goth. pl. tigjus), Gr. δεκάς, *decade*; **swēor** (Goth. swaíhra, Indg. *swékuros), *father-in-law*, beside **sweger**, Gr. ἑκυρά, *mother-in-law*. OHG. **haso** beside OE. **hara**, *hare*; Goth. áusō beside OE. ēare, *ear*.

The Indg. Combinations of Explosives + t or s.

§ 119. 1. The mediae + t or s became tenues + t or s in Indo-Germanic.

2. The Indg. mediae aspiratae + t became tenues + t in early prim. Germanic.

3. The Indg. tenues aspiratae and mediae aspiratae + s had in prim. Germanic the same development as the original tenues + s.

Then pt, kt, qt; ps, ks, qs were shifted to ft, χt; fs, χs at the same time as the original Indg. tenues became voiceless spirants (§ 109). And tt, ts became ss. ss then became simplified to s after long syllables, and before and after consonants. So that for purely practical purposes the above soundlaws may be thus formulated:—Every labial + t or s became ft, fs; every guttural + t or s became χt, χs; every dental + t or s became ss, s.

This explains the frequent interchange between p, ƀ (b), and

§ 119] *Indg. Combinations of Explosives* 71

f; between k, ʒ (g), and h; and between t, þ, đ (d), and ss, s in forms which are etymologically related

p, ƀ (b)—f. OE. scieppan, Goth. skapjan, *to create*, beside OE. ge-sceaft, *creature*, Goth. ga-skafts, *creation*; Goth. giban, OHG. geban, *to give*, beside Goth. fra-gifts, *a giving, espousal*, OE. OHG. gift, *gift*; OHG. weban, *to weave*, beside English weft; OS. thurƀan, *to need*, beside pret. thorfta.

k, ʒ (g)—h. OE. wyrcan, Goth. waúrkjan, *to work*, beside pret. and pp. OE. worhte, worht, Goth. waúrhta, waúrhts; OE. þyncan, Goth. þugkjan, *to seem*, beside pret. and pp. OE. þūhte, þūht, Goth. þūhta, *þūhts; OE. magon, OHG. magun, *they may, can*, beside pret. OE. meahte, Goth. OHG. mahta; OE. bycgan, Goth. bugjan, *to buy*, beside pret. and pp. OE. bohte, boht, Goth. baúhta, baúhts; OE. bringan, Goth. briggan, *to bring*, beside pret. and pp. OE. brōhte, brōht, Goth. brāhta, *brāhts.

t, þ, đ (d)—ss, s. OE. Goth. witan, *to know*, beside pret. OE. wisse, Goth. wissa; OE. sittan, Goth. sitan, *to sit*, beside OE. sess, *seat*; OE. cweþan, Goth. qiþan, *to say*, beside Goth. ga-qiss, *consent*.

ss became s after long syllables, and before and after consonants, as OE. Goth. witan, *to know*, beside OE. wīs, *wise*, Goth. unweis, *unlearned*; OE. etan, *to eat*, beside ǣs, *carrion*; OE. hȳdan, *to hide*, beside hūs, from *χūtso-, *house*; OE. mōt, *I may*, beside OHG. pret. muosa.

In verbal forms we often meet with st instead of ss (s). In such cases the st is due to the analogy of forms where t was quite regular, e. g. regular forms were Goth. last, *thou didst gather*, inf. lisan; Goth. slōht, *thou didst strike*, inf. slahan; OE. meaht, *thou canst*, inf. magan (see § 109, notes); then after the analogy of such forms were made OE. wāst for *wās, Goth. wáist for *wáis, *thou knowest*; OE. mōst for *mōs, *thou art allowed*; regular forms were pret. sing. OE. worhte, Goth. waúrhta, OHG. worhta, beside inf. OE. wyrcan, Goth. waúrkjan, OHG. wurken, *to work*; then after the analogy of such forms were made OE. wiste beside wisse, OHG. wista beside wissa, *I knew*; OE. mōste for *mōse (= OHG. muosa), *I was allowed*.

Assimilation of Consonants.

§ 120. -md- became -nd-, as OE. Goth. hund from Indg. *kmtóm = Gr. ἑ-κατόν, *hundred*; OE. scand, Goth. skanda, *shame, disgrace*, beside OE. scamian, Goth. skaman, *to be ashamed*; OE. sund, *a swimming*, beside swimman, *to swim*.

§ 121. -nw- became -nn-, as OE. cinn, Goth. kinnus, from Indg. *genw-: Gr. γένυ-s, *chin, cheek*; OE. Goth. rinnan from *rinwan-, *to run, flow*, cp. Skr. riṇvámi, *I let flow*; OE. þynne, cp. Lat. tenuis, Skr. fem. tanvī́, *thin*.

§ 122. -ln- became -ll-, as OE. full, Goth. fulls = Lithuanian pìlnas, Indg. *plnós, *full*; OE. hyll = Lat. collis from *klnís, *hill*; OE. wull, Goth. wulla = Lith. vìlna, *wool*

§ 123. -đl- became -ll-, as OE. steall from *stađla-, Indg. *stədhlo-, *stall*, beside staþol, *base, foundation*. The ll was simplified to l after long vowels, as OE. ǣlan from *aidlan-, *to burn*: Gr. αἴθω, *I burn*.

§ 124. Prim. Germanic ƀn, đn, ʒn = Indg. pn⸗, tn⸗, kn⸗, qn⸗ (by Verner's law, § 115), and bhn⸗, dhn⸗, ghn⸗, ghn⸗, became ƀƀ, đđ, ʒʒ before the principal accent, and then later they became bb, dd, gg; and in like manner Indg. bn⸗, dn⸗, gn⸗, gn⸗ became bb, dd, gg. And these mediae were shifted to pp, tt, kk at the same time as the original Indg. mediae became tenues (§ 110). These geminated consonants were simplified to p, t, k after long syllables. Examples are:—
OE. cropp, *crop (of birds)*, O.Icel. kroppr, *body, trunk*, from *grbhn⸗; OE. hnæpp, from *χnaƀn⸗, or *χnabn⸗, *basin, bowl*; OE. hoppian, O.Icel. hoppa, from *χoƀn⸗, Indg. *qupn⸗; OE. OS. topp, O.Icel. toppr, from *toƀn⸗, *top, summit*; OE. hēap, from *χauƀn⸗, *heap*; OE. cnotta, from *knođn⸗, beside OHG. chnodo, chnoto, *knot*; OE. hwīt, Goth. ƕeits, from *χwiđn⸗, *white*; OE. bucc, O.Icel. bokkr, prim. form *bhug-

nós, *buck*; OE. liccian, from *leʒn-, *to lick*, cp. Gr. λίχνος, *lickerish, dainty*; OE. locc, O.Icel. lokkr, prim. form *lugnós, *lock*; OE. lōcian, from *lōʒn-, *to look*.

The Loss of Consonants.

§ 125. Original final -m became -n, and then it, as also Indg. final -n, disappeared in dissyllabic and polysyllabic words during the prim. Germanic period. For examples, see § 80. 1.

§ 126. Guttural n (ŋ) disappeared before χ with lengthening and nasalization of the preceding vowel. For examples, see § 20.

§ 127. The consonants, which arose from the Indg. final explosives (t, d), disappeared in prim. Germanic, except after a short accented vowel. For examples, see § 80. 2.

§ 128. Postconsonantal w disappeared before u, as OE. sund, *a swimming*, beside inf. swimman, *to swim*, O.Icel. pp. sumenn; OE. pp. sungen, beside inf. swingan, *to swing*. In verbal forms the w was mostly reintroduced in the pret. pl. and pp. after the analogy of forms which regularly had w, e.g. pret. pl. swummon, swungon, swullon, pp. swummen, swungen (beside the regular form sungen), swollen, beside inf. swimman, *to swim*, swingan, *to swing*, swellan, *to swell*. On the loss of w in the prim. Germanic combinations χw, kw, ʒw, see § 114.

Other Consonant Changes.

§ 129. Indg. z + media became s + tenuis, as Goth. asts, OHG. ast = Gr. ὄζος, from *ozdos, *branch, twig*; OE. OHG. nest, Lat. nīdus, from *ni-zdos, *nest*, related to root *sed-, *sit*; OE. masc, OHG. masca, *mesh, net*, cp. Lithuanian mezgù, *I tie in knots*.

Indg. z + media aspirata became z + voiced spirant, as OE. meord, Goth. mizdō, *pay, reward*, cp. O.Bulgarian mĭzda, Gr. μισθός, *pay*; OE. mearg, OHG. marg, O.Bulgarian mozgŭ, *marrow*, root *mesgh-.

§ **130.** Initial χ became an aspirate (written h) before vowels, as OE. Goth. OS. **hund**, OHG. **hunt**, from *χunđan, prim. form *kmtóm, *hundred*. Some scholars assume that it also became an aspirate medially between vowels. Upon this assumption it would be difficult to account for the breaking in forms like OE. **slēan** from *sleahan, older *slaχan-, Goth. **slahan**, *to strike, slay*. See §§ 51, 144.

§ **131.** Initial and medial sr became str, as OE. **strēam**, O.Icel. **straumr**, OS. OHG. **strōm**, *stream*, cp. Skt. **srávati**, *it flows*; OE. **sweostor**, Goth. **swistar**, OS. **swestar**, OHG. **swester**, *sister*, with t from the weak stem-form as in the Goth. dat. sing. **swistr** = prim. Germanic *swestri, cp. Skr. dat. **svásrē**; O.Icel. **fōstr**, OE. **fōstor**, *food, sustenance*, cp. Goth. **fōdjan**, OE. **fēdan**, *to feed*.

§ **132.** The remaining Indg. consonants suffered no further material changes which need be mentioned here. Summing up the results of §§ 109–31, we arrive at the following system of consonants for the close of the prim. Germanic period:—

		Labial.	Inter-dental.	Dental.	Palatal and Guttural.
Explosives	voiceless	p		t	k
	voiced	b		d	g
Spirants	voiceless	f	þ	s	χ
	voiced	ƀ	đ	z	ʒ
Nasals		m		n	ŋ
Liquids				l, r	
Semivowels		w			j (palatal)

To these must be added the aspirate h.

CHAPTER VII

SPECIAL WEST GERMANIC CHANGES OF THE PRIM. GERMANIC CONSONANTS

§ 133. Prim. Germanic z from Indg. s by Verner's law (§ 115) became r medially, and disappeared finally, as OE. māra, OS. OHG. mēro = Goth. máiza, *greater*; pp. OE. coren, OS. OHG. gi-koran, beside OE. inf. cēosan, *to choose*; OE. herian = Goth. hazjan, *to praise*; OE. dēor, OS. dior, OHG. tior, Goth. dius (gen. diuzis), prim. Germanic *đeuzan, *deer, wild animal*; OE. dæg, OS. dag, OHG. tag = Goth. dags, O.Icel. dagr, prim. Germanic *đaʒaz, *day*; pl. OE. giefa, OS. geƀa, OHG. gebā = Goth. gibōs, O.Icel. gjafar, prim. Germanic *ʒeƀōz, *gifts*; pl. OE. guman, OS. gumon, OHG. gomon = Goth. gumans, O.Icel. gumar, prim. Germanic *ʒomaniz, *men*.

§ 134. Prim. Germanic đ (§§ 113, 115) became d, which was shifted to t in OHG., as OE. fæder, OS. fadar, OHG. fater, beside O.Icel. faðer, *father*; OE. OS. word, OHG. wort, beside O.Icel. orð, *word*; pp. OE. worden, OS. wordan, OHG. wortan, beside OE. inf. weorþan, *to become*.

§ 135. All single consonants, except r, were doubled after a short vowel before a following j. This j was mostly retained in OS., but generally disappeared in OE. and OHG. ƀj, đj, ʒj became bb, dd, gg (generally written cg in OE.). Examples are: OE. hliehhan, OHG. hlahhan = Goth. hlahjan, *to laugh*; OE. lecgan, OS. leggian, OHG. leggen = Goth. lagjan, *to lay*; OE. settan, OS. settian = Goth. satjan, *to set*; OE. biddan, OS. biddian, OHG. bitten = Goth. bidjan, *to pray, ask*; OE. sibb = Goth. sibja, *relationship*; OE. hell = Goth. halja, *hell*; gen. OE. cynnes = Goth. kunjis, *of a race, generation*. But OE. OS. nerian, OHG. nerien = Goth. nasjan, *to save*; OE. herian = Goth. hazjan, *to praise* (§ 151).

NOTE.—The j in the combination ji had disappeared before the West Germanic doubling of consonants took place, e. g. in the 2. and 3. pers. sing. of the pres. indicative, as OE. legest, legeþ, OS. legis, legid, OHG. legis, legit = Goth. lagjis, lagjiþ, beside inf. OE. lecgan, OS. leggian, OHG. leggen, Goth. lagjan, *to lay*.

§ 136. p, t, k, and h (= χ) were also doubled in West Germanic before a following r or l. The doubling regularly took place in the inflected forms (as gen. OE. OS. OHG. bittres, OE. æpples, OS. apples), and was then generally extended to the uninflected forms by levelling, as OE. bitter (biter), OS. OHG. bittar, cp. Goth. báitrs, *bitter*; OE. hlŭttor (hlūtor), OS. hluttar, OHG. hlūttar, cp. Goth. hlūtrs, *clear, pure*; OE. snottor (snotor), OS. OHG. snottar, cp. Goth. snutrs, *wise*; OE. æppel (æpl), OS. appul, cp. O.Icel. epli, *apple*; OE. wæccer beside wæcer, wacor, *watchful*; O.Nth. tæhher beside WS. tēar from *teahur, older *taχur, *tear*.

§ 137. Doubling of consonants by the assimilation of post-consonantal n to the preceding consonant also regularly took place in the weak declension of nouns, as sing. nom. *lapõ, *lappet*, acc. *lapan(un), beside gen. pl. *lapnõ(n) > *lappõ(n), cp. §§ 246-54. This interchange between the single and double consonants gave rise to levelling in a twofold direction, so that one or other of the forms was extended to all cases; thus in OE. the forms with double consonants were generalized in words like ebba, *ebb*; frogga, *frog*; lappa (læppa), *lappet*; and the forms with single consonant in words like boga, *bow*; dropa, *drop*; nefa, *nephew*.

CHAPTER VIII

THE OE. DEVELOPMENT OF THE PRIMITIVE GERMANIC CONSONANT-SYSTEM

§ 138. Before entering upon the history of the individual consonants in OE., it will be well to treat here several consonant changes which are best dealt with collectively, viz. the voicing and unvoicing of consonants, the vocalization of consonants, assimilation, metathesis, the loss of consonants, the simplification of double consonants, and the doubling of single consonants.

1. THE VOICING OF CONSONANTS.

§ 139. The voiceless spirants f, þ, s became the voiced spirants ƀ, ð, z medially between voiced sounds in simple words, although the f, þ, s were retained in writing (see § 6), as cēafl, *jaw*; ofen, *oven*; wulfas, *wolves*; brōþor, *brother*; āþas, *oaths*; eorþe, *earth*; fæþm, *embrace, fathom*; nosu, *nose*; bōsm, *bosom*; gen. hūses: nom. hūs, *house*.

2. THE UNVOICING OF CONSONANTS.

§ 140. The voiced spirants ƀ, ȝ became the voiceless spirants f, χ before voiceless sounds and finally, as pret. geaf, *he gave*: inf. giefan; healf, *half*; hlāf, *loaf*; burh, *city*, dāh, *dough*, bēah, *ring, bracelet*, beside gen. burge, dāges, bēages; stīhst beside older stīgest, *thou ascendest*. ng became nc before voiceless consonants, but the g was generally restored through association with forms where g was regular, as brincst, *thou bringest*, brincþ, *he brings*, beside bringst, bringþ with g restored from other forms of the verb.

d became t before and after voiceless consonants. When two dentals thus came together, they became tt which were simplified to t finally and after consonants. And interconsonantal t generally disappeared before s. Examples are: **bitst** beside **bidest**, *thou prayest*; **bint** from **bindþ*, older **bindeþ**, *he binds*; **bit, bitt** from **bidþ*, older **bideþ**, *he prays*; **gesynto** from **gesundiþu*, *health*; **īecte** (Goth. **áukida*), *he increased*; **bin(t)st**, older **bindest**, *thou bindest*. The d was often restored from forms where it was regular, as **findst : findan**.

3. The Vocalization of Consonants.

§ 141. When w and j came to stand finally after consonants through the loss of case-endings, they became -u and -i, later -o, -e, as **bealu, -o,** *evil*, **gearu, -o,** *ready*, beside gen. **bealwes, gearwes**; acc. **here** (Goth. **hari**) from **χarj(an)*, *army*.

In late OE. palatal g became i which combined with a preceding æ, e to form a diphthong, as **dæi**, *day*, **wei**, *way*, beside older **dæg, weg**; and -ig became -i through the intermediate stage -ī, as **æni**, *any*, **hefi**, *heavy*, beside older **ænig, hefig**. On vocalic l, m, n, r, see § 96.

4. Assimilation.

§ 142. s or l + r became ss, ll, as **lǣssa** from **lǣs(i)ra*, *smaller*; fem. gen. dat. sing. **þisse** (OHG. **desera**) from **þisre*, *of* or *to this*; gen. pl. **þissa** from **þisra*; **sēlla** beside **sēlra**, *better*. hr and rs became rr, as **hīerra**, *higher*, **nēarra**, *nearer*, beside older **hīehra, nēahra**; **wierrest**, *worst*, beside **wiersa**, *worse*. þs became ss, as **bliss**, *bliss*, **liss**, *favour*, beside **blīþs, līþs**. In late OE. þd became dd, as **cȳdde** beside older **cȳþde**, *he made known*. fn, fm became mn, mm in late OE., as **emn** (Goth. **ibns**), *even*; **stemn** (Goth. **stibna**), *voice*, beside older **ef(e)n, stef(e)n**; **wĭmman** beside older **wīfman**, *woman*.

5. Metathesis.

§ 143. Antevocalic r often became postvocalic by metathesis when a short vowel was followed by n, nn, s, or s + consonant, as **ærn** (Goth. **razn**), *house*; **forsc** (OHG. **frosk**), *frog*; **hors** (O.Icel. **hross**), *horse*; **iernan** (Goth. **rinnan**), *to run*; **biernan**

(Goth. brinnan), *to burn*; gærs (Goth. gras), *grass*. Medial sc often underwent metathesis to cs (written x), especially in late WS., as axe, *ashes*, āxian, *to ask*, fixas, *fishes*, beside asce, āscian, fiscas. sp sometimes became ps and vice versa in late OE., as æps, *aspen*, wæsp, *wasp*, beside æsp, wæps. sl became ls in unstressed syllables, as rǣdels (OS. rādislo), *riddle*; byrgels (OS. burgisli), *tomb*; brīdels, *bridle*.

6. The Loss of Consonants.

§ 144. w disappeared before u and e (= older i), as clēa from *cla(w)u, *claw*, sceadu from *scad(w)u, *shadow*, beside gen. clawe, sceadwe ; neut. pl. fēa from *fa(w)u, *few* (see § 69) ; sǣ from *sā(w)i-, older *saiwi- (Goth. sáiws), *sea* ; gierepþ from prim. Germanic *ȝarwiþ, *he prepares*, pret. gierede from prim. Germanic *ȝarwidǣ-, *he prepared*, beside inf. gierwan. The w was often reintroduced after the analogy of forms where w was regular, as clawu with w from the gen. and dat. clawe. w often disappeared in the second elements of compounds, as hlāford from hlāfweard, *lord*; nāuht beside older nā-wuht, *naught*, and in certain verbal forms with the negative prefix, ne, as næs, *was not*, nǣron, *were not*, nāt, *knows not*, nolde, *would not*, nyton, *they know not* = ne wæs, &c.

Medial j disappeared after original long closed syllables or syllables which became long by the West Germanic doubling of consonants (§ 135), as dēman (Goth. dōmjan), *to judge*; hild from *hildju, *war*; biddan = Goth. bidjan, *to pray*; hell = Goth. halja, *hell*.

m and n disappeared before f, þ, s with lengthening of the preceding vowel, as fīf, Goth. fimf, *five*; sōfte, OHG. samfto, *softly*; ōsle, OHG. amsala, *ousel*; ōþer, Goth. anþar, *other*; cūþ, Goth. kunþs, *known*; ūs, Goth. uns, *us*, see § 73.

Final -n generally disappeared in verbal forms before the pronouns wē, wit; gē, git, as binde wē, *let us bind*. On the loss of final -n in Nth. see *OE. Grammar*, § 288. n sometimes disappeared between consonants, as elboga, *elbow*; sæterdæg, *Saturday*, beside elnboga, sæterndæg.

The guttural ŋ disappeared in an unstressed syllable when preceded by n in a stressed syllable in the course of the OE. period, as cynig, *king*, penig, *penny*, beside older cyniŋg, peniŋg.

d disappeared in the combination ldl, as sellic beside seldlic (OS. seldlīc), *strange, wonderful*. t often disappeared between consonants, as fæsnian, *to fasten*, rihlīce, *justly*, beside fæstnian, rihtlīce. þ disappeared before st, as cwist, *thou sayest*, wierst, *thou becomest*, beside older cwiþest, wierþest.

ʒ often disappeared after palatal vowels before a following dental or consonantal n with lengthening of the preceding vowel, as brīdel, *bridle*, mæden, *maiden*, rīnan, *to rain*, þēnian, *to serve*, beside older brigdel, mægden, rignan, þegnian, see § 72.

Medial χ disappeared before s + consonant, between a vowel and a following liquid or nasal, between a liquid and a following vowel, and between vowels, as fȳst from *fūχstiz, *fist*; wæsma, wæstm, *growth*, beside weaxan (OHG. wahsan), *to grow*. ēorod from *eohrād, *troop*; hēla from *hōhila, *heel*; ȳmest (Goth. áuhmists), *highest*. fēolan (Goth. fĭlhan), *to penetrate, hide*; gen. mēares beside nom. mearh, *horse*. ēa (OHG. aha), *water, river*; slēan (Goth. slahan), *to slay*. sēon (OHG. sehan), *to see*. See §§ 68, 74–5.

h often disappeared with ne and habban, as nabban, *not to have*, næbbe, *I have not*, næfde, *I had not*. It also disappeared in the second element of compounds which were no longer felt as such in OE., as bēot from *bi-hāt, *boast*; frēols, from *frī-hals, *freedom*; līcuma beside older līc-hama, *body*.

7. THE SIMPLIFICATION OF DOUBLE CONSONANTS.

§ 145. Medial double consonants were simplified before and after other consonants; they were also simplified in pronunciation finally, although often retained in writing; also in unstressed syllables in late OE. Examples are: pret. sing. cyste, fylde, ypte, beside inf. cyssan, *to kiss*; fyllan, *to fill*, yppan, *to reveal*;

third pers. sing. pres. indic. fielþ, swimþ, winþ, beside inf. feallan, *to fall*, swimman, *to swim*, winnan, *to fight*. Pret. sing. gewielde from *gewield-de, gyrde from *gyrd-de, reste from *rest-te, sende from *send-de, beside inf. gewieldan, *to subdue*, gyrdan, *to gird*, restan, *to rest*, sendan, *to send*. buc, *buck*, eal, *all*, man, *man*, beside bucc, eall, mann. cg was always preserved in writing in order to show that it was an explosive and not a spirant, as brycg, *bridge*, mycg, *midge*. Late OE. atelic, *terrible*, bliccetan, *to glitter*, forgiefenes, *forgiveness*, gen. pl. ōþera, *other*, beside older atollic, bliccettan, forgiefennes, ōþerra.

8. THE DOUBLING OF CONSONANTS.

§ 146. Consonants were doubled during the OE. period before a following r or l with shortening of a preceding long vowel or diphthong, as blæddre, *bladder*, deoppra, *deeper*, hwittra, *whiter*, beside older blǣdre, dēopra, hwītra; gen. miccles beside older micles, nom. micel, *great*. In words like attor, *poison*, foddor, *food*, beside older ātor, fōdor, the doubling of the consonant went out from the inflected forms, as gen. ātres, which regularly became attres and from which a new nom. attor was formed. Cp. § 136.

THE SEMIVOWELS.

w

§ 147. Germanic w (written uu, u, ƿ in OE. manuscripts) remained initially before vowels, and generally also initially before and after consonants, as OE. OS. Goth. witan, OHG. wiʒʒan, *to know*, and similarly wæter, *water*; wilde, *wild*; winter, *winter*; wlanc, *proud*; wrītan, *to write*; cwēn, *queen, wife*; sweostor, *sister*; twā, *two*.

§ 148. Medial w generally remained before vowels, as OE. OS. OHG. spīwan, Goth. speiwan, *to vomit, spit*; sāwol, Goth. sáiwala, *soul*; blāwan, *to blow*; cnāwan, *to know*; rōwan, *to row*; meowle, Goth. mawilō, *maiden*; spearwa, *sparrow*; gen. cneowes, snāwes, gearwes, beside nom. cnēo, *knee*, snā, *snow*, gearu, *ready*.

§ 149. When w came to stand at the end of a word or syllable, it became vocalized to u (later o). The u then combined with a preceding short vowel to form a diphthong, but disappeared after long stems, long vowels, and diphthongs, as bealu (later bealo), *evil, calamity*, nearu, *narrow*, beside gen. bealwes, nearwes. Nom. cnēo, *knee*, trēo, *tree*, beside gen. cneowes, treowes. But the w was mostly reintroduced into the nom. sing. from the inflected forms, especially after long vowels and long diphthongs, as cnēow, snāw, strēaw, beside the regular forms cnēo, snā, strēa, *straw*. And conversely from the new nom. was sometimes formed a new gen., as cnēowes, trēowes beside older cneowes, treowes. For the loss of w, see § 144.

j

§ 150. Germanic initial j (= i consonant) had become a palatal spirant like the y in NE. yon in the oldest period of the language, and was generally written g, ge, also i, gi before u, as gēar, Goth. jēr, *year*; geoc, iuc, Goth. juk, *yoke*; geong, giong, giung, iung, Goth. juggs, *young*; giest, *yeast*; gingra, *younger*.

§ 151. It remained (written g, ge) medially between vowels when the first element was a long vowel or diphthong, as frīgea older frīegea, Goth. frául̲ja, *lord, master*; dat. hīege (Goth. háuja), īege, beside nom. hīeg, *hay*, īeg, *island* with -g from the inflected forms; fēog(e)an, *to hate*. It also remained (written i, g; ig, eg, also ige before a) after r in the combination short vowel + r, as herian, hergan, herigan, heregan, herigean, Goth. hazjan, *to praise*; gen. sing. heries, herges, heriges = Goth. harjis, *of an army*. The i, e in ig, eg represent a vocalic glide which was developed between the r and the j; and the e in the pl. herigeas merely indicates the palatal nature of the preceding g.

For medial -ij-, see § 69; for the loss of medial -j-, see § 135; for Germanic -ī = Indg. -eje, see § 85. 3; and for the vocalization of final -j, see § 141.

The Liquids.

§ 152. Germanic l and r remained, as lecgan, Goth. lagjan, *to lay*; stelan, Goth. stilan, *to steal*; sceal, Goth. skal, *shall*; and similarly land, *land*; lǣdan, *to lead*; ealu, *ale*; slǣpan, *to sleep*; blōd, *blood*; hlāford, *lord*; feallan, *to fall*; tellan, *to tell*; cōl, *cool*; full, *full*. rēad, Goth. ráuþs, *red*; here, Goth. harjis, *army*; fæder, Goth. fadar, *father*; and similarly rīdan, *to ride*; rūm, *room*; beran, *to bear*; duru, *door*; feorran, *from afar*; fȳr, *fire*. West Germanic medial r from older z (§ 133) also remained, as betra, māra = Goth. batiza, *better*; máiza, *greater*.

For vocalic l, r, see § 96; for metathesis, see § 143; and for assimilation, see § 142.

The Nasals.

§ 153. Germanic m and n generally remained, as mōna, Goth. mēna, *moon*; nama, Goth. namō, *name*; dumb, Goth. dumbs, *dumb*; and similarly mann, *man*; mōdor, *mother*; cuman, *to come*; climban, *to climb*; hām, *home*; rūm, *room*. Final -m, when an element of inflexion, became -n in late OE., as dat. pl. dagon, sunun beside older dagum, sunum. OE. Goth. niman, *to take*; nefa, *nephew*; findan, *to find*; grēne, *green*; spinnan, *to spin*; stān, *stone*; synn, *sin*.

For vocalic m, n, see § 96; and for the loss of m, n, see § 144.

§ 154. Germanic guttural ŋ (written g in Gothic and n in the other languages) only occurred medially before g and k (written c in OE.). In OE. it remained guttural or became palatal according as the following g, c remained guttural or became palatal, cp. §§ 166, 169. Examples are: bringan, Goth. briggan, *to bring*; drincan, Goth. drigkan, *to drink*; geong, Goth. juggs, *young*. benc from *baŋkiz, *bench*; lengra (OHG. lengiro), *longer*; þencan, Goth. þagkjan, *to think*.

For the loss of ŋ in unstressed syllables, see § 144.

The Labials.

§ 155. Germanic p (§ 110) was of rare occurrence, especially initially. Most of the words beginning with p in OE. are Latin or Greek loanwords. p remained in OE., as pād, Goth. páida, *cloak*; pening, O.Icel. penningr, *penny*; slǣpan, Goth. slēpan, *to sleep*; stæppan, *to step*; dēop, Goth. diups, *deep*; scip, Goth. skip, *ship*. peru (Lat. pirum), *pear*; pund (Lat. pondō), *pound*; pic (Lat. acc. picem), *pitch*; pinsian (Lat. pensāre), *to weigh, consider*.

§ 156. Germanic b (§ 112) and West Germanic bb (§§ 135, 137) remained, as beran, Goth. baíran, *to bear*; blind, Goth. blinds, *blind*; dumb, Goth. dumbs, *dumb*; climban, *to climb*; lamb, *lamb*. sibb, Goth. sibja, *relationship*; habban, *to have*; ebba, *ebb*.

§ 157. Germanic ƀ (written f) remained medially between voiced sounds (§ 113), as giefan, Goth. giban, *to give*; seofon, Goth. sibun, *seven*; sealfian, Goth. salbōn, *to anoint*; stefn, Goth. stibna, *voice*; hæfde, Goth. habáida, *he had*; gen. wīfes (OHG. wībes) beside nom. wīf, *wife*.

For the unvoicing of ƀ to f, see § 140; and for the assimilation of ƀm, ƀn to mm, mn, see § 142.

§ 158. Germanic f remained initially, medially before voiceless consonants, and finally, as fæder, Goth. fadar, *father*; fīf, Goth. fimf, *five*; gesceaft, Goth. gaskafts, *creature*; and similarly fōt, *foot*; feþer, *feather*; æfter, *after*; ceaf, *chaff*; hōf, *he raised*.

fj became bb, as hebban, Goth. hafjan, *to raise*.

For the voicing of f to ƀ between voiced sounds, see § 139.

The Dentals.

§ 159. Germanic t remained, as tōþ, Goth. tunþus, *tooth*; etan, Goth. itan, *to eat*; neaht, Goth. nahts, *night*; and similarly tellan, *to tell*; tīd, tīma, *time*; hatian, *to hate*; sittan, *to sit*; fōt, *foot*; hāt, *hot*; sceatt, *money, tribute*.

For the loss of t between consonants, see § 144.

§ **160.** Germanic d (§ 112) and West Germanic d (§ 134) generally remained, as dæg, Goth. dags, *day*; dohtor, Goth. daúhtar, *daughter*; OE. Goth. bindan, *to bind*. fæder, Goth. fadar, *father*; biddan, Goth. bidjan, *to pray*; cwǣdon, *they said*; dēad, Goth. dáuþs, *dead*.

For the unvoicing of d to t before and after voiceless consonants, see § 140.

§ **161.** Germanic þ generally remained initially, medially when doubled, and finally, as þencan, Goth. þagkjan, *to think*; oþþe, eþþa, Goth. aíþþáu, *or*; āþ, Goth. acc. áiþ, *oath*; and similarly þancian, *to thank*; þēof, *thief*; þunor, *thunder*; moþþe, *moth*; smiþþe, *smithy*; clāþ, *cloth*; mūþ, *mouth*; tōþ, *tooth*.

For the voicing of medial þ to đ, see § 139.

§ **162.** Germanic medial lþ became ld. The ld then became extended to the final position by levelling. Examples are: fealdan, Goth. falþan, *to fold*; wilde, Goth. wilþeis, *wild*; wuldor, Goth. wulþus, *glory*. Gen. goldes (= Goth. *gulþis), dat. golde (= Goth. gulþa), from which a new nom. gold for *golþ (= Goth. gulþ) was formed; and similarly beald, *bold*; eald, *old*; feld, *field*.

§ **163.** Germanic þl generally remained in Anglian, but became dl after long vowels in WS., as nǣdl (Anglian nēþl), *needle*; wǣdl (Anglian wēþl), *poverty*.

§ **164.** The combinations tþ, dþ became tt, which were simplified to t finally and after consonants, as bit(t) from *bitþ, older bīteþ, *he bites*; it(t) from *itþ, older iteþ, *he eats*. bit(t) from *bidþ, older bideþ, *he prays*; bint from *bindþ, older bindeþ, *he binds*; gesynto from *gesundiþu, *health*; mittȳ from mid þȳ, *when, while*.

The combinations s, ss + þ became st, as cīest from cīesþ, older cīeseþ, *he chooses*; hafastu = hafas + þū, *hast thou*. cyst from older cysseþ, *he kisses*.

For the assimilation of þs, þd to ss, dd, see § 142; and for the loss of þ before st, see § 144.

The Sibilant s.

§ 165. Germanic s remained initially, medially in combination with voiceless consonants, and finally, as sēcan, Goth. sōkjan, *to seek*; gāst, OHG. geist, *spirit*; and similarly sǣd, *seed*; sittan, *to sit*; slǣpan, *to sleep*; smæl, *small*; sunu, *son*; strēam, *stream*; assa, *ass*; sweostor, *sister*; gærs, *grass*; gōs, *goose*; wæs, *was*.

For the voicing of **s** to **z** between voiced sounds, see § 139; and for the metathesis of **s**, see § 143.

The Gutturals.

k

§ 166. Germanic k, generally written c in OE., remained a guttural initially before consonants and before the guttural vowels ă, ŏ, ŭ, and their umlauts æ (e), ǣ, e, ē (œ̄), y, ȳ, but became a palatal before the palatal vowels, æ, ǣ (ē) = Germanic ǣ, e (= Germanic e), ē (= Germanic ē); ea, eo, io, from Germanic a, e, i by breaking (§§ 51-3), ēa, ēo, īo, i, ī, and their umlauts e, ie (= i-umlaut of ea, io), īe (= i-umlaut of ēa, īo), see § 57.

Germanic medial k and kk remained guttural when originally followed by a guttural vowel, as bucca, *he-goat*; macian from *makōjan, *to make*; sacu, *strife*; geoc, prim. Germanic *jukan, *yoke*; but became palatal when originally followed by an i or j, as bryce from *brukiz, *breach*; sēcan = Goth. sōkjan, *to seek*; þeccan from *þakjan, *to cover*.

The guttural and palatal c often existed side by side in different forms of the same word, as pret. pl. curon, pp. coren, beside inf. cēosan, *to choose*; brecan, *to break*, beside bricþ from *brikiþ, *he breaks*.

Both the guttural and the palatal k were generally written c in OE. When c was palatal it was often written ce, ci medially before a following guttural vowel, with e, i to indicate the palatal nature of the c, as þencean, *to think*. Examples are:

1. Guttural c: cēlan from *kōljan, *to cool*; cemban from *kambjan, *to comb*; cynn, Goth. kuni, *race, generation*; cnēo, Goth. kniu, *knee*; and similarly camb, *comb*; cēpan, *to keep*; cōl, *cool*; coss, *kiss*; cuman, *to come*; cyning, *king*; cȳþan, *to make known*. climban, *to climb*; cræft, *craft*; cwēn, *queen*. æcer, Goth. akrs, prim. Germanic *akraz, *field*; nacod, Goth. naqaþs, *naked*; and similarly bacan, *to bake*; sprecan, *to speak*; sticca, *stick*. macian from *makōjan, *to make*, and similarly liccian, *to lick*; lōcian, *to look*; þancian, *to thank*. drincan, *to drink*. bucc, O.Icel. bokkr, *buck*; blæc, prim. Germanic *blakaz, *black*; and similarly āc, *oak*; bæc, *back*; bōc, *book*; flocc, *flock*; sēoc, *sick*; þanc, *thought*.

2. Palatal c: cēapian, Goth. káupōn, *to trade, traffic*; cēosan, Goth. kiusan, *to choose*; cinn, Goth. kinnus, *chin*; and similarly ceaf, *chaff*; cealc, *chalk*; ceald, *cold*; cealf, *calf*; ceorfan, *to carve, cut*; cēowan, *to chew*; cīese, *cheese*; cild, *child*. bēc from *bōkiz, *books*; þenc(e)an, Goth. þagkjan, *to think*; and similarly birce, *birch*; flicce, *flitch*; þync(e)an, *to seem*; stenc, *smell, odour*.

OE. final c became palatal when preceded by ĭ, as ic, *I*; hwelc from *hwa-līk, *which*; pic, *pitch*; swelc from *swa-līk, *such*.

NOTE.—cs was generally written x, as æx beside older æces, *axe*; rīxian beside rīcsian, *to rule*.

§ 167. In the oldest period of the language sc, like c (§ 166), was guttural or palatal, but some time during the OE. period the guttural sc became palatal, except in loanwords. It was often written sce, sci before a following guttural vowel with e, i to indicate the palatal nature of the sc. Examples are: sc(e)acan, *to shake*; scand, *disgrace*; scēap, *sheep*; scearp, *sharp*; scieran, *to shear*; scip, *ship*; scrūd, *dress, garment*; scūr, *shower*; scyldig, *guilty*; wascan, *to wash*; fisc, *fish*. But scōl (Lat. schola), *school*; scinn (O.Icel. skinn), *skin*.

For the metathesis of sc, see § 143.

g

§ 168. Germanic ȝ became g after n during the prim. Germanic period (§ 112). ȝj (§ 135) and ȝn (§ 137) became gg in West Germanic. The gg from ȝn remained guttural in OE., as dogga, *dog*; frogga, *frog*; but the gg from ȝj became palatal, and was generally written cg, also cge, cgi before a guttural vowel, as pl. secg(e)as beside sing. secg, *man*, gen. secges, dat. secge. Germanic ȝ remained a spirant in all other positions in the oldest period of OE.

Germanic initial and medial ȝ became differentiated in prehistoric OE. into a guttural and a palatal voiced spirant under the same conditions as those by which Germanic k became differentiated into a guttural and palatal explosive (§ 166).

The guttural and palatal ȝ often existed side by side in different forms of the same word, as pl. gatu beside sing. geat, *gate*; pret. pl. guton, pp. goten, beside inf. gēotan, *to pour out*.

Initial guttural ȝ remained in the oldest period of the language, but had become the voiced explosive g before the end of the OE. period. Initial palatal ȝ (written g) remained a spirant (= the y in NE. yon) and fell together with Germanic initial j (§ 150). This explains why Germanic initial j was written g in OE. Examples are:—

1. Guttural ȝ: gōd, Goth. gōþs, *good*; OE. Goth. guma, *man*; græs, Goth. gras, *grass*; and similarly gaderian, *to gather*; gāt, *goat*; gatu, *gates*; gōs, *goose*; gylden, *golden*; grund, *ground*.

2. Palatal ȝ: geaf, Goth. gaf, *he gave*; gēotan, Goth. giutan, *to pour out*; giefan, Goth. giban, *to give*; and similarly gēafon, *they gave*; geat, *gate*; geolu, *yellow*; gieldan, *to repay, yield*; giest, *guest*; gift, *marriage gift*.

§ 169. The g in the combination ng remained guttural or became palatal according as it was originally followed by a guttural vowel or a palatal vowel or j. It also remained guttural before consonants:—

1. Guttural ŋg: bringan, Goth. briggan, *to bring*; cyning from *kuningaz, *king*; and similarly englisc, *English*; finger, *finger*; singan, *to sing*; þing, *thing*.

2. Palatal ŋg, often written nge medially before guttural vowels with e to denote the palatal nature of the g: seng(e)an from *saŋgjan, *to singe*; and similarly, streng, *string*; lengra, *longer*; steng, *pole*.

For the change of ŋg to nc before voiceless consonants, see § 140.

§ 170. Medial ȝ remained a guttural spirant before original guttural vowels, but became a palatal spirant when originally followed by a palatal vowel or j. It also became palatal between OE. palatal vowels:—

1. Guttural ȝ: ēage, Goth. áugō, *eye*; stīgan, Goth. steigan, *to ascend*; and similarly dragan, *to draw*; dagian from *daȝōjan, *to dawn*; boga, *bow*; fugol, *bird*; lagu, *law*; dagas, *days*.

2. Palatal ȝ, often written ge before a following guttural vowel: bīegan from *bauȝjan, *to bend*; ege, Goth. agis, *fear*; and similarly eglan, *to molest*; hyge, *mind*. fægen, *glad*; nægel, *nail*; gen. sing. dæges, *of a day*.

For the unvoicing of ȝ to h (= χ), see § 140; and for the loss of ȝ, see § 144.

§ 171. Medial -igi-, -ige- were contracted to -ī-, as īl beside igil, *hedgehog*; sīþe from *sigiþe, *scythe*; līst beside ligest, *thou liest*.

§ 172. When Germanic ȝ came to stand finally in OE., it is probable that it became a voiceless spirant (χ) just as in Goth. OS. and prehistoric O.Icel., but that the g (= ȝ) was mostly restored again through the influence of the inflected forms. After liquids and long vowels the restoration of the g was merely orthographical, but the further history of the sound in OE. shows that after palatal vowels it was restored in pronunciation as well. The h (= χ) seldom occurs in early OE., but is common in late OE. especially after liquids and long vowels, as mearh, *marrow*, bealh, *he became angry*, beside mearg, bealg; and similarly **beorh**, *hill*; **burh**, *city*; **sorh**, *sorrow*. **dāh**, *dough*, **plōh**, *plough*, beside **dāg**, **plōg**; and similarly **flēah**, *he flew*; **stāh**, *he ascended*; **genōh**, *enough*; **troh** beside **trog**, *trough*.

For the vocalization of palatal **g**, see § 141.

h, χ.

§ 173. Initial χ had become an aspirate before vowels already in prim. Germanic (§ 130). In OE. it also became an aspirate initially before consonants except in the combination χw. The spirant remained in the combination χw and has been preserved in many Scottish dialects down to the present day. Examples are: **habban**, Goth. **haban**, *to have*; and similarly **hand**, *hand*; **hēafod**, *head*; **hungor**, *hunger*; &c.

hlāf, Goth. **hláifs**, *loaf, bread*; and similarly **hnīgan**, *to bend down*; **hnutu**, *nut*; **hring**, *ring*; **hladan**, *to load*; **hlid**, *lid*.

hwā, Goth. **ƕas**, *who*; and similarly **hwæl**, *whale*; **hwǣte**, *wheat*; **hwīl**, *space of time*; **hwīt**, *white*.

For the loss of **h** in compounds, see § 144.

§ 174. Medial χ (written h) remained in OE. before voiceless consonants, and when doubled. It was guttural or palatal according as it was originally followed by a guttural or palatal vowel or j, as **brōhte**, Goth. **brāhta**, *he brought*; **dohtor**, Goth. **daúhtar**, *daughter*; and similarly **bohte**, *he bought*; **cnieht**, **cniht**, *boy*; **eahta**, *eight*; **þōhte**, *he thought*. **pohha**, *pocket*; **tiohhian**, *to think, consider*.

Dat. **dehter** from *dohtri beside nom. **dohtor**, *daughter*; **hliehhan**, Goth. **hlahjan**, *to laugh*; **līehtan**, Goth. **liuhtjan**, *to give light*; **siehþ**, OHG. **sihit**, *he sees*.

For the loss of medial χ, see § 144.

§ 175. χs became ks (written x), as **oxa**, Goth. **aúhsa**, *ox*; **siex**, Goth. **saíhs**, *six*; **weaxan**, OHG. **wahsan**, *to grow*.

§ 176. Final χ (written h) remained, as **hēah**, OHG. **hōh**, *high*; **seah**, OHG. **sah**, *he saw*; **þurh**, Goth. **þaírh**, *through*; and similarly **feoh**, *cattle, property*; **scōh**, *shoe*; **sleah**, *slay thou*; **holh**, *hollow*; **furh**, *furrow*.

ACCIDENCE
CHAPTER IX
NOUNS

§ 177. In OE. as in the oldest periods of the other Germanic languages, nouns are divided into two great classes, according as the stem originally ended in a vowel or a consonant. Nouns whose stems originally ended in a vowel belong to the vocalic or so-called strong declension. Those whose stems originally ended in -n belong to the weak declension. All other consonantal stems will be put together under the general heading, 'Minor Declensions'. Both the stem- and case-endings of nouns underwent so many changes partly in prim. Germanic and partly in the prehistoric period of OE. that it is rarely possible from an OE. nominative singular alone to determine the original stem of any given noun, because in some classes of nouns not only original case-endings, but also stem-endings regularly disappeared, see §§ 80–8. The only method by which the learner can gain an extensive and accurate knowledge of the declension of nouns is by reading OE. texts and by learning the gender, genitive singular, and nominative plural of nouns as they occur in the course of his reading.

§ 178. OE. nouns have two numbers: singular and plural; three genders: masculine, feminine, and neuter, as in the other old Germanic languages from which the gender of nouns in OE. does not materially differ; five cases: Nominative, Accusative, Genitive, Dative, and Instrumental. The dat. is generally used for the instr. in OE., so that this case is omitted in the paradigms. The vocative is like the nominative. The nom. and acc. singular of masculine and feminine nouns are alike except in the ō- and the n-stems. The nom. and acc. plural are always alike. Traces of an old locative occur in what is called the uninflected dat. sing. of **hām**, *home*. In Northumbrian both the declension and gender of nouns fluctuated considerably as compared with the other dialects.

A. The Vocalic or Strong Declension.

1. The a-Declension.

§ 179. The a-declension comprises masculine and neuter nouns only, and corresponds to the Latin and Greek o-declension (Lat. masc. -us, neut. -um; Gr. masc. -ος, neut. -ον), for which reason it is sometimes called the o-declension. The a-declension is divided into pure a-stems, ja-stems, and wa-stems.

a. Pure a-Stems.

§ 180. *Masculine.*

Sing.

Nom. Acc.	stān, *stone*	dæg, *day*	mearh, *horse*
Gen.	stānes	dæges	mēares
Dat.	stāne	dæge	mēare

Plur.

Nom. Acc.	stānas	dagas	mēaras
Gen.	stāna	daga	mēara
Dat.	stānum	dagum	mēarum

Note.—The gen. sing. ended in **-æs** in the oldest period of the language, and in late OE. occasionally in **-as, -ys**. The regular nom. pl. ending would be **-e** (§ 86); the **-as** is probably a prim. OE. shortened pronominal form representing the **-ās** in **þās**, *these* (§ 310), just as prim. Germanic had the pronominal ending of the gen. sing. from the simple demonstrative pronoun, which accounts for the preservation of the final **-s** in both cases. For a similar pronominal ending of the nom. pl. of these stems, cp. Latin **lupī**, Gr. λύκοι with **-ī, -οι** = OE. **-ā** in **þā**, and Goth. **-ái** in **þái** (§ 309). For other suggested explanations of the OE. **-as**, see *OE. Grammar*, § 334. In late OE. the dat. pl. ended in **-un, -on, -an** (§ 153).

§ 181. Like **stān** are declined by far the greater majority of monosyllabic a-stems, as **ǣl**, *eel*; **āþ**, *oath*; **bār**, *boar*; **bāt**, *boat*; **bēam**, *tree*; **beard**, *beard*; **bolt**, *bolt*; **camb**, *comb*; **cēap**, *price*; **clāþ**, *cloth*; **clūt**, *patch*; **cocc**, *cock*; **cræft**, *skill*; **dōm**, *doom*; **earm**, *arm*; **eorl**, *nobleman*; **fisc**, *fish*; **fox**, *fox*; **gāst**, *spirit*; **geard**, *yard*; **hām**, *home*; **hlāf**, *loaf*; **hring**, *ring*; **hund**, *dog*; **mōr**, *moor*; **mūþ**, *mouth*; **pott**, *pot*; **rāp**, *rope*; **rūm**, *room*; **strēam**, *stream*; **þēof**, *thief*; **weall**, *wall*; **weg**, *way*.

§ 182. Like **dæg** are declined **hwæl**, *whale*; **pæþ**, *path*; **stæf**, *staff*, see §§ 29–30; and **mǣg**, *kinsman*, pl. **māgas** (§ 45) beside **mǣgas** with **ǣ** from the singular.

Like **mearh** are declined **ealh**, *temple*; **eolh**, *elk*; **fearh**, *pig*, *boar*; **healh**, *corner*; **sealh**, *willow*; **seolh**, *seal*; **wealh**, *foreigner*, see § 76. **scōh**, *shoe*, gen. **scōs**, dat. **scō**; pl. **scōs**, gen. **scōna** with -na after the analogy of n-stems (§ 247), dat. **scōm**, **scōum** (§ 68); and similarly **slōh** (also fem. and neut.), *slough*, *mire*; **eoh** (also neut.), *horse*.

§ 183. SING.

Nom. Acc.	cyning, *king*	engel, *angel*	fugol, *bird*	heofon, *heaven*
Gen.	cyninges	engles	fugles	heofones
Dat.	cyninge	engle	fugle	heofone

PLUR.

Nom. Acc.	cyningas	englas	fuglas	heofonas
Gen.	cyninga	engla	fugla	heofona
Dat.	cyningum	englum	fuglum	heofonum

On the retention or loss of the medial vowel in the inflected forms of dissyllabic words, see §§ 96–8; and on pl. forms like **heofenas** beside **heofonas**, see § 100.

§ 184. Like **cyning** are declined **æcer**, *field*; **hærfest**, *autumn*; **hengest**, *horse*; &c.; and derivative nouns ending in -aþ (-oþ), -dōm, -els, -hād, and in -ing, -ling with concrete meaning, as **drohtaþ**, *way of life*; **fiscoþ**, *fishing*; **cynedōm**, *kingdom*; **fǣtels**, *tub*; **cildhād**, *childhood*; **hǣring**, *herring*; **feorþling**, *farthing*.

§ 185. Like **engel** are declined **angel**, *fish-hook*; **bealdor**, *prince*; **blōstm**, *blossom*; **bōsm**, *bosom*; **brēmel**, *bramble*; **dēofol**, *devil*; **dryhten**, *lord*; **ealdor**, *prince*; **finger**, *finger*; **hleahtor**, *laughter*; **māþum**, *treasure*; **morgen**, *morning*; **þȳmel**, *thimble*.

§ 186. Like **fugol** are declined **botm**, *bottom*; **fæþm**, *embrace*; **hæg(e)l, hagol**, *hail*; **ofen**, *oven*; **nægl**, *nail*; **reg(e)n**, *rain*; **þeg(e)n**, *thane*.

§ 187. Like **heofon** are declined **bydel**, *beadle*; **bulluc**, *bullock*; **cradol**, *cradle*; **eofor**, *boar*; **hafoc, heafuc**, *hawk*; **hamor**, *hammer*; **heorot**, *hart*; **mattuc**, *mattock*; **metod**, *Creator*; **pearroc**, *park*; **rodor**, *sky*; **sadol**, *saddle*; **þunor**, *thunder*.

§ 188. *Neuter.*

Sing.

Nom. Acc.	word, *word*	hof, *dwelling*	fæt, *vessel*
Gen.	wordes	hofes	fætes
Dat.	worde	hofe	fæte

Plur.

Nom. Acc.	word	hofu, -o	fatu, -o
Gen.	worda	hofa	fata
Dat.	wordum	hofum	fatum

The inflexion of the neuter **a**-stems only differs from the masculine in the nom. and acc. plural which in prim. Germanic ended in -ō. The -ō became -u in prehistoric O.E., and then disappeared after long stem-syllables (§ 85. 1). In the nouns with short stem-syllables the -u became -o at an early period, and then in late OE. -a.

§ 189. Like **word** are declined a large number of monosyllables with long stem, as **bān**, *bone*; **bearn**, *child*; **bēor**, *beer*; blōd, *blood*; brēost, *breast*; corn, *corn*; dēor, *wild animal*; fām, *foam*; fleax, *flax*; folc, *folk*; gēar, *year*; gearn, *yarn*; gold, *gold*; hors, *horse*; hūs, *house*; īs, *ice*; land, *land*; lēaf, *leaf*; līn, *flax, linen*; morþ, *murder*; nest, *nest*; sār, *pain*; scēap, *sheep*; sweord, *sword*; þing, *thing*; weorc, *work*; wīf, *woman*. And similarly words with a prefix, as behāt, *promise*.

§ 190. Like hof are declined broþ, *broth*; ceaf, *chaff*; col, *coal*; dor, *door*; geoc, *yoke*; god, *god* (*heathen*); hol, *hole*; loc, *lock*; and similarly words with a prefix, as bebod, gebod, *command*. geat (§ 56), *gate*, pl. gatu beside geatu with ea from the singular. On plurals like cliofu, *cliffs*, gebeodu, *prayers*, beside clifu, gebedu, see § 59.

§ 191. Like fæt are declined bæc, *back*; bæþ, *bath*; bræs, *brass*; dæl, *dale*; gærs, older græs, *grass*; glæs, *glass*; sæp, *sap*; þæc, *thatch, roof*; wæl, *slaughter*; &c. See §§ 29–30.

§ 192. flāh, *fraud*, gen. flās, dat. flā; þēoh, *thigh*, gen. þēos, dat. þēo, pl. þēoh, gen. þēona with -na after the analogy of the n-stems (§ 253); holh, *hollow, hole*, gen. hōles, dat. hōle, pl. holh, see § 74. feoh, *cattle*, gen. fēos, dat. fēo (originally u-stem).

§ 193. SING.

Nom. Acc.	tungol, *star*	wæter, *water*	hēafod, *head*
Gen.	tungles	wæteres	hēafdes
Dat.	tungle	wætere	hēafde

PLUR.

Nom. Acc.	tungol	wæter	hēafodu
Gen.	tungla	wætera	hēafda
Dat.	tunglum	wæterum	hēafdum

On the loss or retention of the medial vowel in the inflected forms, see §§ 97–8; and on the loss or retention of the -u in the plural, see § 85. 1. In the later period of the language there was great fluctuation in the formation of the plural and in the loss or retention of the medial vowel, as nom. acc. pl. tunglu, wæt(e)ru, hēafdu beside older tungol, wæter, hēafodu; gen. sing. wætres beside older wæteres.

§ 194. Like tungol are declined ātor, *poison*; bēacen, *beacon*; fōdor, *fodder*; morþor, *murder*; spātl, *saliva*; tācen, *token*; wǣpen, *weapon*; wuldor, *glory*; wundor, *wonder*.

§ 195. Like wæter are declined brægen, *brain*; gamen, *game, sport*; mægen, *strength*; reced, *house, hall*; weder, *weather*; weorod, werod, *troop*, pl. weredu (§ 100) beside werod. setl, *seat*, pl. setlu beside setl.

§ 196. Like hēafod are declined clīewen, clīwen, *ball of thread, clew*; mǣden, mǣgden, *maiden*; nīeten, *animal*.

b. ja-Stems.

§ 197. In the ja-stems it is necessary to distinguish between those stems which were originally long and those which became long by the West Germanic doubling of consonants (§ 135). The j caused umlaut of the stem-vowel and then disappeared in the inflected forms except after r (§§ 57, 151). When it came to stand finally after the loss of prim. Germanic -az, -an (§ 84) it became vocalized to -i which remained in the oldest period of the language, and then later became -e (§ 141); cp. here, *army*, ende, *end*, beside Goth. acc. hari, andi. The OE. forms with double consonants in the nom. acc. singular are all new formations from the inflected forms. The regular forms would be *sege, *man*, *dyne, *noise*, neut. *cyne (Goth. kuni), *race, generation*, instead of secg, dynn, cynn.

Masculine.

§ 198. Sing.

Nom. Acc.	secg, *man*	ende, *end*
Gen.	secgeʒ	endeʒ
Dat.	secge	ende

Plur.

Nom. Acc.	secg(e)as	endas
Gen.	secg(e)a	enda
Dat.	secg(e)um	endum

The masculine ja-stems have the same inflexional endings as the pure a-stems (§ 180). On the (e) in the plural of secg, see § 168.

§ 199. Like secg are declined bridd, *young bird*; cnyll, *knell*; dyn(n), *noise*; hrycg, *back, ridge*; hyll, *hill*; mycg, *midge*; wecg, *wedge*. See § 135.

§ 200. The j (written i, ig; also ige before a guttural vowel, § 151) remained medially after r preceded by a short vowel, as nom. acc. here, *army*; gen. heries, herges, heriges; dat. herie, herge, herige; pl. nom. acc. herias, hergas, herigas, herigeas; gen. heria, heriga, herigea; dat. herium, herigum. Forms without j also occur occasionally, as gen. heres, dat. here, pl. heras.

§ 201. Like ende are declined esne, *servant*; hierde, *shepherd*; hwǣte, *wheat*; lǣce, *physician*; mēce, *sword*; and the nomina agentis, as bæcere, *baker*; sǣdere, *sower*.

§ 202. *Neuter.*

SING.

Nom. Acc.	cyn(n), *race*	wīte, *punishment*	wēsten, *desert*
Gen.	cynnes	wītes	wēstennes
Dat.	cynne	wīte	wēstenne

PLUR.

Nom. Acc.	cyn(n)	wītu	wēstennu
Gen.	cynna	wīta	wēstenna
Dat.	cynnum	wītum	wēstennum

The neuter ja-stems had the same endings as the masculine except in the nom. acc. plural. The nom. acc. plural ended in prim. Germanic in -jō which became -ju in prim. OE. The j regularly disappeared after causing umlaut of the preceding vowel. And then the -u being preceded by a long syllable also disappeared (§ 85. 1). The nom. acc. plural of the originally short stems is regularly developed from the prim. Germanic form, as cyn(n) from *kunjō. But the -u in the originally long stems and in words containing a suffix is not the preservation of the prim. OE. -u. Such nouns owe their final -u to the analogy of the nom. acc. pl. of short a-stems (§ 85. 1). That forms like wītu, wēstennu are new formations is proved by the simple fact that from a prim. Germanic point of view these nouns ought to have the same ending in OE. as the fem. nom. singular of the jō-stems (§ 221). In late OE. the double consonants in words containing a suffix were generally simplified in the inflected forms, and the medial vowel was also occasionally syncopated, as gen. wēstenes, pl. wēstenu, beside wēstnu.

§ 203. Like cyn(n) are declined bedd, *bed*; nebb, *beak*; nett, *net*; ribb, *rib*; witt, *understanding*. See § 135.

§ 204. Like wīte are declined ǣrende, *errand*; ierfe, *inheritance*; ierre, *anger*; rīce, *kingdom*; stīele, *steel*; neut. nouns with the prefix ge-, as gefilde, *plain*; getimbre, *building*. flicce, *flitch*, stycce, *piece*, prim. Germanic *flikkja-, *stukkja-.

§ 205. Like wēsten are declined neut. derivative nouns ending in -en, -et, as fæsten(n), *fortress*; sǣwet(t), *sowing*.

c. wa-STEMS.

§ 206.   *Masculine.*

SING.

Nom. Acc. bearu, -o, *grove*   þēo(w), *servant*
    Gen. bearwes   þeowes
    Dat. bearwe   þeowe

PLUR.

Nom. Acc. bearwas   þeowas
    Gen. bearwa   þeowa
    Dat. bearwum   þeowum

In the inflected forms the masc. wa-stems have the same endings as the pure a-stems (§ 180). The nom. acc. singular bearu, þēo are regularly developed from the prim. Germanic forms *ƀarwaz, -an, *þewaz, -an (see §§ 84, 141). After a long vowel the -u from -w regularly disappeared, as in snā, *snow*, from *snaiwaz, -an. At a later period the w of the inflected forms was levelled out into the nom. acc. singular, whence þēow, snāw beside older þēo, snā. And then later from þēow was often formed a new gen. þēowes beside the regular þeowes. On forms like gen. bearuwes beside bearwes, see § 102.

§ 207. Like þēo, þēow are declined bēaw, *gadfly*; dēaw (also neut.), *dew*; lārēow, *teacher*; lāttēow, *leader*; þēaw, *custom*.

§ 208. *Neuter.*

Sing.

Nom. Acc.	bealu, -o, *evil*	cnēo(w), *knee*
Gen.	bealwes	cneowes
Dat.	bealwe	cneowe

Plur.

Nom. Acc.	bealu, -o	cnēo(w)
Gen.	bealwa	cneowa
Dat.	bealwum	cneowum

The neuter wa-stems have the same endings as the masculine except in the nom. acc. plural. The nom. acc. plural bealu, cnēo are from older *beal(w)u, *kne(w)u (§ 149), whereas the nom. acc. sing. bealu, cnēo are from older *bealw-, *knew- (§ 141). What has been said in § 206 about the history of the w also applies to the neuters. On forms like gen. bealuwes beside bealwes, see § 102.

§ 209. Like bealu are declined c(w)udu, *cud*; teoru, *tar*; meolu, melu, *meal, flour*; searu, *device*; smeoru, *fat*.

§ 210. Like cnēo, cnēow are declined anclēow, *ankle*; bēow, *barley*; gehlōw, *lowing, bellowing*; gehrēow, *lamentation*; hlēo(w), *protection, covering*; strēa(w), *straw*; trēo(w), *tree*.

2. The ō-Declension.

§ 211. The ō-declension contains feminine nouns only and corresponds to the Latin and Greek ā-declension, for which reason it is sometimes called the ā-declension. The ō-declension is divided into pure ō-stems, jō-stems, and wō-stems.

a. Pure ō-Stems.

§ 212. Sing.

Nom.	giefu, -o, *gift*	ār, *honour*
Acc.	giefe	āre
Gen.	giefe	āre
Dat.	giefe	āre

Plur.

Nom. Acc.	giefa, -e	āra, -e
Gen.	giefa, (-ena)	āra, (-na, -ena)
Dat.	giefum	ārum

On the loss or retention of the -u in the nom. sing., see § 85. 1.

The normally developed ending of the nom. acc. pl. is -e, which was regularly preserved in the Anglian dialects (§ 86), whereas -a is the usual ending in WS. and Ken. The ending -a in these dialects is due to the analogy of the fem. u-declension (§ 245). After the analogy of words like duru, hand : pl. dura, handa, to words like giefu, ār were formed pl. giefa, āra. The regular ending of the gen. pl. is -a, but in late OE. the gen. pl. often ended in -(e)na after the analogy of the n-stems (§ 250). Short stems with a often have æ beside a in the acc. gen. and dat. sing., as læþe, ræce, beside laþe, race.

§ 213. Like giefu are declined caru, *care*; daru, *injury*; faru, *journey* ; laþu, *invitation* ; lufu, *love* ; racu, *account, narrative* ; sacu, *strife* ; talu, *tale, number* ; wracu, *revenge*; &c.

§ 214. Like ār are declined a large number of nouns, as

æsp, *aspen-tree*; bǣr, *bier*; beorc, *birch-tree*; brōd, *brood*; gād, *goad*; glōf, *glove*; heord, *herd*; hwīl, *space of time*; lār, *learning*; mearc, *boundary*; rōd, *cross*; scofl, *shovel*; sorg, *sorrow*; wund, *wound*; &c.

§ 215. SING.

Nom.	firen, *crime*	sāwol, *soul*
Acc.	firene	sāwle
Gen.	firene	sāwle
Dat.	firene	sāwle

PLUR.

Nom. Acc.	firena, -e	sāwla, -e
Gen.	firena	sāwla
Dat.	firenum	sāwlum

In originally trisyllabic words the final -u regularly disappeared in the nom. sing. when the stem-syllable and the medial syllable were short, but remained when the stem-syllable was long and the medial syllable short (§ 85. 1). Then after the analogy of words like firen, the final -u was also dropped in words like sāwol. The medial vowel regularly disappeared in the inflected forms after long stems, but remained after short (§§ 97–8). The nouns of this class do not have the ending -(e)na in the gen. plural.

§ 216. Like firen are declined bisen, bisn, *example*; byden, *bushel*; feter, *fetter*; feþer, *feather*; netel, *nettle*; spinel, *spindle*; stefn, *voice*.

§ 217. Like sāwol are declined ādl, *disease*; ceaster, *city, fortress*; frōfor (also masc.), *consolation*; nǣdl, *needle*; wōcor, *increase, usury*.

§ 218. Nom. strenþu, -o, *strength* leornung, *learning*
Acc. Gen. Dat. strengþe leornunge, -a

The fem. abstract nouns ending in prim. Germanic -iþō (Goth. -iþa, -ida, OHG. -ida) regularly syncopated the medial i (§ 98) and in the oldest period of the language retained the final -u in the nom. (§ 85. 1). Then at a later period the -u (-o) was often dropped after the analogy of words like ār (§ 212). At a still later period the nom. with and without the final -o came to be used for all cases. The abstract nouns in -ung regularly syncopated the final -u in the nom. (§ 85. 1). The ending -a was due to the analogy of the fem. u-declension (§ 245).

§ 219. Like strengþu are declined cȳþþu, cȳþ(þ), *native country*; fǣhþ(u), *feud*; mǣgþ(u), *family, kindred*; þīefþ(u), *theft*; &c.

§ 220. Like leornung are declined ǣfnung, *evening*; lēasung, *falsehood*; wēnung, *hope, expectation*; &c.

b. jō-STEMS.

§ 221. SING.

Nom.	hen(n), *hen*	gierd, *rod*
Acc.	henne	gierde
Gen.	henne	gierde
Dat.	henne	gierde

PLUR.

Nom. Acc.	henna, -e	gierda, -e
Gen.	henna	gierda
Dat.	hennum	gierdum

It is necessary to distinguish between those stems which were originally long and those which became long by the West Germanic doubling of consonants (§ 135). The j regularly disappeared after causing umlaut of the preceding vowel, and then the -u in the nom. sing. being preceded by a long stem also disappeared (§ 85. 1), so that the endings of the jō-stems are the same as those of the ō-stems except that the gen. pl. never has the ending -(e)na.

§ 222. Like hen(n) are declined brycg, *bridge*; cribb, *crib*; crycc, *crutch*; ecg, *edge*; hell, *hell*; sciell, *shell*; secg, *sword*; sibb, *relationship*; syll, *threshold*; synn, *sin*; wynn, *joy*. See § 135.

§ 223. Like **gierd** are declined **æx**, *axe*; **bliþs**, *bliss*; **hild**, *war, battle*; **hind**, *doe*; **nift**, *niece*; **rest**, *rest*; **spræc**, *speech, language*; **wylf**, *she-wolf*; &c.

§ 224.

	Sing.	Plur.
Nom.	byrþen(n), *burden*	byrþenna, -e
Acc.	byrþenne	byrþenna, -e
Gen.	byrþenne	byrþenna
Dat.	byrþenne	byrþennum

In originally trisyllabic words the final -u in the nom. sing. also regularly disappeared after the medial syllable which became long by the West Germanic doubling of consonants (§§ 85. 1, 135). The nouns ending in -en(n) sometimes took -u again in the nom. sing. after the analogy of the short ō-stems (§ 212). In late OE. the double consonants were often simplified in the inflected forms.

§ 225. Like byrþen(n) are declined the fem. nouns ending in -en, -en(n), and -es(s), -nes(s), as **biren**, *she-bear*; **fyxen**, *she-fox*; **gyden**, *goddess*; **ræden(n)**, *rule, arrangement*; **hūsræden(n)**, *household*; **hægtes(s)**, *witch*; **cōlnes(s)**, *coolness*; **þrīnes(s)**, *trinity*.

c. wō-Stems.

§ 226.

Sing.		
Nom.	beadu, -o, *battle*	mǣd, *meadow*
Acc. Gen. Dat.	beadwe	mǣdwe
Plur.		
Nom. Acc.	beadwa, -e	mǣdwa, -e
Gen.	beadwa	mǣdwa
Dat.	beadwum	mǣdwum

In the inflected forms the wō-stems had the same endings as the ō-stems except that they never had the ending -(e)na in the gen. plural. In the nom. sing. the Germanic ending -wō regularly became -wu, then the w disappeared before the -u

(§ 144). The -u remained after consonants preceded by an original short vowel, but disappeared after consonants preceded by a long vowel (§ 85. 1). When the -u was preceded by a it combined with it to form a diphthong, as clēa from *cla(w)u, *claw*, þrēa from *þra(w)u, *threat* (§ 69), pl. nom. acc. clēa, dat. clēam from *cla(w)um; beside the regular nom. sing. forms clēa, þrēa, new nominatives clawu, þrawu were made from the stem-form of the oblique cases. The final -u from older -w also regularly disappeared after long vowels and diphthongs (§ 149), but the w was restored again from the inflected forms already in the oldest period of the language, as hrēow, *repentance*; stōw, *place*; trēow, *faith, truth*. On forms like gen. beaduwe beside beadwe, see § 102.

§ 227. Like beadu are declined sceadu, *shadow*; sinu, sionu, *sinew*; and the plurals frætwa, -e, *ornaments*; geatwa, -e, *armaments, armour*.

§ 228. Like mǣd are declined blōd(es)lǣs, *blood-letting, bleeding*; lǣs, *pasture*.

3. Feminine Abstract Nouns in -īn.

§ 229. This declension comprises the fem. abstract nouns formed from adjectives, as brǣdu, *breadth* : brād, *broad*; strengu, *strength* : strang, *strong*; Goth. managei, *multitude* : manags, *many*. The nouns of this category had originally the stem-ending -īn and were declined according to the weak declension as in Gothic managei, gen. manageins. The -ī, -īn- regularly became -i, -in- in prehistoric OE. (§ 85. 3), and then the i caused umlaut of the stem-vowel. This umlaut of the stem-vowel is the only characteristic feature preserved in the historic period of the language of the nouns belonging to this class. In the prehistoric period of OE. this class of nouns was remodelled on analogy with the short ō-stems (§ 212), so that the nom. came to end in -u, later -o, and the oblique cases of the singular in -e. At a later period the new nominative came to be used for all forms of the singular and for the nom. acc. plural. Few nouns belonging to this class have a plural.

Sing.		Plur.
Nom.	strengu, -o, *strength*	strenga, -e ; -u, -o
Acc.	strenge, -u, -o	,,
Gen.	,,	strenga
Dat.	,,	strengum

§ 230. Like **strengu** are declined **bieldu**, *boldness*; **bierhtu**, *brightness*; **engu**, *narrowness*; **fyllu**, *fullness*; **hǣlu**, *health*; **hǣtu**, *heat*; **menigu, mengu**, *multitude*; **þīestru**, *darkness*; &c.

4. The i-Declension.

§ 231. The i-declension comprises masculine, feminine, and neuter nouns, and corresponds to the Latin and Greek i-declension (nom. masc. and fem. Lat. -is, Gr. -ις; acc. -im, -ιν; neut. nom. acc. -e, -ι). The masculine and feminine i-stems were originally declined alike in the sing. and plural as in Latin and Greek, but with the exception of a few plurals, chiefly names of peoples, the masculines came to be inflected after the analogy of the a-stems (§ 180) in early OE.

a. Masculine.

§ 232. Sing.

Nom. Acc.	wine, *friend*	giest, *guest*
Gen.	wines	giestes
Dat.	wine	gieste

Plur.

Nom. Acc.	wine, -as	giestas
Gen.	wina, wini(ge)a	giesta
Dat.	winum	giestum

The Germanic endings -iz, -in of the nom. and acc. sing. regularly became -i in prehistoric OE. (§ 84). The -i caused umlaut of the stem-vowel and then disappeared after long stems, but remained after short stems and later became -e. The regular ending of the gen. sing. would be -e (§ 90), the -es is from the a-stems. The dat. sing. ended in -i (later -e) in the oldest OE. and corresponded to the Germanic ending -ī (§ 85. 3). The prim. Germanic nom. pl. ending -īz regularly became -i, later -e (§ 87), which remained in the oldest period of the language. But at an early period the nom. pl. was re-formed after the analogy of the masc. a-stems and then later the old ending -e was only preserved in a few plurals, especially in names of peoples, as **Dene**, *Danes*; **Engle**, *the English*; **Mierce** (gen. **Miercna**), *Mercians*; **Norþhymbre**, *Northumbrians*; **Seaxe** (gen. **Seaxna**), *Saxons*; **ielde**, *men*; **ielfe**, *elves*; **līode, lēode**, *people*; **stede**, *places*. The Germanic gen. pl. ending -(i)jõn regularly became -(i)ja (§ 88. 2) which has only been preserved in a few words with short stems, as **Deni(ge)a, wini(ge)a**. The ending -a is from the gen. pl. of the a- and consonantal stems. The dat. pl. would regularly have ended in -im, but it had -um from the other classes of nouns. Apart from the few words mentioned above, the long i-stems have the same endings as the masc. a-stems and are only distinguishable from them by the presence or absence of umlaut.

§ 233. Like **wine** are declined a large number of nouns, as **bile**, *beak, bill*; **byre**, *son*; **ciele**, *cold*; **dene**, *valley*; **dyne**, *din*; **hæle** (orig. cons. stem, see § 261), *man, hero*; **hege**, *hedge*; **hype**, *hip*; **mere** (orig. neut.), *lake, pool*; **ryge**, *rye*; **sele**, *hall*; masc. verbal abstract nouns, as **bite**, *bite*; **cwide**, *saying, speech*; **cyme**, *advent*; **cyre**, *choice*; **flyge**, *flight*; **ryne**, *course*; **stige**, *ascent*; abstract nouns ending in -scipe, as **bēorscipe**, *feast*; **gōdscipe**, *goodness*; and a number of nouns originally belonging to the neut. os-, es-declension (§ 266), as **bere**, *barley*; **ege**, *fear*; **hete**, *hate*; **sige**, *victory*. **hyse** (pl. **hys(s)as**), *youth, son*; **ile** (pl. **il(l)as**), *sole of the foot*; **mete** (pl. **mettas**), *food*, form their pl. after the analogy of the ja-stems (§ 198).

§ 234. Like **giest** are declined a large number of nouns, as **æsc**, *ash-tree*; **dǽl**, *part*; **ent**, *giant*; **fierst**, *period of time*;

hyht, *hope*; līeg, *flame*; lyft (also fem.), *air*; mǣw, *sea-gull*; sǣl (also fem.), *time*; smīec, *smoke*; streng, *string*; þyrs, *giant*; wyrm, *worm*; masc. verbal abstract nouns, as drenc, *drink*; flyht, *flight*; hlīep, *leap*; hwyrft, *turning, circuit*; slieht, *slaughter*.

§ 235. sǣ, prim. Germanic *saiwiz, *sea*, gen. sǣs, dat. sǣ, pl. nom. acc. sǣs, gen. *sǣwa, dat. sǣm beside the new formation sǣwum; also fem. gen. dat. sǣ beside sǣwe; drȳ, *magician*, gen. drȳs, dat. drȳ, pl. nom. acc. drȳas, dat. drȳum. See § 68.

b. Feminine.

§ 236.

	Sing.	Plur.
Nom. Acc.	cwēn, *queen*	cwēne, -a
Gen.	cwēne	cwēna
Dat.	cwēne	cwēnum

The nom. acc. and gen. singular were regularly developed from the corresponding prim. Germanic forms *kwǣniz, *kwǣnin, *kwǣnaiz. The dat. sing. had -e after the analogy of the ō-stems, the regular form would have been *cwēn (see § 85. 3). The nom. pl. cwēne regularly had -e from prim. Germanic -īz (§ 87). The gen. and dat. pl. were new formations as in the masc. i-stems. In early Nth., and then later in WS. and Ken., the acc. sing. often had -e after the analogy of the ō-stems; and in like manner the nom. acc. pl. often had -a already in early OE. All the fem. short i-stems went over into the ō-declension in the prehistoric period of the language.

§ 237. Like cwēn are declined bēn, *prayer*; benc, *bench*; brȳd, *bride*; cȳf, *tub*; fierd, *army*; fȳst, *fist*; glēd, *live coal*; hȳd, *hide, skin*; hȳf, *hive*; tīd, *time*; wǣd, *garment*; wēn, *hope*; wyrt, *vegetable, herb*; ȳst, *storm*; and fem. verbal abstract nouns, as ǣht, *property*; cyst, *choice*; dǣd, *deed*; ēst, *favour*; hǣs, *command*; meaht, miht, *might, power*; scyld, *guilt*; spēd, *success*; wist, *food, sustenance*; wyrd, *fate*.

NOTE.—ǣ, prim. Germanic *aiwiz, *divine law*, generally remains uninflected in the sing. and in the nom. acc. pl., but beside the gen. dat. sing. ǣ there also exists ǣwe from which a new nom. ǣw was formed.

§ 238. A certain number of nouns, which originally belonged to the fem. i-stems, partly or entirely became neuter and were then declined like cynn (§ 202) or hof (§ 188) in the singular, and like hof in the plural. Such nouns are : fulwiht, fulluht, *baptism*; grīn, *snare, noose*; oferhygd, *pride*; wiht, wuht, *thing, creature*; nouns with the prefix ge-, as gebyrd, *birth*; gecynd, *nature, kind*; gehygd, *mind*; gemynd, *memory*; gesceaft, *creation*; geþeaht, *thought*; geþyld, *patience*; gewyrht, *merit, desert*; pl. gedryhtu, *elements*; giftu, *gifts*. In late OE. other fem. i-stems also sometimes took the neut. plural ending -u, -o.

c. Neuter.

§ 239. Sing. Plur.

Nom. Acc. spere, *spear*   speru, -o
Gen. speres   spera
Dat. spere   sperum

The neuter i-stems had originally the same endings as the masculine except in the nom. acc. sing. and plural. The nom. acc. sing. ended in -i which regularly disappeared after long stems, but remained after short stems, and then later became -e (§ 83). The nom. acc. pl. ended in -ī which would regularly have become -i, later -e, after short stems, and disappeared after long stems. The nom. acc. pl. ending -u (-o) was due to the influence of the short neut. a-stems. The endings of the other cases are of the same origin as those of the masc. short i-stems. The regular form of the nom. acc. sing. would be *spire (§ 21. 2) if spere originally belonged to the neuter i-declension.

§ 240. Like spere are declined ofdæle, *downward slope, descent*; oferslege, *lintel*; orlege, *fate*; sife, *sieve*. All these nouns probably belonged originally to the os-, es-declension (§ 266).

A certain number of neuter nouns which originally belonged

partly to the neut. ja-declension (§ 202), and partly to the os-, es-declension, are declined like spere, except that the stem-syllable being long the final -e disappeared in the nom. acc. singular. Such nouns are: flǣsc, *flesh*; flīes, *fleece*; hǣl, *health*; hilt (also masc.), *hilt*; lǣn, *loan*; sweng, *blow*; gefēg, *joining, joint*; gegrynd, *plot of ground*; gehlȳd, *noise*; genyht, *sufficiency*; geresp, *blame*; gewēd, *fury, madness*; geswinc, *labour, affliction*.

5. THE u-DECLENSION.

§ 241. The u-declension comprises masculine and feminine nouns, and corresponds to the Latin and Greek u-declension (Lat. -us, Gr. -υς; acc. -um, -υν). A large number of the masc. and fem. u-stems passed over entirely into the a- and ō-declensions respectively in the prehistoric period of the language, and the other masc. and fem. nouns ending in a consonant have the case-endings of the a- and o-declensions beside the regular case-endings, especially in the gen. sing. and in the plural. During the OE. period the -u (-o) of the nom. acc. sing. was often extended to the dat. sing. and nom. acc. pl. in the short stems; and likewise the -a of the gen. and dat. sing. to the nom. acc. And in late OE. the short stems also often formed their gen. sing. and nom. acc. pl. after the analogy of the a-stems. On the loss or retention of -u (-o) in the nom. acc. singular, see § 83.

a. Masculine.

§ 242. SING.

Nom. Acc.	sunu, -o, *son*	feld, *field*
Gen.	suna	felda
Dat.	suna	felda

PLUR.

Nom. Acc.	suna	felda
Gen.	suna	felda
Dat.	sunum	feldum

§ 243. Like sunu are declined bregu, *prince, ruler*; heoru, *sword*; lagu, *sea, flood*; magu, *son, man*; medu, meodu (gen. meda beside medwes), *mead*; sidu, *custom*; spitu, *spit*; wudu, *wood*.

§ 244. Like feld are declined eard, *native country*; ford, *ford*; gār, *spear*; hād, *rank, order*; hearg, *temple*; sēaþ, *pit, spring*; weald, *forest*; sumor, *summer*; æppel (gen. æp(p)les, pl. ap(p)la beside æp(p)las, and neut. ap(p)lu), *apple*; winter (pl. neut. wintru beside winter), *winter*.

b. Feminine.

§ 245. SING.

Nom. Acc.	duru, -o, *door*	hand, *hand*
Gen.	dura	handa
Dat.	dura	handa

PLUR.

Nom. Acc.	dura	handa
Gen.	dura	handa
Dat.	durum	handum

Beside the regular gen. and dat. sing. dura, there also occurs dyre, dyru with i-umlaut after the analogy of the i-declension. And in the long stems the nom. acc. sing. was sometimes used for the gen. and dative. To the short stems also belongs nosu, *nose*; and to the long stems: cweorn (also ō-declension), *hand-mill*; flōr (also masc.), *floor*; and originally also cin(n), Goth. kinnus, *chin*.

B. THE WEAK DECLENSION (N-STEMS).

§ 246. The weak declension comprises masculine, feminine, and neuter nouns, and corresponds to the Latin and Greek declension of n-stems, as Lat. nom. homō (OE. guma), *man*, sermō, *discourse*, acc. homin-em (OE. guman), sermōn-em; Gr. nom. ποιμήν, *shepherd*, ἡγεμών, *leader*, acc. ποιμέν-α, ἡγεμόν-α.

a. *Masculine.*

§ 247. SING.

Nom.	guma, *man*	frēa, *lord*
Acc.	guman	frēan
Gen.	guman	frēan
Dat.	guman	frēan

PLUR.

Nom. Acc.	guman	frēan
Gen.	gumena	frēana
Dat.	gumum	frēa(u)m

§ 248. Like **guma** are declined a large number of nouns, as **ǣrendra**, *messenger*; **apa**, *ape*; **assa**, *ass*; **bana**, *slayer*; **bera**, *bear*; **boga**, *bow*; **bucca**, *he-goat*; **cnapa**, *boy*; **cruma**, *crumb*; **dogga**, *dog*; **fola**, *foal*; **frogga**, *frog*; **gealga**, *gallows*; **haca**, *hook*; **hara**, *hare*; **hunta**, *hunter*; **mōna**, *moon*; **nama**, *name*; **nefa** (dat. pl. also **nefenum**), *nephew*; **oxa** (pl. **œxen, exen,** beside **oxan,** dat. also **oxnum**), *ox*; **plega**, *play*; **slaga**, *slayer*; **spearwa**, *sparrow*; **þūma**, *thumb*; **wita**, *sage, wise man*; **wyrhta**, *worker*.

§ 249. Like **frēa** are declined **flēa**, *flea*; **gefā**, *foe*; **(ge)fēa**, *joy*; **lēo**, *lion*; **rā**, *roe*; **twēo**, *doubt*; **wēa**, *woe*; and the pl. **Swēon**, *Swedes.* See § 68.

b. *Feminine.*

§ 250. SING.

Nom.	tunge, *tongue*	bēo, *bee*
Acc.	tungan	bēon
Gen.	tungan	bēon
Dat.	tungan	bēon

PLUR.

Nom. Acc.	tungan	bēon
Gen.	tungena	bēona
Dat.	tungum	bēom

§ 251. Like tunge are declined a large number of nouns, as ǣsce, *inquiry*; asse, *she-ass*; asce, *ash, cinders*; bēce, *beech-tree*; blǣdre, *bladder*; burne, *stream, brook*; cēace, *cheek, jaw*; cirice, *church*; crāwe, *crow*; cuppe, *cup*; cwene, *woman*; fiþele, *fiddle*; heorte, *heart*; hlǣfdige, *lady*; meowle, *maiden*; molde, *earth*; moþþe, *moth*; pīpe, *pipe*; sunne, *sun*; swealwe, *swallow*; wicce, *witch*; wuduwe, *widow*; and nomina agentis ending in -estre, as hlēapestre, *dancer*; lǣrestre, *teacher*; sangestre, *songstress*.

The fem. nouns with short stems began to form their nom. sing. after the analogy of the ō-stems (§ 212) already in early OE., as cinu, *chink*, spadu, *spade*, wicu (wucu), *week*, beside cine, spade, wice (wuce).

§ 252. Like bēo are declined cēo, *jackdaw, chough*; flā, *arrow*; sēo, *pupil of the eye*; slā, slāh, *sloe*; tā, *toe*; þō, *clay*. See § 68.

c. *Neuter.*

§ 253. SING.   PLUR.
Nom. Acc. ēage, *eye*   ēagan
Gen.   ēagan   ēagena
Dat.   ēagan   ēagum

§ 254. Like ēage are only declined ēare, *ear*; wange (also with strong forms), *cheek*.

C. MINOR DECLENSIONS.

1. MONOSYLLABIC CONSONANT STEMS.

a. *Masculine.*

§ 255. SING.   PLUR.
Nom. Acc. fōt, *foot*   fēt
Gen.   fōtes   fōta
Dat.   fēt   fōtum

§ 256. Like fōt are declined tōþ, *tooth*; man(n) (beside manna, acc. mannan, n-declension), *man*; and wifman, wimman, *woman*.

b. Feminine.

§ 257. SING.

Nom. Acc.	bōc, *book*	hnutu, *nut*
Gen.	bēc; bōce	*hnyte; hnute
Dat.	bēc	hnyte

PLUR.

Nom. Acc.	bēc	hnyte
Gen.	bōca	hnuta
Dat.	bōcum	hnutum

In nouns belonging to this class the stem-vowels ā, ō, u, ū were regularly mutated to ǣ, ē (Nth. œ̄), y, ȳ in the gen. dat. sing. and nom. acc. plural. In nearly all the nouns belonging to this class, beside the gen. sing. with umlaut there exists a form ending in -e without umlaut which was made after the analogy of the ō-stems (§ 212). In late OE. the dat. sing. was often like the nominative. hnutu is the original acc. (§ 84).

§ 258. Like bōc are declined āc, *oak*; brōc, *trousers*; burg, *city* (gen. dat. sing. and nom. acc. pl. byrig beside byrg (§ 102), also declined like cwēn (§ 236), but without i-umlaut); cū, *cow* (also gen. sing. cūe, cūs; nom. acc. pl. cȳ, cȳe, gen. cūa, cūna, cȳna); dung, *prison*; gāt, *goat*; gōs, *goose*; grūt, *coarse meal, groats*; lūs, *louse*; meol(u)c, *milk*; mūs, *mouse*; neaht, niht, *night* (also gen. dat. sing. nihte; adv. gen. nihtes, ānes nihtes, *at night, by night*, formed after the analogy of dæges); turf, *turf*; furh, *furrow* (gen. sing. fūre beside fyrh, pl. gen. fūra, dat. fūrum, § 74); sulh, *plough* (gen. sing. sūles on analogy with a-stems, pl. gen. sūla, dat. sūlum); þrūh, *trough* (dat. pl. þrūm, § 144); wlōh, *fringe*.

§ 259. Like hnutu are declined hnitu, *nit*; studu, stuþu, *pillar*.

c. Neuter.

§ 260. The only remnant of this class is scrūd, *garment*, dat. scrȳd; gen. scrūdes and late OE. dat. scrūde were formed after the analogy of the neut. a-stems (§ 188), and also the pl. nom. acc. scrūd, gen. scrūda, dat. scrūdum.

2. STEMS IN -þ.

§ 261. Of the nouns which originally belonged to this class only four have been preserved: masc. hæleþ, *hero, man*, mōnaþ, *month*; fem. mæg(e)þ, *maiden*; neut. ealu, *ale*. They were all originally neut. nouns ending in -t which regularly disappeared finally in prim. Germanic in the nom. acc. sing. (§ 80. 2). The old nom. acc. sing. was preserved in hæle which passed over into the i-declension, and in ealu. In hæleþ, mōnaþ, and mæg(e)þ the þ of the inflected forms was levelled out into the nom. acc. singular. The gen. and dat. sing. of hæleþ and mōnaþ were formed on analogy with the a-declension (§ 183); and beside the nom. acc. pl. hæleþ, mōnaþ, there also exist hæleþas, mōn(e)þas. Those forms which did not originally have umlaut have been generalized in OE. They are declined as follows:—

SING.

Nom. Acc.	hæleþ	mōnaþ	mæg(e)þ	ealu
Gen.	hælepes	mōn(e)þes	mæg(e)þ	ealoþ
Dat.	hæleþe	mōn(e)þe	mæg(e)þ	ealoþ

PLUR.

Nom. Acc.	hæleþ	mōnaþ	mæg(e)þ	
Gen.	hæleþa	mōn(e)þa	mæg(e)þa	ealeþa
Dat.	hæleþum	mōn(e)þum	mæg(e)þum	

3. STEMS IN -r.

§ 262. To this class belong the nouns of relationship: fæder, *father*; brōþor, *brother*; mōdor, *mother*; dohtor, *daughter*; sweostor, *sister*; and the collective plurals, gebrōþor, gebrōþru, *brethren*; gesweostor, -tru, -tra, *sisters*. gebrōþor and gesweostor were originally neut. collective nouns and were declined like wīte (§ 202), whence the plural endings gebrōþru, gesweostru, -tra, which were afterwards extended to the plural of mōdor and dohtor.

SING.

Nom. Acc.	fæder	brōþor	mōdor
Gen.	fæder, -eres	brōþor	mōdor
Dat.	fæder	brēþer	mēder

PLUR.

Nom. Acc.	fæderas	brōþor, -þru	mōdor, -dru, -dra
Gen.	fædera	brōþra	mōdra
Dat.	fæderum	brōþrum	mōdrum

SING.

Nom. Acc.	dohtor	sweostor
Gen.	dohtor	sweostor
Dat.	dehter	sweostor

PLUR.

Nom. Acc.	dohtor, -tru, -tra	sweostor
Gen.	dohtra	sweostra
Dat.	dohtrum	sweostrum

fæderes and fæderas were formed after the analogy of the a-stems (§ 183). In late OE. the dat. mēder, dehter were often used for the gen. and vice versa.

4. THE MASCULINE STEMS IN -nd.

§ 263. SING.

Nom. Acc.	frēond, *friend*	wīgend, *warrior*
Gen.	frēondes	wīgendes
Dat.	frīend, frēonde	wīgende

PLUR.

Nom. Acc.	frīend, frēond, -as	wīgend, -e, -as
Gen.	frēonda	wīgendra
Dat.	frēondum	wīgendum

The nouns of this class are old isolated present participles, and originally had the same case-endings as the other consonantal stems. But in OE. as in the other Germanic languages they underwent various new formations. The OE. present participles themselves had passed over into the ja-declension of adjectives (§ 289) in the oldest period of the language.

The nom. sing. was a new formation with d from the inflected forms, cp. Lat. ferēns from *ferenss older *ferents (§ 119). The gen. and dat. sing. and the nom. acc. pl. in -es, -e, -as were formed after the analogy of the masc. a-stems (§ 180). The dat. frīend with umlaut is from *frīondi older *frijōndi; and the nom. pl. frīend is also from *frīondi older *frijōndiz. The nom. and gen. pl. endings -e, -ra are adjectival (§ 271).

§ 264. Like frēond are declined fēond, *enemy*; tēond, *accuser*; the compound noun gōddōnd (pl. -dōnd, beside -dēnd), *benefactor*; and the collective plurals gefīend, *enemies*; gefrīend, *friends*, which were originally neuter collective nouns and declined like wīte (§ 202).

§ 265. Like wīgend are declined āgend, *owner*; beswīcend, *deceiver*; hǣlend, *Saviour*; helpend, *helper*; hettend, *enemy*; ner(i)gend, *Saviour*; wealdend, *ruler*.

5. STEMS IN -os, -es.

§ 266. This class of nouns corresponds to the Greek neuters in -ος, Latin -us, as Gr. γένος, *race*, gen. γένεος older *γένεσος, Lat. genus, gen. generis, pl. genera. A fairly large number of nouns originally belonged to this class, but owing to various levellings and new formations, some of which took place in the prehistoric period of all the Germanic languages, nearly all the nouns belonging here went over into other declensions in OE.; see *OE. Grammar*, § 419.

§ 267. The few remaining nouns formed their gen. and dat. sing. after the analogy of the neuter a-stems (§ 188). The cases of the plural were regularly developed from the corresponding prim. Germanic forms.

Sing.

Nom. Acc.	lamb, *lamb*	cealf, *calf*	ǣg, *egg*
Gen.	lambes	cealfes	ǣges
Dat.	lambe	cealfe	ǣge

Plur.

Nom. Acc.	lambru	cealfru	ǣgru
Gen.	lambra	cealfra	ǣgra
Dat.	lambrum	cealfrum	ǣgrum

Beside lamb there also occurs lombor and sometimes lemb; in late OE. the pl. was lamb, lamba, lambum after the analogy of the neut. a-stems. Beside the Anglian sing. calf there also occurs cælf, celf with i-umlaut.

§ 268. Like lamb are declined cild (pl. cild beside cildru), *child*; speld, *splinter, torch*; pl. brēadru, *crumbs*.

CHAPTER X

ADJECTIVES

A. The Declension of Adjectives.

§ 269. In OE., as in the other old Germanic languages, the adjectives are declined as strong or weak. They have three genders, and the same cases as nouns with the addition of an instrumental in the masc. and neut. singular.

The strong form is used predicatively in the positive and superlative degrees, and when the adjective is used attributively without any other defining word, as wæs sēo fǣmne geong, *the woman was young*; þā menn sindon gōde, *the men are good*; þus wǣron þā latestan fyrmeste, *thus were the last, first*. In the vocative the weak form exists beside the strong, as þū lēofa dryhten, *thou dear Lord*; þū riht cyning, *thou just king*.

The weak form is used after the definite article, and after demonstrative and possessive pronouns, as se ofermōda cyning, *the proud king*; þæs ēadigan weres, *of the blessed man*; þes ealda mann, *this old man*; on þissum andweardan dæge, *on this present day*; mīn lēofa sunu, *my dear son*; þurh þīne æþelan hand, *through thy noble hand*. In poetry the weak form often occurs where in prose the strong form would be used.

eall, *all*; fēawe, *few*; genōg, *enough*; manig, *many*; and ōþer, *second*, were always declined according to the strong declension; and ordinal numerals except ōþer, comparatives, and superlatives except the nom. acc. neut. in -est, -ost, and ilca, *same*, are declined according to the weak declension. All other adjectives can be declined according to either declension.

When the same adjective refers to nouns of different genders, it is put in the neut. plural.

1. The Strong Declension.

§ 270. The endings of the strong declension are partly nominal and partly pronominal; the latter are printed in italics for blind, *blind*, and glæd, *glad*. The nominal endings are those of the a-, ō-declensions. The strong declension is divided into pure a-, ō-stems, ja-, jō-stems, and wa-, wō-stems, like the corresponding nouns. The original i- and u-stems passed over almost entirely into this declension in prehistoric OE. The ja-, jō-stems and the wa-, wō-stems only differ from the pure a-, ō-stems in the masc. and fem. nom. singular and the neut. nom. acc. singular.

a. Pure a-, ō-Stems.

§ 271.

Sing.	*Masc.*	*Neut.*	*Fem.*
Nom.	blind, *blind*	blind	blind
Acc.	blind*ne*	blind	blinde
Gen.	blindes	blindes	blind*re*
Dat.	blind*um*	blind*um*	blind*re*
Instr.	blinde	blinde	

	Masc.	Neut.	Fem.
PLUR.			
Nom. Acc.	blinde	blind	blinda, -e
Gen.	blindra	blindra	blindra
Dat.	blindum	blindum	blindum
SING.			
Nom.	glæd, *glad*	glæd	gladu, -o
Acc.	glædne	glæd	glade
Gen.	glades	glades	glædre
Dat.	gladum	gladum	glædre
Instr.	glade	glade	
PLUR.			
Nom. Acc.	glade	gladu, -o	glada, -e
Gen.	glædra	glædra	glædra
Dat.	gladum	gladum	gladum

On the interchange between æ and a in the declension of glæd, see § 29, note 1; on the loss or retention of the -u, -o in the fem. nom. sing. and the nom. acc. neut. plural, see § 85. 1. In late WS. the masc. nom. acc. pl. form was generally used for the neuter and often for the feminine; and occasionally the -u of the short stems was extended to the long.

§ 272. Like blind are declined the monosyllabic adjectives with long stems, as beald, *bold*; brūn, *brown*; dēad, *dead*; dēop, *deep*; genōg (genōh), *enough*; gōd, *good*; grēat, *large*; hāl, *whole, sound*; lang, *long*; sār, *sore*; sēoc, *sick*; wāc, *weak*; wǣt, *wet*; wīs, *wise*; wrāþ, *wroth, angry*; compound and derivative adjectives ending in -cund, -feald, -fæst, -full, -lēas, -weard, as æþelcund, *of noble origin*; ānfeald, *single*; ārfæst, *virtuous*; andgietful(1), *intelligent*; bānlēas, *boneless*; andweard, *present*. For the simplification of the double consonants in the inflected forms of adjectives like eall, *all*; full, *full*, see § 145.

§ 273. Like glæd are declined the monosyllabic adjectives with short stems, as bær, *bare*; blæc, *black*; smæl, *small*; dol, *foolish*; til, *good*; wan, *wanting*; adjectives with the suffixes -lic and -sum, as ānlic, *solitary*; angsum, *troublesome*.

§ 274.

	Masc.	Neut.	Fem.
Sing.			
Nom.	hēah, *high*	hēah	hēa
Acc.	hēa(n)ne	hēah	hēa
Gen.	hēas	hēas	hēa(r)re
Dat.	hēa(u)m	hēa(u)m	hēa(r)re
Instr.	hēa	hēa	
Plur.			
Nom. Acc.	hēa	hēa	hēa
Gen.	hēa(r)ra	hēa(r)ra	hēa(r)ra
Dat.	hēa(u)m	hēa(u)m	hēa(u)m

hēanne, hēarra, hēarre were due to the assimilation of hn and hr; and hēane, hēara, hēare arose from the regular loss of h before n, r (§ 144). In hēaum the u was restored after the analogy of forms like gladum, blindum. The instr., masc. and fem. nom. pl., and fem. acc. singular hēa were from older *hēahe; and the neut. nom. acc. pl. and fem. nom. singular from older *hēahu; masc. and neut. gen. sing. from *hēahes. See § 68. Late OE. forms like gen. hēages, dat. hēage, nom. pl. hēage beside older hēas, hēa(u)m, hēa were formed after the analogy of such words as gen. gefōges, genōges beside nom. gefōh, genōh (§ 172).

§ 275. Like hēah are declined fāh, *hostile*; nēah, *near*; rūh, *rough*; tōh, *tough*. sceolh, *awry, squinting*, and þweorh, *cross, perverse*, dropped the h and lengthened the diphthong in the inflected forms, as gen. scēoles, þwēores, cp. § 76.

§ 276.

	Masc.	Neut.	Fem.
Sing.			
Nom.	manig, *many*	manig	manig
Acc.	manigne	manig	manige
Gen.	maniges	maniges	manigre
Dat.	manigum	manigum	manigre
Instr.	manige	manige	

	PLUR.	*Masc.*	*Neut.*	*Fem.*
Nom. Acc.		manige	manig	maniga, -e
Gen.		manigra	manigra	manigra
Dat.		manigum	manigum	manigum
	SING.			
Nom.		hālig, *holy*	hālig	hāligu, -o
Acc.		hāligne	hālig	hālge
Gen.		hālges	hālges	hāligre
Dat.		hālgum	hālgum	hāligre
Instr.		hālge	hālge	
	PLUR.			
Nom. Acc.		hālğe	hāligu, -o	hālga, -e
Gen.		hāligra	hāligra	hāligra
Dat.		hālgum	hālgum	hālgum

On the loss or retention of the medial vowel in the inflected forms, see §§ 97–8; and on the loss or retention of the -u, -o in the fem. nom. sing. and the neut. nom. acc. pl., see § 85. 1. In adjectives ending in -en, -er, the combinations -enne (masc. acc. sing.), -erra (gen. pl.), and -erre (fem. gen. dat. sing.) were often simplified to -ene, -era, -ere especially in late OE. (§ 145).

§ 277. Like **manig** are declined the dissyllabic adjectives with short stems, as **bysig**, *busy*; **efen**, *even*; **fægen**, *glad*; **fæger**, *fair*; **micel**, *large, great*; **nacod**, *naked*; **open**, *open*; **sicor**, *sure*; **yfel**, *evil*; pp., as **boren**, *borne*; **coren**, *chosen*; **legen**, *lain*, see § 290.

§ 278. Like **hālig** are declined the dissyllabic adjectives with long stems, as **ācol**, *timid*; **āgen**, *own*; **bit(t)er**, *bitter*; **cildisc**, *childish*; **ēadig**, *rich, happy*; **geōmor**, *sad*; **gylden**, *golden*; **lȳtel**, *little*; **ōþer**, *second*; **snottor**, *wise*; pp., as **bunden**, *bound*; **holpen**, *helped*, see § 290.

b. ja-, jō-STEMS.

§ 279. In the ja-, jō-stems it is necessary to distinguish between those stems which were originally long and those which became long by the West Germanic doubling of consonants (§ 135). The latter class were declined in OE. like the pure a-, ō-stems ending in double consonants (§ 272); such are: **gesibb**, *akin, related*; **midd**, *middle*; **nytt**, *useful*. The regular form of the nom. sing. masc. and neut. of a word like **midd** would be *mide, see § 197.

§ 280.

Sing.	*Masc.*	*Neut.*	*Fem.*
Nom.	wilde, *wild*	wilde	wildu, -o
Acc.	wildne	wilde	wilde
Gen.	wildes	wildes	wildre
Dat.	wildum	wildum	wildre
Instr.	wilde	wilde	
Plur.			
Nom. Acc.	wilde	wildu, -o	wilda, -e
Gen.	wildra	wildra	wildra
Dat.	wildum	wildum	wildum

The only difference in declension between the original long ja-, jō-stems and the long pure a-, ō-stems is in the masc. nom. sing., neut. nom. acc. sing. and plural, and the fem. nom. singular. **wilde** (masc. nom. sing.) is regularly developed from prim. Germanic *wilþjaz, and the neut. nom. acc. sing. from *wilþjan (§§ 84, 141); **wildu** (fem. nom. sing. and neut. nom. acc. plural) was formed on analogy with the short pure a-stems (§ 271), the regular form would be *wild (see § 85. 1). Double consonants were simplified before or after other consonants (§ 145), as masc. acc. sing. **þynne**, *thin*, **fǣcne**, *deceitful*, **ierne**, *angry*, from *þynnne, *fǣcnne, *iernne; fem. gen. dat. sing. **gīfre**, *greedy*, **ierre** from *gīfrre, *ierrre. When **n, r** came to stand between two consonants the first of which was not a nasal or liquid, they became vocalic and then developed an **e** before them, as masc. acc. sing. **gīferne** from *gīfrne; fem. gen. dat. sing. **fǣcenre** from *fǣcnre. Nearly all the old long i- and u-stems went over into this declension in prehistoric OE.

§ **281.** Like **wilde** are declined a large number of adjectives, as **æþele**, *noble*; **blīþe**, *joyful*; **cēne**, *bold*; **clǣne**, *clean*; **dīere, dēore**, *dear*; **fǣge**, *fated*; **frēo** (§ 69), *free*; **gesīene**, *visible*; **getrīewe**, *faithful*; **grēne**, *green*; **ierre**, *angry*; **līþe**, *gentle*; **milde**, *mild*; **nīewe, nīwe** (§ 62), *new*; **ofersprǣce**, *loquacious*; **rīpe**, *ripe*; **smēþe**, *smooth*; **strenge**, *strong*; **þriwintre**, *three years old*; **þynne**, *thin*; **wierþe**, *worthy*; adjectives ending in -bǣre, -ede, -wende, as **hālbǣre**, *wholesome*; **hōcede**, *shaped like a hook*; **lufwende**, *amiable*; and the present participles (§ 289).

c. wa-, wō-Stems.

§ **282.**

Sing.	*Masc.*	*Neut.*	*Fem.*
Nom.	gearu, -o, *ready*	gearu, -o	gearu, -o
Acc.	gearone	gearu, -o	gearwe
Gen.	gearwes	gearwes	gearore
Dat.	gearwum	gearwum	gearore
Instr.	gearwe	gearwe	

Plur.

Nom. Acc.	gearwe	gearu, -o	gearwa, -e
Gen.	gearora	gearora	gearora
Dat.	gearwum	gearwum	gearwum

w became vocalized to u (later o) when final and before consonants in prehistoric OE. (§ 149); whence masc. nom. sing., neut. nom. acc. sing. **gearu** from *ʒarw-az, -an. The u had become o before consonants in the oldest period of the language, as **gearone, gearora**. The fem. nom. sing. and neut. nom. acc. pl. are from older *ʒarwu with loss of w before the following u (§ 144). The dat. **gearwum** for *gearum was a new formation made from forms like **gearwes, gearwe**, where the w was regular. On forms like gen. **gearuwes, gearowes** beside **gearwes**, see § 102.

§ **283.** Like gearu are declined calu, *bald*; fealu, *fallow*; geolu, *yellow*; mearu, *tender*; nearu, *narrow*; salu, sealu, *dusky, dark*; &c.

§ **284.** The adjectives which had a long vowel or long diphthong in the stem reintroduced the w into the nominative from the inflected forms (§ 149) and then came to be declined like pure long a-, ō-stems (§ 271); such are: gedēaw, *dewy*; gehlēow, *sheltered*; gesēaw, *succulent*; glēaw, *wise*; hrēaw, *raw*; slāw, *slow*; þēow, *servile*. fēawe (fēa), *few*, neut. fēa from *fawu, fem. fēawa; gen. fēara, fēawera (§ 102), dat. fēam, fēaum, fēawum.

d. i-Stems.

§ **285.** Of the adjectives which originally belonged to this class, the long stems took final -i (later -e) from analogy with the short stems and then both classes went over into the ja-declension in prehistoric OE. The old short i-stems are still recognizable by the fact that they do not have double consonants in the stem-syllable. Examples are: bryce, *brittle*; gemyne, *remembering*; swice, *deceitful*; and of old long i-stems: blīþe (Goth. bleiþs), *joyful*; brȳce (Goth. brūks), *useful*; clǣne, *clean*; gemǣne (Goth. gamáins), *common*; grēne, *green*; swēte, *sweet*; &c.

e. u-Stems.

§ **286.** Of the adjectives which originally belonged to this class only three have preserved traces of the old u-declension, namely nom. sing. cwicu, c(w)ucu, *alive*, masc. acc. sing. cucone, nom. wlacu, *warm, tepid*, and the WS. isolated inflected form fela, feola (Nth. feolu, -o), *much, many*. And even cwicu, wlacu generally have nom. cwic, wlæc and are declined like short pure a-stems. All the other adjectives passed over into the a-, ja-, or wa-declension in prehistoric OE., as heard (Goth. hardus), *hard*; egle (Goth. aglus), *troublesome*; twelfwintre (Goth. twalibwintrus), *twelve years old*; þyrre (Goth. þaúrsus), *dry, withered*; glēaw (Goth. glaggwus), *wise*.

2. THE WEAK DECLENSION.

§ 287. The weak declension of adjectives has the same endings as the weak declension of nouns, except that the adjectives generally have the strong ending -ra (§ 271) instead of -(e)na in the gen. plural. Beside the regular dat. pl. ending -um there also occurs at an early period -an which was taken over from the nom. acc. plural. In trisyllabic adjectives the medial vowel remained after short stems, but disappeared after long stems, as wacora, wacore, *vigilant*, beside hālga, hālge, *holy* (§§ 97–8). On adjectives like hēa, *high*, gen. hēan, see § 274. In like manner are declined the ja- and wa-stems, as wilda, wilde, *wild*; gearwa, gearwe, *ready*.

§ 288.

Sing.	*Masc.*	*Neut.*	*Fem.*
Nom.	blinda, *blind*	blinde	blinde
Acc.	blindan	blinde	blindan
Gen.	blindan	blindan	blindan
Dat.	blindan	blindan	blindan

Plur.			
Nom. Acc.	blindan	blindan	blindan
Gen.	blindra, -ena	blindra, -ena	blindra, -ena
Dat.	blindum	blindum	blindum

3. THE DECLENSION OF PARTICIPLES.

§ 289. In the parent language the stem of the present participle ended in -nt, as in Lat. ferent-, Gr. φέροντ-, *bearing*. The masc. and neut. were originally declined like consonant stems (§ 263). The fem. nom. originally ended in -ī which was shortened to -i (§ 85. 3) in prehistoric OE. (cp. Goth. frijōndi, fem. *friend*). The -i of the feminine was extended to the masculine and neuter, which was the cause of their passing over into the ja-declension (§ 279). In OE. the pres. participle was declined strong or weak like an ordinary adjective. When used predicatively it often had the uninflected form for all genders in the nom. and accusative.

§ 290. The past participle, like the present, was declined strong or weak like an ordinary adjective. When strong it was declined like **manig** or **hālig** (§ 276) according as the stem-syllable was short or long ; and similarly when it was declined weak (§ 288). When used predicatively it generally had the uninflected form for all genders. A small number of past participles of strong verbs have i-umlaut of the stem-vowel, because in prim. Germanic, beside the ordinary ending -énaz = Indg. -énos, there also existed -íniz = Indg. -énis, hence forms like **ǣgen** beside **āgen**, *own* ; **cymen** beside **cumen**, *come* ; **slegen** beside **slægen, slagen**, *slain* ; **tygen** from *tuȝiniz beside **togen** from *tuȝenaz, *drawn*. See § 326.

B. THE COMPARISON OF ADJECTIVES.

I.

§ 291. In prim. Germanic the comparative was formed from the positive by means of the two suffixes -iz-, -ōz- (= prim. OE. -ir-, -ōr-, § 115), to which were then added the endings of the weak adjectives. In prim. OE. polysyllabic derivative adjectives and compound adjectives had the suffix -ōr-, and the great majority of uncompounded pure a-stems also had it, but the ja-stems had only -ir-. During the prehistoric period of OE. the i in -ir- caused umlaut of the stem-syllable (§ 57), and then along with the ō in the suffix -ōr- disappeared, leaving only -r- for all classes of adjectives, so that, except in the ja-stems, the presence or absence of umlaut is the only indication as to which of the two prim. Germanic suffixes the -r- goes back.

In prim. Germanic the superlative was formed from the positive by means of the two suffixes -ist-, -ōst- (= OE. -est-, -ost-), to which were then added the endings of the strong or weak adjectives. The adjectives which had -iz- in the comparative had -ist- in the superlative, and those which had

-ōz- in the comparative had -ōst- in the superlative. In OE. the adjectives which had i-umlaut in the comparative generally had -est-, but sometimes also -ost- in the superlative, and those which did not have umlaut in the comparative generally had -ost- (rarely -ust-, -ast-). In Gothic the superlative had both the strong and the weak declension, but in OE. it generally had only the weak except in the nom. acc. neuter which had both forms -est, -ost, beside -este, -oste. In late OE. the medial vowel was often syncopated, as in lengsta beside older lengesta. On the interchange of the medial vowel in forms like lēofesta beside lēofosta, *dearest*, see § 100.

Examples are :—

earm, *poor*	earmra	earmost
grim(m), *grim*	grimra	grimmost
hālig, *holy*	hāligra	hāligost
lēof, *dear*	lēofra	lēofost
glæd, *glad*	glædra	gladost (§ 30)
nēah, *near*	nēahra, nēarra (§ 142)	nīehst (§ 57)
clǣne, *clean*	clǣnra	clǣnest
īeþe, *easy*	īeþra	īeþest

Only a small number of a-stems have umlaut in the comparative and superlative, of which the most common are :—

brād, *broad*	brǣdra beside brādra	brǣdest
eald, *old*	ieldra (Goth. alþiza)	ieldest
feorr, *far*	fierra	fierrest
geong, *young*	giengra, gingra	giengest, gingest
grēat, *great*	grīetra	grīetest
hēah, *high*	hīehra, hīerra (§ 142), beside hēahra	hīehst
lang, *long*	lengra	lengest
sceort, *short*	sciertra	sciertest
strang, *strong*	strengra	strengest

2. Irregular Comparison.

§ 292. The following adjectives form their comparatives and superlatives from a different root than the positive:—

gōd, *good*	bet(e)ra, bettra (§ 146)	bet(e)st
	sēlra, sēlla (§ 142)	sēlest
lȳtel, *little*	lǣssa (cp. § 142)	lǣst
micel, *great*	māra	mǣst
yfel, *evil*	wiersa	wierrest (§ 142), wierst

NOTE.—In a few words comparative and superlative adjectives were formed from adverbs: ǣr, *before*, ǣrra, *former, earlier*, ǣrest, *first*; **fyrest** from *furist-, *first*, related to **fore**, *before*; **furþra**, *higher, greater*, related to **forþ**, *forth*.

§ 293. In a number of words the comparative was formed from an adverb or preposition, with a superlative in -um-, -uma (prim. Germanic -umō̃), cp. Lat. optimus, *best*, summus, *highest*. The simple superlative suffix was preserved in OE. **forma** (Goth. fruma), *first*, beside **fore**, *before*; **hindema**, *last, hindmost*, beside **hindan**, *behind*; and **meduma, medema**, *midway in size*, related to **midd**, *middle*. But in prehistoric OE., as in Gothic, to -um- was added the ordinary superlative suffix -ist- which gave rise to the double superlative suffix -umist-, as Goth. frumists, *first*; hindumists, *hindmost*. In OE. -umist- became -ymist- (§ 57), later -imest-, -emest-, -mest-, as

æfter, *after*	æfterra	æftemest
ēast, *eastwards*	ēasterra	ēastmest
fore, *before*		forma, fyrmest
inne, *within*	innerra	innemest
lǣt, *late*	lǣtra	lǣtemest beside lǣtest
midd, *middle*		medema, midmest
nioþan, *below*	niþerra	ni(o)þemest
norþ, *northwards*	norþerra, nyrþra	norþmest

sīþ, *late*	sīþra	sīþemest beside sīþest
sūþ, *southwards*	sūþerra, sȳþerra	sūþmest
ufan, *above*	uferra / yferra	ufemest / yfemest
ūte, *without*	ūterra / ȳterra	ūt(e)mest / ȳt(e)mest
west, *westwards*	westerra	westmest

C. NUMERALS.

1. CARDINAL AND ORDINAL.

§ 294.

ān, *one*	forma, formest(a) / fyrmest(a), fyrest(a), ǣrest(a)
twā (§ 295), *two*	ōþer, æfterra
þrī (§ 295), *three*	þridda
fēower, *four*	fēo(we)rþa
fīf, *five*	fīfta
siex, six, *six*	siexta, sixta
seofon, *seven*	seofoþa
eahta, *eight*	eahtoþa
nigon, *nine*	nigoþa
tīen, tȳn, tēn, *ten*	tēoþa
en(d)le(o)fan, *eleven*	en(d)le(o)fta
twelf, *twelve*	twelfta
þrēotīene, *thirteen*	þrēotēoþa
fēowertīene, *fourteen*	fēowertēoþa
fīftīene, *fifteen*	fīftēoþa
siex-, sixtīene, *sixteen*	siex-, sixtēoþa
seofontīene, *seventeen*	seofontēoþa
eahtatīene, *eighteen*	eahtatēoþa
nigontīene, *nineteen*	nigontēoþa
twěntig, *twenty*	twěntigoþa
ān and twěntig, *twenty-one*	

þrītig, *thirty*	þrītigoþa
fēowertig, *forty*	fēowertigoþa
fīftig, *fifty*	fīftigoþa
si(e)xtig, *sixty*	si(e)xtigoþa
hundseofontig, *seventy*	hundseofontigoþa
hundeahtatig, *eighty*	hundeahtatigoþa
hundnigontig, *ninety*	hundnigontigoþa
hundtēontig hund, hundred } *hundred*	hundtēontigoþa
hundendleofantig hundendlufontig } 110	hundendleofantigoþa hundendlufontigoþa
hundtwelftig, 120	hundtwelftigoþa
tū hund, hundred, 200	
þrēo hund, hundred, 300	
þūsend, *thousand*	

§ 295. The cardinals 1 to 3 were declinable in all cases and genders. ān was declined according to the strong (§ 271) or weak declension (§ 288) of adjectives. The strong masc. acc. sing. is generally ǣnne (shortened later to ænne, enne) from prim. Germanic *aininōn, beside the less common form ānne from *ainanōn. Strong pl. forms are rare, but they occur occasionally, meaning *each, all, every one,* as ānra gehwilc, *each one*. When declined weak it means *alone, solus.*

	Masc.	*Neut.*	*Fem.*
Nom. Acc.	twēgen, *two*	tū, twā	twā
Gen.	{ twēg(e)a twēgra	twēg(e)a twēgra	twēg(e)a twēgra
Dat.	twǣm, twām	twǣm, twām	twǣm, twām

Like **twēgen** is also declined **bēgen** (shortened later to **beggen**), neut. **bū**, fem. **bā** (Goth. masc. bái), *both*. Also in the combination masc. and fem. **bā twā**, neut. **bū tū**, often written in one word **būtū**, *both*.

	Masc.	Neut.	Fem.
Nom. Acc.	þrī, þrīe, *three*	þrīo, þrēo	þrīo, þrēo
Gen.	{ þrīora	þrīora	þrīora
	{ þrēora	þrēora	þrēora
Dat.	þrim	þrim	þrim

§ 296. The cardinal numbers 4 to 19 generally remained uninflected when they stood before a noun, whereas, if they stood after a noun or were used as nouns, they were declined according to the i-declension: nom. acc. masc. and fem. -e, neut. -u (-o); gen. -a, dat. -um, as of **fīf hlāfum**, *from five loaves*; **mid fēawum brōþrum, þæt is, seofonum oþþe eahtum**, *with seven or eight brothers*; **fīfa sum**, *one of five*.

§ 297. The ending -tig of the decades was originally a noun meaning *decade*, whence **twēntig** from **twēgen + tig**, lit. *two decades*, with a following noun in the gen. case (cp. Goth. **twái tigjus**, *twenty*, dat. **twáim tigum**). The OE. decades could be used both substantively and adjectively. When used as substantives their gen. ended in -es; when used as adjectives they were either uninflected or formed their gen. in -ra, -a, and dat. in -um. **hund**, *hundred*, and **þūsend**, *thousand*, being nouns, governed a following noun in the gen. case. **hund** was generally uninflected, but occasionally it had a dat. ending -e, -um. **hundred** had a pl. form **hundredu, -o**, when used absolutely. **þūsend** was a neut. noun and was often inflected as such.

2. Other Numerals.

§ 298. The multiplicative numeral adjectives were formed from the cardinals and the suffix -feald, as **ānfeald**, *single*, **twie-, twifeald**, *twofold*, **þrie-, þrifeald**, *threefold*, **fēowerfeald**, *fourfold*, &c., **manigfeald**, *manifold*, which were declined as ordinary adjectives. The first element of **twifeald, þrifeald** was sometimes inflected, as dat. **twǣmfealdum, þrimfealdum**.

§ 299. Of the old adverbial multiplicatives only three

occur: ǣne (rare in gen. form ǣnes), *once*; tuwa, twiwa, twywa, *twice*; þriwa, þrywa, *thrice*. The remaining multiplicatives, and often also *once, twice, thrice*, were expressed by sīþ, *going, way*, and the cardinals, as ǣne sīþa or on ǣnne sīþ, twǣm sīþum (Goth. twáim sinþam), fīf sīþum (Goth. fimf sinþam), &c.

§ 300. *For the first, second, third, &c. time*, were expressed by sīþ and the ordinals, as forman sīþe, ōþre sīþe, þriddan sīþe, fīftan sīþe, &c.

§ 301. The distributive numerals were ān-, ǣnlīepige, *one each*; be twǣm or twǣm and twǣm, be þrim or þrim and þrim, fēower and fēower, þūsendum and þūsendum, &c.

§ 302. OE. also had numerals like NHG. anderthalb, dritt(e)halb, lit. (*one and*) *the second half*, (*two and*) *the third half*. This method of expressing numbers goes back to the prim. Germanic period, and was originally common in all the Germanic languages. Originally both elements of the compound were inflected, but at a later period the compound, when used before nouns, became uninflected like other cardinal numerals, as ōþer healf hund daga, 150 *days*; þridda healf, *two and a half*, fēo(we)rþa healf, *three and a half*; cp. Gr. τρίτον ἡμιτάλαντον, *two talents and a half*, lit. *third half talent*.

CHAPTER XI

PRONOUNS

1. Personal.

§ 303.   *First Person.*

	Sing.	Dual.	Plur.
Nom.	ic, *I*	wit	wě
Acc.	mec, mě	unc, uncit	ūsic, ūs
Gen.	mīn	uncer	ūser, ūre
Dat.	mě	unc	ūs

§ 304. *Second Person.*

	Sing.	Dual.	Plur.
Nom.	þū, *thou*	git	gē
Acc.	þec, þē̆	inc, incit	ēowic, ēow, īow
Gen.	þīn	incer	ēower, īower
Dat.	þē̆	inc	ēow, īow

§ 305. *Third Person.*

Sing.

	Masc.	Neut.	Fem.
Nom.	hē̆, *he*	hit	hīo, hēo
Acc.	hine, hiene	hit	hīe
Gen.	his	his	hiere, hire
Dat.	him	him	hiere, hire

Plur. all Genders.

Nom. Acc.	hīe, hĭ
Gen.	hiera, hira, hiora, heora
Dat.	him

§ 306. In forms marked with both long and short vowels, as in mē̆, wē̆, hē̆, &c., those with long vowels were the accented, and those with short vowels the unaccented forms. In the pronouns of the first and second persons the gen. case singular, dual, and plural is the same as the uninflected forms of the corresponding possessive pronouns (§ 308). The c in the acc. forms mec, þec, ūsic, ēowic goes back to a prim. Germanic emphatic particle *ke = the -γε in Gr. ἐμέγε. The acc. forms with c only occur in the oldest records and in poetry. unc, inc are old accusatives also used for the dative. The pronoun of the third person is originally a demonstrative pronoun formed from the Indg. stem *ki-, *this*, which occurs in Lat. ci-s, ci-ter, *on this side*. The acc. fem. form hīe (later also hī, hig, § 5, note 1) was often used for the nominative, and vice versa hīo, hēo for hīe. In the plural the masc. form was used for all genders, but sometimes the old fem. sing. hīo, hēo was used instead of it. The gen. pl. forms hiora, heora are due to o/a-umlaut (§ 59. 2). All the forms with ĭ often had y̆ in late WS.

2. Reflexive.

§ 307. The personal pronouns were used to express the reflexive, to which self (declined strong and weak), *self*, was often added to emphasize them.

3. Possessive.

§ 308. The possessive pronouns are: mīn, *my*, þīn, *thy*, sīn (mostly used in poetry, see below), *his, her, its*, which were declined in the sing. and plural, all genders, like blind (§ 271); uncer, *of us two*, incer, *of you two*, ūser, *our*, ēower, *your*, like hālig (§ 276), and ūre, *our*, like wilde (§ 280) except that the fem. nom. sing. was ūre not *ūru; in the fem. gen. dat. sing. and gen. pl. ūrre, ūrra, the rr was often simplified to r. In those cases which had syncope of the medial vowel, the sr became ss (cp. § 142) in the declension of ūser, and then the ss was sometimes extended by analogy to the other cases, as nom. sing. ūsser, masc. acc. sing. ūsserne beside the regular forms ūser, ūserne.

Instead of sīn the gen. of the personal pronoun was generally used except in poetry, as in Lat. eius, gen. pl. eōrum, eārum.

4. Demonstrative.

§ 309. The simple demonstrative pronoun sĕ, þæt, sīo (sēo), *the, that*, was declined as follows:—

Sing.	*Masc.*	*Neut.*	*Fem.*
Nom.	sĕ	þæt	sīo, sēo
Acc.	þone	þæt	þā
Gen.	þæs	þæs	þǣre
Dat.	þǣm, þām	þǣm, þām	þǣre
Instr.		þȳ, þon	

Plur. all Genders.

Nom. Acc. þā
Gen. þāra, þǣra
Dat. þǣm, þām

For þone late OE. has þæne, þane; for þæs Anglian has þes (= Goth. þis, OHG. des); for the gen. sing. þǣre from *þaizjōz Merc. and Ken. have þere (= Goth. þizōs), and for the dat. þǣre from *þaizjai they have þere (= Goth. þizai); dat. sing. þǣm from an old instrumental form *þaimi beside þām with the ā from the plural forms þā, þāra, and similarly the dat. pl. þām beside the regular form þǣm from *þaimiz, and conversely gen. pl. þǣra with ǣ from the dat. þǣm. The instr. þȳ, þon were chiefly used before the comparative of adverbs and as a factor in adverbial conjunctional phrases like the Goth. instr. þē, as þon mā, *the more*, cp. Goth. ni þē haldis, *none the more*; for þȳ, for þon, *because, on that account*.

§ 310. The compound demonstrative pronoun þĕs, þis, þīos (þēos), *this*, was originally formed from the simple demonstrative + the deictic particle *-se, *-si. For the origin and explanation of the various forms of this pronoun, see *OE. Grammar*, § 466. It is declined as follows:—

Sing.	*Masc.*	*Neut.*	*Fem.*
Nom.	þĕs	þis	þīos, þēos
Acc.	þisne	þis	þās
Gen.	þis(s)es	þis(s)es	þisse
Dat.	þis(s)um	þis(s)um	þisse
Instr.		þȳs, þīs	

Plur. all Genders.

Nom. Acc. þās
Gen. þissa
Dat. þis(s)um

The medial -ss- was often simplified to -s-. In the dat sing.

and pl. Anglian has þios(s)um, þeos(s)um with u-umlaut (§ 59. 1) beside þis(s)um. Fem. gen. and dat. sing. þisse from older *þisre, gen. pl. þissa from older *þisra (§ 142); in late OE. there also occur þissere, þissera with -re, -ra from the simple demonstrative, beside þisre, þisra with syncope of the medial vowel and simplification of the ss.

§ 311. ilca, *same*, which only occurs in combination with the def. art., as sē ilca, þæt ilca, sēo ilca, *the same*, is always declined weak.

self, seolf, sylf, silf, *self*, was declined according to the strong or weak declension. In combination with the def. art., as sē selfa, it meant *the selfsame*. See also § 307.

5. Relative.

§ 312. A relative pronoun proper did not exist in prim. Germanic. The separate Germanic languages expressed it in various ways. In OE. it was expressed by the relative particle þe alone or in combination with the personal or the simple demonstrative pronoun, and for the third person also by the simple demonstrative pronoun alone, as

ic hit eom, þe wiþ þē sprece, *it is I who speak with thee*; idesa scēnost þe on woruld cōme, *the fairest one of ladies who came into the world*; gē þe yfle synt, *ye who are evil*.

wē þās word sprecaþ, þe wē in carcerne sittaþ, *we who sit in prison speak these words*; saga hwæt ic hātte, þe ic lond rēafige, *say what I am called, I who lay waste the land*; þæt se mon ne wāt, þe him on foldan fægrost limpeþ, *the man to whom on earth the fairest happens knows not that*.

sē þe brȳd hæfþ, sē is brȳdguma, *he who hath the bride is the bridegroom*; gehȳre, sē þe ēaran hæbbe, *let him hear who hath ears*; þæt þe ācenned is of flǣsce, þæt is flǣsc, *that which is born of the flesh is flesh*.

se mon-dryhten, sē ēow þā māþmas geaf, *the lord who gave you the treasures*; þonne tōdǣlaþ hī his feoh þæt tō lāfe biþ, *then they divide his property which is left*.

6. Interrogative.

§ 313. The simple interrogative pronoun had no independent form for the feminine, and was declined in the singular only.

	Masc.	Neut.
Nom.	hwă	hwæt
Acc.	hwone	hwæt
Gen.	hwæs	hwæs
Dat.	hwǣm, hwām	hwǣm, hwām
Instr.		hwȳ, hwī

Beside **hwone** there also rarely occurs **hwane**, and in late OE. **hwæne**. **hwām** was a new formation with **ā** from **hwā**. Beside **hwȳ, hwī** there also occur **hwon (hwan)** in such adverbial phrases as **for hwon, tō hwon**, *why?*, and **hū**, *how?*

§ 314. **hwæþer**, *which of two?*, and **hwelc, hwilc, hwylc**, *what sort of?*, were declined according to the strong declension of adjectives.

7. Indefinite.

§ 315. OE. had the following indefinite pronouns:— **ǣghwā**, *each one, every one*, from **ā**, *ever* + **gi** + **hwa**; and similarly **ǣghwæþer**, *each of two, both*; **ǣghwelc, ǣghwilc**, *each one, every one*. **ǣlc**, *each, every*; **ǣnig**, *any*, **nǣnig**, *not any one, no one*; **æthwā**, *each*; **āhwā**, *any one*; **āhwæþer, ōhwæþer, āwþer, ōwþer**, *one of two*, **nāhwæþer, nōhwæþer, nāwþer, nōwþer**, *neither of two*; **ān**, *some one, a certain one*, in plur. *each, every, all*, **nān**, *no one*, **nānþing**, *nothing*; **āwiht, ōwiht, āwuht, ōwuht, āht, ōht**, *anything*; **nāwiht, nōwiht, nāwuht, nōwuht, nāht, nōht**, *nothing*; **gehwā**, *each one, every one*; **gehwæþer**, *each of two, both*; **gehwilc**, *each, every one*; **hwelchwugu**, *any, some, some one*; **hwæthwugu**, *somewhat, something*; **lōc, lōca** + pronoun **hwā, hwæþer**, as **lōc hwæþer þǣra gebrōþra**, *whichever of the two brothers*, **bide me lōce hwæs þū wille**, *ask me for whatever thou wilt*; **man**, *one*; **nāt+hwā, hwelc**, *some one*

I know not who, which; samhwilc, *some*; sum, *some one*; swā ... swā, *as* swā hwā swā, *whosoever, whoever*, swā hwæt swā, *whatsoever, whatever*, swā hwæþer swā, *whichever of two*, swā hwelc swā, *whichever*; swelc, swilc, *such*; þyslic, þuslic, þyllic, þullic, *such*.

CHAPTER XII

VERBS

§ 316. The OE. verb has the following independent forms:— One voice (active), two numbers, three persons, two tenses (present and preterite), two complete moods (indicative and subjunctive, the latter originally the optative), besides an imperative which is only used in the present tense; one verbal noun (the present infinitive), a present participle with active meaning, and one verbal adjective (the past participle).

The simple future was generally expressed by the present tense as in the oldest periods of the other Germanic languages, but already in OE. the present forms of bēon, *to be*, sculan, *shall*, willan, *will*, with the infinitive began to be used to express the future. In the oldest OE. the perfect of transitive verbs was formed by means of the forms of habban, *to have*, and the past participle, and that of intransitive verbs by means of wesan, *to be*, and the past participle. At a later period habban came to be used to form the perfect of intransitive verbs also. The only trace of the old passive voice preserved in OE. is hātte (Goth. háitada), *is* or *was called*, pl. hātton. Otherwise the passive was expressed by the forms of bēon, wesan, *to be*, occasionally also by weorþan, *to become*, and the past participle.

§ 317. The OE. verbs are divided into two great classes:— Strong and Weak. The strong verbs form their preterite (originally perfect) and past participle by means of ablaut (§ 103). The weak verbs form their preterite by the addition of a syllable containing a dental (**-de**, **-te** = Goth. -da, -ta), and their past participle by means of a dental suffix (**-d**, **-t** = Goth. -þ, -t).

Besides these two great classes of strong and weak verbs, there are a few others which will be treated under the general heading of *Minor Groups*.

The strong verbs were originally further subdivided into reduplicated and non-reduplicated verbs. In OE. the reduplication almost entirely disappeared in the prehistoric period of the language (§ 355). The non-reduplicated verbs are divided into six classes according to the six ablaut-series (§ 103). The originally reduplicated verbs are put together in this book and called class VII. Strong verbs could have either the strong or weak grade of ablaut in the present; in the former case they are called imperfect presents (as **cēosan**, *to choose*; **helpan**, *to help*; **etan**, *to eat*; &c.), and in the latter case aorist presents (as **lūcan**, *to close*; **murnan**, *to mourn*; **cuman**, *to come*; &c.).

A. Strong Verbs.

§ 318. We are able to conjugate an OE. strong verb when we know the four stems, as seen (1) in the infinitive or first pers. sing. pres. indicative, (2) first pers. sing. pret. indicative, (3) pret. pl. indicative, (4) the past participle. The conjugation of **beran**, *to bear*, **helpan**, *to help*, **bindan**, *to bind*, **rīdan**, *to ride*, **cēosan**, *to choose*, **weorpan**, *to throw*, **faran**, *to go*, **biddan**, *to pray*, **feallan**, *to fall*, **tēon**, *to draw*, **slēan**, *to slay*, and **fōn**, *to seize*, will serve as models for all strong verbs, because in addition to verbal endings, one or other of them illustrates such phenomena as umlaut (§ 57), the interchange between **i** and **e** in the pres. indic. of verbs belonging to classes III, IV, and V (§ 21. 2), breaking (§§ 51–5), vowel contraction (§ 68), vowel syncope (§ 319), the simplification of double consonants (§ 145), Verner's law (§ 115), and the consonant changes in the second and third pers. sing. of the pres. indicative (§ 319).

Present.

Indicative.

Sing.	1.	bere	helpe	binde	rīde
	2.	bir(e)st	hilpst	bintst	rītst
	3.	bir(e)þ	hilpþ	bint	rīt(t)
Plur.		beraþ	helpaþ	bindaþ	rīdaþ

Subjunctive.

Sing.	bere	helpe	binde	rīde
Plur.	beren	helpen	binden	rīden

Imperative.

Sing.	2.	ber	help	bind	rīd
Plur.	2.	beraþ	helpaþ	bindaþ	rīdaþ

Infinitive.

beran	helpan	bindan	rīdan

Participle.

berende	helpende	bindende	rīdende

Preterite.

Indicative.

Sing.	1.	bær	healp	band	rād
	2.	bǣre	hulpe	bunde	ride
	3.	bær	healp	band	rād
Plur.		bǣron	hulpon	bundon	ridon

Subjunctive.

Sing.	bǣre	hulpe	bunde	ride
Plur.	bǣren	hulpen	bunden	riden

Participle.

boren	holpen	bunden	riden

Present.

Indicative.

Sing. 1.	cēose	weorpe	fare	bidde
2.	cīest	wierpst	fær(e)st	bitst
3.	cīest	wierpþ	fær(e)þ	bit(t)
Plur.	cēosaþ	weorpaþ	faraþ	biddaþ

Subjunctive.

Sing.	cēose	weorpe	fare	bidde
Plur.	cēosen	weorpen	faren	bidden

Imperative.

Sing. 2.	cēos	weorp	far	bide
Plur. 2.	cēosaþ	weorpaþ	faraþ	biddaþ

Infinitive.

cēosan	weorpan	faran	biddan

Participle.

cēosende	weorpende	farende	biddende

Preterite.

Indicative.

Sing. 1.	cēas	wearp	fōr	bæd
2.	cure	wurpe	fōre	bæde
3.	cēas	wearp	fōr	bæd
Plur.	curon	wurpon	fōron	bædon

Subjunctive.

Sing.	cure	wurpe	fōre	bæde
Plur.	curen	wurpen	fōren	bæden

Participle.

coren	worpen	faren	beden

Present.

Indicative.

Sing.	1.	fealle	tēo	slēa	fō
	2.	fielst	tīehst	sliehst	fēhst
	3.	fielþ	tīehþ	sliehþ	fēhþ
Plur.		feallaþ	tēoþ	slēaþ	fōþ

Subjunctive.

Sing.	fealle	tēo	slēa	fō
Plur.	feallen	tēon	slēan	fōn

Imperative.

Sing.	2.	feall	tēoh	sleah	fōh
Plur.	2.	feallaþ	tēoþ	slēaþ	fōþ

Infinitive.

feallan	tēon	slēan	fōn

Participle.

feallende	tēonde	slēande	fōnde

Preterite.

Indicative.

Sing.	1.	fēoll	tēah	slōh, slōg	fēng
	2.	fēolle	tuge	slōge	fēnge
	3.	fēoll	tēah	slōh, slōg	fēng
Plur.		fēollon	tugon	slōgon	fēngon

Subjunctive.

Sing.	fēolle	tuge	slōge	fēnge
Plur.	fēollen	tugen	slōgen	fēngen

Participle.

feallen	togen	slægen	fangen

The Endings of Strong Verbs.

§ 319. Pres. Indicative: The original ending of the first pers. sing. was -ō (cp. Lat. ferō, Gr. φέρω, *I bear*), which became -u (later -o) in prim. OE. (§ 85. 1). The -u (-o) regularly remained after short stems, and disappeared after long stems, as beru, -o beside *help, *bind, but already in prehistoric OE. the verbs with long stems took -u again after the analogy of those with short stems. The Anglian dialects mostly preserved the -u (-o), but in early WS. and Ken. its place was taken by -e from the present subjunctive. The personal endings of the second and third pers. sing. and the third pers. pl. of strong verbs which originally had the principal accent on the stem-syllable were in prim. Germanic -z, -đ, -nd (§§ 82, 134) = Indg. -si, -ti, -nti, but the personal endings of the corresponding persons of the aorist presents (i. e. strong verbs with the weak grade of ablaut in the present) and of the first class of weak verbs were: ´s, ´þ, ´nþ, which became generalized in prehistoric OE., cp. § 115. The oldest OE. ending of the second pers. sing. is -s, as biris, bindis, later bires, bindes (§ 93. 3). The ending -st arose partly from analogy with the preterite-present forms wāst, þearft, scealt, &c., and partly from a false etymological division of the pronoun from the verb to which it was often attached enclitically, thus birisþu became biristu, from which birist was extracted as the verbal form. The ending -st occurs earliest in the contracted verbs like tīehst, sliehst, &c. The oldest OE. ending of the third pers. sing. is -þ, as biriþ, bindiþ, later bir(e)þ, bint (§ 164). The -eþ appears as -es in late Nth.

In the second and third pers. sing. the medial -i- (-e-) was regularly syncopated after long stems, hilpst, hilpþ, tīehst, tīehþ, and remained after short stems, as birest, bireþ, færest, færeþ (§ 93. 3), but there are many exceptions to this rule, especially in WS. and Ken., owing to new formations in both directions, as bindest, bindeþ, hilpest, hilpeþ, &c., and on the other hand birst, birþ, færst, færþ, &c. In Anglian the forms without syncope were almost entirely generalized, but in WS. and Ken. syncope was practically general except after a liquid or a nasal.

The syncope of the -e- in the second and third pers. sing. gave rise to various consonantal changes: Double consonants were simplified before the personal endings (§ 144), as fielst, fielþ, spinst, spinþ, beside inf. feallan, *to fall*, spinnan, *to spin*.

d became t before -st, as bintst, bitst, rītst. d and t+-þ became tt (common in the older period of the language), later t, as bint, bit(t), rīt(t); birst, it(t), beside inf. berstan, *to burst*, etan, *to eat*, see §§ 140, 164. Forms like bindest, bidst; bindeþ, bid(e)þ, &c., were new formations after the analogy of forms which regularly had d.

After a long vowel, diphthong, or liquid, g became h before -st, -þ (§ 140), as stīhst, stīhþ, inf. stīgan, *to ascend*; flīehst, flīehþ, inf. flēogan, *to fly*; swilhst, swilhþ, inf. swelgan, *to swallow*, but the g was often restored from forms which regularly had g.

s, ss, st + -st, -þ became -st (§§ 144, 164), as cīest; cyst beside inf. wv. cyssan, *to kiss*, birst beside birstest, birsteþ (new formations); x (= hs) + -st, -þ became -xt, as wiext beside inf. weaxan, *to grow*. In verbs of this type the second and third pers. sing. regularly fell together.

þ disappeared before -st (§ 144), as cwist, wierst, beside inf. cweþan, *to say*, weorþan, *to become*. Forms like cwiþst, wierþst were new formations after the analogy of the other forms of the present. þ + -þ became -þ, as cwiþ, wierþ.

The forms of the first and second pers. plural had disappeared in the oldest period of the language, their place having been taken by the form of the third person. The ending of the third pers. is -þ, as beraþ, bindaþ, where -a-þ goes back to prim. Germanic -á-nþ (= Indg. o-nti, cp. Gr. Doric φέροντι, *they bear*), which regularly became -a-þ in OE. (§ 94. 3).

§ 320. Pres. subjunctive: this tense is properly an old optative which came to be used in place of the original subjunctive in prim. Germanic. The original endings were sing. -oi-, -oi-s, -oi-t; third pers. pl. -oi-nt = prim. Germanic -ai- (§ 17), -ai-z (§ 115), -ai (§ 80. 2); ai-n (§ 80. 2). The -z disappeared in prim. West Germanic (§ 133). Then ai became æ (through the intermediate stage ǣ), see § 89, which remained in the oldest OE., and afterwards became e. In this manner all the original forms of the sing. became alike, as bere, and the pl. had -en, as beren. Beside -en there also occurs in late WS. -an, and also -un, -on taken over from the pret. pl. indicative. The final -n of the plural disappeared in WS. and Ken. when a personal pronoun of the first or second pers. came immediately after the verb, as bere wĕ, wit, gĕ, git. Then bere wĕ, &c., came to be used for the indicative and imperative.

§ 321. Imperative: The original ending of the second pers. sing. was -e which regularly disappeared (§ 81), whence ber = Gr. φέρε. On the -e in forms like bide beside its absence in ber, &c., see § 85. 3. In OE. the third pers. pl. of the present indicative was used for the second pers. plural. The first pers. pl. is generally expressed by the pres. subjunctive.

§ 322. Pres. participle: The oldest OE. ending is -ændi, -endi, later -ende. On the inflexion of the present participle, see § 289.

§ 323. Infinitive: The inf. is originally a nomen actionis formed by means of the suffix -ono- to which was added the nom. acc. neut. ending -m, thus the original form of beran was *bhéronom, the -onom of which regularly became -an in OE. (§§ 17, 80. 1). In prim. West Germanic the inf. was inflected in the gen. and dat. sing. like an ordinary noun of the ja-declension (§ 202), gen. -ennes, dat. -enne. The inflected forms of the inf. are sometimes called the gerund. The gen. disappeared in prehistoric OE. The dat. tō berenne generally became -anne through the influence of the inf. ending -an. Beside -enne, -anne, there also occur in late OE. -ene, -ane (§ 145), and -ende with d from the pres. participle.

§ 324. Pret. indicative: The pret. indic. is morphologically an old perfect, which already in prim. Germanic was chiefly used to express the past tense. The original endings of the perf. sing. were -a, -tha, -e, cp. Gr. οἶδα, *I know*, οἶσθα, οἶδε. The -a and -e regularly disappeared in prim. Germanic (§ 81), whence OE. first and third pers. sing. bær, band, &c. The ending of the second pers. singular would regularly have become -þ (§ 111) in OE., except after prim. Germanic s, f, χ where it regularly became -t (§ 109, notes), as in Goth. last, *thou didst gather*, slōht, *thou didst slay*, þarft (OE. þearft), *thou needest*. This -t became generalized in prim. Germanic, as Goth. O.Icel. namt, *thou tookest*. But in the West Germanic languages the old ending was only preserved in the preterite-present verbs, as OE. þearft, *thou needest*, scealt, *thou shalt*, meaht, *thou mayest*, &c., see § 383. The third pers. pl. ended originally in -nt (with vocalic n) which regularly became -un in prim. Germanic (§§ 17, 80. 2). -un remained in the oldest OE. and then later became -on, and in late OE. -an beside -on occurs, whence bǣron, bundon, &c.

§ 325. Pret. subjunctive: This tense is properly an old optative which came to be used in place of the original subjunctive in prim. Germanic. The prim. Germanic endings of the sing. were: -ī (§ 80. 1), -ī-z (§ 115), -ī (§ 80. 2); third pers. pl. -ī-n (§ 80. 2) from earlier -ī-m, -ī-s, -ī-t; -ī-nt. The endings of the sing. would regularly have become -i in the oldest OE. The -i would have caused umlaut in the stem-syllable and then have disappeared after long stems and have remained (later -e) after short stems. Regular forms would have been *bynd, *hylp, *fēr, &c., but *cyre, *tyge, &c. The pl. ending -ī-n would regularly have become -i-n (later -e-n) with umlaut in the stem-syllable, as *bynden, *cyren, &c. But real old pret. subjunctive forms have only been preserved in OE. in a few isolated instances as in the preterite-presents, dyge, scyle, þyrfe. In OE. the old endings of the pres. subjunctive came to be used for the preterite some time before the operation of i-umlaut. This accounts for the absence of umlaut in the OE. pret. subjunctive, as bunde, bunden. Already in early OE. the pret. subjunctive also began to take the endings of the pret. indicative. The final -n of the plural disappeared in WS. and Ken. when a personal pronoun of the first or second person came immediately after the verb, as bǣre wē, wit, gē, git. Then later bǣre wē, &c., came to be used also for the indicative.

§ 326. Past participle: Prim. Germanic had two endings of the pp., viz. -én-az, -ín-iz (= Indg. -én-os, -én-is), which regularly fell together in -en in OE., but they were still kept apart in the oldest period of the language, the former being -æn (-en), and the latter -in, see § 290.

GENERAL REMARKS ON THE STRONG VERBS.

§ 327. Present indicative: On the interchange between i in the second and third pers. sing. and e in the other forms of the present in verbs belonging to classes III, IV, and V, as hilpst, hilpþ: helpan, *to help*; bir(e)st, bir(e)þ: beran, *to bear*; cwist, cwiþ: cweþan, *to say*, see § 21. 2. i-umlaut took place in the second and third pers. sing. of all verbs containing a vowel or diphthong capable of having umlaut. On the i-umlaut in verbs of class VI, as fær(e)st, fær(e)þ, see § 58, note 2. On the Anglian forms of the second and third pers. sing. of verbs like cēosan, tēon, see § 57, note 5. The regular forms of the second and third pers. sing. were often remodelled on analogy with the other forms of the present, especially in Anglian, as help(e)st, help(e)þ; fealst, fealþ, feallest, fealleþ; weorpest, weorpeþ, beside older hilpst, hilpþ; fielst, fielþ; wierpst, wierpþ.

On u- or o/a-umlaut of a, e in the first pers. sing., and the pl. in the non-WS. dialects, see § 59. On the breaking of Germanic a to ea, as in feallan, healp, wearp, and of e to eo, as in weorpan, see §§ 51-2. On the vowel contraction in the present of contracted verbs, see § 68.

Strong verbs like biddan, *to pray*, hliehhan, *to laugh*, licgan, *to lie down*, had single medial consonants in the second and third pers. sing., as bitst, bit(t); hliehst, hliehþ; lig(e)st, lig(e)þ, see § 135, note.

§ 328. Infinitive: On the o/a-umlaut in the non-WS. dialects, see § 59.

§ 329. Pret. indicative: OE. only preserved the old pret. (originally perfect) of the second pers. sing. in the preterite-present verbs (§ 383). In all other strong verbs the second pers. sing. was formed direct from the pret. subjunctive, which accounts for the absence of i-umlaut in the stem-syllable and the preservation of the final -e after both short and long stems, as ride, cure, &c., and bǣre, hulpe, bunde, &c.

On the question of u-umlaut in the plural of verbs belonging to class I, see § 59. 1.

§ 330. Past participle: The ending of the pp. has already been explained in § 290. In prim. Germanic the prefix *ʒi- was added to the past participle to impart to it a perfective meaning. Verbs which were already perfective in meaning, such as bringan, *to bring*, cuman, *to come*, niman, *to take*, weorþan, *to become*, did not originally have it. But in OE. the simple pp. generally had ge-, irrespectively as to whether it was perfective or imperfective in meaning. On past participles which have i-umlaut, see § 290.

§ 331. On the parts of strong verbs which exhibit Verner's law in OE., see § 115.

The Classification of the Strong Verbs.

Class I.

§ 332. The verbs of this class belong to the first ablaut-series (§ 103) and therefore have ī in all forms of the present, ā in the first and third pers. sing. of the preterite, and i in the pret. plural and pp., thus:

bīdan, *to await*   bād   bidon   biden

And similarly a large number of other verbs, as ætwītan, *to blame, reproach*; bītan, *to bite*; drīfan, *to drive*; gewītan, *to depart*; glīdan, *to glide*; rīdan, *to ride*; scīnan, *to shine*; slīdan, *to slide;* slītan, *to slit;* strīdan, *to stride;* wrītan, *to write.* stīgan, *to ascend,* pret. sing. **stāg** beside **stāh** (§ 172); and similarly hnīgan, *to incline;* sīgan, *to sink.*

§ 333. snīþan, *to cut*   snāþ   snidon   sniden

And similarly līþan, *to go;* scrīþan, *to go, proceed.* See § 115. In ārīsan, *to arise;* gerīsan, *to befit;* mīþan, *to avoid;* wrīþan, *to twist,* the s, þ of the present was extended to all forms of the verb.

§ 334. tīon, tēon, *to accuse*   tāh   tigon   tigen

tīon, tēon, from older *tīohan, *tīhan (§§ 55, 68); on the g in the pret. pl. and pp., see § 115. The verbs of this type often formed their pret. and pp. after the analogy of class II (§ 335), as tēah, tugon, togen; and similarly lēon, *to lend;* sēon (pp. also siwen, § 114. 5), *to strain;* þēon, *to thrive,* wrēon, *to cover.*

Class II.

§ 335. The verbs of this class belong to the second ablaut-series (§ 103) and therefore have ēo in the present, ēa in the first and third pers. sing. of the preterite, u in the pret. plural, and o in the pp., thus:

bēodan, *to offer*   bēad   budon   boden

And similarly many other verbs, as clēofan, *to cleave asunder;* crēopan, *to creep;* drēopan, *to drip;* gēotan, *to pour;* rēocan, *to smoke, reek;* scēotan, *to shoot;* smēocan, *to smoke.* drēogan, *to endure,* pret. sing. drēag beside drēah (§ 172); and similarly flēogan, *to fly;* lēogan, *to tell lies.* brēowan, *to brew,* pret. sing. brēaw (cp. § 149); and similarly cēowan, *to chew;* hrēowan, *to repent of, rue.*

§ 336. cēosan, *to choose*   cēas   curon   coren

And similarly drēosan, *to fall;* forlēosan, *to lose;* frēosan, *to freeze;* hrēosan, *to fall;* sēoþan (sudon, soden), *to boil.* See § 115.

§ 337. tēon, *to draw*   tēah   tugon   togen

tēon (Goth. tiuhan) from *tēohan (§ 68); on the g in the pret. pl. and pp., see § 115; and similarly flēon, *to flee*.

§ 338. Here belong also the aorist presents with weak grade vowel in all forms of the present (§ 317):

brūcan, *to use*   brēac   brucon   brocen

And similarly dūfan, *to dive*; lūcan, *to lock*; slūpan, *to slip*; sūcan, *to suck*; sūpan, *to sup*. būgan, *to bend*, pret. sing. bēag beside bēah (§ 172); and similarly smūgan, *to creep*; sūgan, *to suck*.

Class III.

§ 339. The verbs of this class belong to the third ablaut-series (§ 104), and include the strong verbs having a medial nasal or liquid + consonant, and a few others in which the stem-vowel is followed by two consonants other than a nasal or liquid + consonant.

§ 340. Verbs with nasal + consonant have i in all forms of the present, a, o (§ 46) in the first and third pers. sing. of the preterite, and u in the pret. pl. and pp., thus:

bindan, *to bind*   band (bond)   bundon   bunden

And similarly with many other verbs, as climban, *to climb*; drincan, *to drink*; findan (pret. sing. also funde), *to find*; gelimpan, *to happen*; grindan, *to grind*; onginnan, *to begin*; rinnan, *to run, flow*; sincan, *to sink*; singan, *to sing*; slincan, *to slink, creep*; spinnan, *to spin*; stingan, *to sting*; swingan, *to swing*; swimman, *to swim*; windan, *to wind*.

NOTE.—In the two verbs corresponding to Goth. brinnan, *to burn*, and rinnan, *to run*, the metathesis of the r (§ 143) took place earlier than breaking, whence Anglian biorna(n), beorna(n), iorna(n), eorna(n), see § 53. In WS. we have biernan (later birnan, byrnan), barn (born, later bearn), burnon, burnen; and iernan, arn (orn, later earn), urnon, urnen. biernan, iernan were new formations made from the third pers. sing. biern(e)þ, iern(e)þ. The new formation was due to the fact that the two verbs were mostly used impersonally.

§ 341. Verbs with l + cons. except lc (§ 342) have e in the

present, ea (§ 51) in the first and third pers. sing. of the preterite, u in the pret. plural, and o in the pp. (§ 23), thus:

helpan, *to help*   healp   hulpon   holpen

And similarly belgan, *to swell with anger*; bellan, *to bellow*; beteldan, *to cover*; delfan, *to dig*; meltan, *to melt*; swelgan, *to swallow*; swellan, *to swell*; sweltan, *to die*. gieldan (§ 56), *to yield*, geald, guldon, golden; and similarly giellan, *to yell*; gielpan, *to boast*.

§ 342. Verbs with lc, r or h + consonant have eo in the present (§ 52), ea in the first and third pers. sing. of the preterite (§ 51), u in the pret. plural, and o in the pp. (§ 23). On the verbs with the combination weo- in the present, see § 63.

weorpan, *to throw*   wearp   wurpon   worpen

And similarly beorcan, *to bark*; beorgan, *to protect*; ceorfan, *to cut, carve*; feohtan, *to fight*; meolcan (late WS. also melcan), *to milk*; sceorpan, *to scrape*; steorfan, *to die*. weorþan, *to become*, wearþ, wurdon, worden (§ 115).

Note.—fēolan from *feolhan (§ 76), *to enter, penetrate*, fealh, fulgon (§ 115) beside the more common form fǣlon made after the analogy of verbs of class IV, folgen; pret. pl. and pp. also fūlon from *fulhon, fōlen from *folhen with h from the present *feolhan.

§ 343.

bregdan, *to brandish*	brægd	brugdon	brogden
stregdan, *to strew*	strægd	strugdon	strogden
berstan, *to burst*	bærst	burston	borsten
þerscan, *to thresh*	þærsc	þurscon	þorscen
frignan, *to ask*	frægn	frugnon	frugnen
murnan, *to mourn*	mearn	murnon	
spurnan (spornan), *to spurn*	spearn	spurnon	spornen

Note.—In bregdan and stregdan, beside the forms with g there also occur forms with loss of g and lengthening of the preceding vowel, as brēdan, brǣd, brūdon, brōden (§ 72). berstan (OHG. brestan) and þerscan (OHG. dreskan) have metathesis of r (§ 143), hence the absence of breaking in the present and the pret. singular. The **i** in **frignan** is due to the influence of the **gn**; beside **frignan** there also occurs **frīnan** (§ 72) to which a new pret. sing. **frān** was formed after the analogy of verbs of class I (§ 332); beside the pret. pl. **frugnon** there also occur **frungon** with metathesis of **gn**, and **frūnon** with loss of **g** (§ 72); and beside the pp. **frugnen** there also occur **frūnen** with loss of **g**, and **frognen**. **murnan** and **spurnan** are aorist presents (§ 317).

Class IV.

§ 344. The verbs of this class belong to the fourth ablaut-series (§ 104), which includes the strong verbs whose stems end in a single liquid or nasal. They have **e** in the present, **æ** in the first and third pers. sing. of the preterite, **ǣ** in the pret. plural (but see § 45), and **o** in the pp., thus:

beran, *to bear*	bær	bǣron	boren

And similarly **cwelan**, *to die*; **helan**, *to conceal*; **stelan**, *to steal*; **teran**, *to tear*; **þweran**, *to stir*. **scieran**, *to shear*, **scear**, **scēaron**, see § 56, **scoren**.

§ 345.

cuman, *to come*	c(w)ōm	c(w)ōmon	cumen (cymen)
niman, *to take*	nōm	nōmon	numen

NOTE.—From the regular forms of the second and third pers. sing. pres. indic. **cym(e)st, cym(e)þ**, the **y** was often extended to other forms of the pres., especially to the pres. subjunctive, as **cyme** beside **cume**; **cuman** is an aorist present (§ 317) from **kwuman*, older **kwoman* (§§ 48, 114. 2) with regular loss of the **w**, after the analogy of which it was often dropped in the pret. pl. **cwōmon** from **kwǣmun*; **c(w)ōm** for **cam*, **com* (§ 114. 2) was a new formation from the plural where the **ō** was regular; **cumen** from **kwumen*, older **kwomen*; on **cymen**, see § 290. **niman** from older **neman* (§ 47); **nōm** was a new formation from the plural which regularly had **ō** (§ 49); beside **nōm, nōmon** there also occur the new formations **nam, nāmon**; **numen** from older **nomen* (§ 48).

Class V.

§ 346. The verbs of this class belong to the fifth ablaut-series (§ 104), which includes the strong verbs whose stems end in a single consonant other than a liquid or a nasal. They have e in the present, æ in the first and third pers. sing. of the preterite, ǣ in the pret. plural, and e in the pp., thus:

metan, *to measure*   mæt   mǣton   meten

And similarly brecan (pp. brocen after the analogy of class IV); cnedan, *to knead*; drepan (pp. also dropen after the analogy of class IV), *to hit, kill*; screpan, *to scrape*; sprecan (late OE. specan), *to speak*; swefan, *to sleep*; tredan, *to tread*; wefan, *to weave*; wegan (pret. pl. wǣgon beside wāgon, see § 45), *to carry*.

§ 347. giefan, *to give*   geaf   gēafon   giefen

And similarly forgietan, *to forget*. See § 56.

§ 348. etan, *to eat*   ǣt   ǣton   eten

And similarly fretan, *to devour*. These two verbs had ǣ in the pret. sing. already in prim. Germanic, cp. Lat. edō, *I eat*, pf. ēdī.

§ 349. cweþan, *to say*   cwæþ   cwǣdon   cweden
       wesan, *to be*   wæs   wǣron

See § 115. genesan, *to be saved*, and lesan, *to collect, gather*, extended the s of the pres. and the pret. singular to all forms.

§ 350. sēon from *seohan (§§ 52, 68), *to see*, seah, sāwon beside sǣgon, sewen beside sawen with a difficult to account for; Anglian gesegen with g from the pret. plural, see § 114. 5; and similarly gefēon, *to rejoice*, gefeah, pret. pl. gefǣgon; plēon, *to risk*, pret. sing. pleah.

§ 351. To this class also belong a few verbs which originally had j in the present (see §§ 21. 2, 135), as

biddan, *to pray*	bæd	bǣdon	beden
sittan, *to sit*	sæt	sǣton	seten
licgan, *to lie down*	læg	lǣgon	legen

The pret. pl. of licgan has lāgon beside lǣgon (see § 45). þicgan, *to receive*, is a weak verb in WS. (§ 371); in poetry it has the strong forms þeah (þāh), þǣgon, þegen. fricgan, *to ask, inquire*, with strong pp. gefrigen, gefrugen.

Class VI

§ 352. The verbs of this class belong to the sixth ablaut-series (§ 103), and have a in the present, ō in the pret. sing. and plural, and æ beside a in the pp. The regular vowel in the pp. is æ (cp. § 29, note 1), the forms with a are new formations made direct from the present and infinitive:—

faran, *to go*   fōr   fōron   færen, faren

And similarly alan, *to grow*; bacan, *to bake*; calan, *to be cold*; galan, *to sing*; grafan, *to dig*; hladan, *to lade, load*; sacan, *to strive, quarrel*; wacan, *to awake, be born*; wadan, *to go*; wascan, *to wash*. gnagan (pret. sing. gnōg beside gnōh (§ 172), *to gnaw*; and similarly dragan, *to draw*. scacan, sceacan, *to shake*, scōc, sceōc, scacen, sceacen, see § 56, note 3; and similarly scafan, sceafan, *to shave, scrape*. standan, *to stand*, stōd, stōdon, standen with n from the present. spannan, *to allure*, pret. spōn beside spēon which was formed after the analogy of verbs of class VII.

§ 353.

slēan, *to strike*   slōg, slōh   slōgon   slægen, slagen

slēan from *sleahan (§§ 51, 68); slōg with g from the plural, beside slōh, slōgon (see § 115); beside slægen, slagen there also occurs slegen with i-umlaut, see § 290; and similarly flēan, *to flay*; lēan, *to blame*; þwēan, *to wash*.

§ 354. To this class also belong a few verbs which originally had j in the present like Goth. hafjan, *to raise*, hlahjan, *to laugh* (see §§ 57, 135):—

hebban, *to raise*	hōf	hōfon	hæfen, hafen
hliehhan, *to laugh*	hlōg, hlōh	hlōgon	
sceþþan, *to injure*	scōd	scōdon	
scieppan, *to create*	scōp	scōpon	sceapen
stæppan, steppan, *to step, go*	stōp	stōpon	stæpen, stapen
swerian, *to swear*	swōr	swōron	sworen

NOTE.—hebban (§ 158) has also weak pret. and pp. in late WS. (hefde, hefod); beside hæfen there also occurs hefen (§ 290). hlōg with g from the plural (§ 115) beside hlōh. The regular WS. form of sceþþan would be scieþþan (§ 56); scōd with d from scōdon (§ 115). On sceapen, see § 56. sworen with o from analogy of verbs of class IV, as in OHG. gisworan.

Class VII.

§ 355. To this class belong those verbs which originally had reduplicated preterites like Goth. haíhald, laílōt: inf. haldan, *to hold*, lētan, *to let*. Traces of the old reduplicated preterites have been preserved in Anglian and in poetry, viz. hĕht, leolc, leort, ondreord, reord, beside inf. hātan, lācan, lǣtan, ondrǣdan, rǣdan, see below. This class of verbs is divided into two sub-divisions according as the preterite had ē or ēo. The preterite sing. and pl. have the same stem-vowel. The stem-syllable of all verbs belonging to this class is long.

Sub-division 1.

§ 356. hātan, *to call*   hēt   hēton   hāten

And similarly lācan, *to play*; scādan, sceādan (§ 56, note 3), *to separate*, pret. scēd beside scēad.

§ 357. lǣtan, *to let, allow*   lēt   lēton   lǣten

And similarly ondrǣdan (WS. also weak pret. ondrǣdde), *to dread, fear*; rǣdan (pret. and pp. mostly weak in WS.: rǣdde, gerǣdd), *to advise*; slǣpan (WS. also weak pret. slǣpte), *to sleep*. blandan, *to mix*, pret. blēnd, pp. blanden.

§ 358. fōn (§ 20), *to seize*, fēng with ng from the plural, fēngon (§ 115), fangen; and similarly hōn, *to hang*.

Sub-division 2.

§ 359. bannan, *to summon*   bēon(n)   bēonnon   bannen

And similarly gangan (pret. also gīeng), *to go*; spannan, *to join, clasp*.

§ 360. fealdan (§ 51), feold feoldon fealden
to fold

And similarly feallan, *to fall*; healdan, *to hold*; stealdan, *to possess*; wealcan, *to roll*; wealdan, *to rule*; weallan, *to boil*; weaxan (originally belonged to class VI), *to grow*.

§ 361. blāwan, *to blow* blēow blēowon blāwen
(cp. § 149)

And similarly cnāwan, *to know*; crāwan, *to crow*; māwan, *to mow*; sāwan, *to sow*; swāpan, *to sweep*; þrāwan, *to turn, twist*; wāwan, *to blow*.

§ 362. bēatan, *to beat* bēot bēoton bēaten

And similarly āhnēapan, *to pluck off*; hēawan, *to hew*; hlēapan, *to leap*.

§ 363. blōtan, *to sacrifice* blēot blēoton blōten

And similarly blōwan, *to bloom, blossom*; hrōpan, *to shout*; hwōpan, *to threaten*; flōwan, *to flow*; grōwan, *to grow*; hlōwan, *to low, bellow*; rōwan (pret. pl. rēon beside rēowon, § 68), *to row*; spōwan, *to succeed*; wēpan (Goth. wōpjan), *to weep*. The pret. of flōcan, *to clap, strike*; swōgan, *to sound*; wrōtan, *to root up*, do not occur.

B. Weak Verbs.

§ 364. The weak verbs, which for the most part are derivative and denominative, form by far the greater majority of all OE. verbs. They are divided into three classes according to the endings of the infinitive, pret. indicative, and past participle. These endings are :—

	Inf.	Pret.	P.P.
Class I.	-an	-ede, -de, -te	-ed, -d, -t
	(Goth. -jan)	(Goth. -ida, -ta)	(Goth. -iþs, -ts)
Class II.	-ian	-ode	-od
	(Goth. -ōn)	(Goth. -ōda)	(Goth. -ōþs)
Class III.	-an	-de	-d
	(Goth. -an)	(Goth. -áida)	(Goth. -áiþs)

General Remarks on the Weak Verbs.

§ 365. The personal endings of the pres. indicative are the same as those of strong verbs. Including the characteristic dental (-d-, -t-) the prim. Germanic endings of the pret. indicative were:—sing. - đōn (-đǣn), -đǣs, -đǣ (§ 80. 2); third pers. plural -đun (§ 134), which regularly became -de, -des, -de; -dun (later -don) in OE., see §§ 80, 85; and similarly in the combinations with -t- which only occurred after voiceless consonants (§ 119). The -t in the OE. second pers. sing. -dest is of the same origin as the -t in the present of strong verbs (§ 319). On the origin of the formation of the preterite, see *OE. Grammar*, § 520.

The endings -e, -en of the pres. and pret. subjunctive are of the same origin as in strong verbs (§§ 320, 325).

The indic. plural was used for the imperative plural just as in the strong verbs (§ 321); for the imperative singular, see the separate classes.

The present participle was declined like an ordinary ja-stem (§ 289), and the pp. in -ed, -od like manig or hālig according as the stem-syllable was short or long (§ 290).

Class I.

§ 366. The verbs of this class are divided into two subdivisions: (*a*) verbs which originally had a short stem-syllable; (*b*) polysyllabic verbs and those which originally had a long stem-syllable. Nearly all the verbs belonging to this class are causative and denominative.

Sub-division (*a*).

§ 367. Formation of the present stem: The present stem of verbs ending in a single consonant, except r, became long (except in the second and third pers. sing. pres. indicative, and second pers. sing. imperative) by the West Germanic law of the doubling of consonants (§ 135). The j had already disappeared in these persons before the operation of the law, for which reason they had single consonants in OE. (§ 135, note).

§ 368. Formation of the pret. and past participle: The j, which caused the doubling of the final consonants in the present stems, never existed in the preterite or past participle, so that these stems ended in single consonants. The pret. generally had the ending -ede from prim. Germanic -iđōn, but verbs whose present stems ended in dd, tt (= West Germanic dj, tj) had -de, -te on analogy with the verbs which originally had long stems (§ 373). On many verbs whose present stems ended in cc, ll (= West Germanic kj, lj), see § 379.

The past participle generally ended in -ed from older -id, prim. Germanic -iđaz from older -iđás = Indg. -itós, as genered, gefremed (cp. § 290). But in WS. and Ken. the verbs whose stems ended in d, t had vowel syncope and assimilation of consonants, as geset(t), masc. acc. sing. gesetne, dat. gesettum, fem. gen. dat. sing. gesetre, beside Anglian geseted, gesetedne, gesettum, gesetedre; gehred(d) beside Anglian gehreded, *rescued*.

The ending -e (older -i) = prim. Germanic -ī, of the imperative singular regularly remained (§ 85. 3).

§ 369. The full conjugation of nerian (Goth. nasjan), *to save*; fremman (Goth. *framjan), *to perform*; and settan (Goth. satjan), *to set*, will serve as models for verbs belonging to sub-division (*a*).

Present.

Indicative.

Sing.	1. nerie	fremme	sette
	2. neres(t)	fremes(t)	setst
	3. nereþ	fremeþ	set(t)
Plur.	neriaþ	fremmaþ	settaþ

Subjunctive.

Sing.	nerie	fremme	sette
Plur.	nerien	fremmen	setten

Imperative.

Sing. 2. nere	freme	sete
Plur. 2. neriaþ	fremmaþ	settaþ

Infinitive.

nerian   fremman   settan

Participle.

neriende   fremmende   settende

Preterite.

Indicative.

Sing. 1.	nerede	fremede	sette
2.	neredes(t)	fremedes(t)	settes(t)
3.	nerede	fremede	sette
Plur.	neredon	fremedon	setton

Subjunctive.

Sing.	nerede	fremede	sette
Plur.	nereden	fremeden	setten

Participle.

genered   gefremed   geseted, geset(t)

§ 370. On forms like nergan, nerigan, nerigean, see § 151. Like nerian are conjugated andswerian, *to answer*; berian, *to make bare*; derian, *to injure*; erian, *to plough*; herian, *to praise*; spyrian, *to pursue*; werian, *to defend*.

In late WS. many of the verbs of this type went over into class II owing to the ending of the infinitive being the same in both classes.

§ 371. Like fremman are conjugated clynnan, *to sound*; dynnan, *to make a noise*; sceþþan (also sv. § 354), *to injure*; sweþþan, *to swathe*; temman, *to tame*; trymman, *to strengthen*; þicgan (in poetry also strong pret. þeah, þāh), *to receive*; wreþþan, *to support*.

In WS. and Ken. most of the verbs whose stems ended in
l, m, n, s, þ were remodelled on analogy with verbs like nerian
with single consonant, as clynian, fremian, helian, *to conceal*,
sweþian, and then later often went over into class II.

§ 372. Like settan are conjugated cnyttan, *to bind, knit*;
hreddan, *to rescue, save*; hwettan, *to whet, incite*; lettan, *to
hinder*; spryttan, *to sprout*; and lecgan, *to lay*.

Sub-division (*b*).

§ 373. The preterite generally ended in -de from older -ide,
the i of which caused umlaut in the stem-syllable and then disappeared (§§ 57, 98). The following points should be noted in
regard to the consonants: (1) Germanic double consonants
were simplified before -de, as fyllan (Goth. fulljan), *to fill*, pret.
fylde (§ 145), pp. gefylled; (2) þ+d became dd in late WS.,
as cȳþan, *to make known*, pret. cȳþde, pp. gecȳþed, later cȳdde
(§ 142), pp. gecȳd(d) with dd from the inflected forms; (3) -de
became -te after voiceless consonants (§ 140), as cyssan, *to kiss*,
pret. cyste, pp. gecyssed; grētan, *to greet*, pret. grētte, pp.
gegrēted; (4) the d in -de disappeared after consonant+d or t
(§ 145), as sendan, *to send*, pret. sende, pp. gesend(ed);
fæstan, *to make fast*, pret. fæste, pp. gefæst(ed).

Verbs which would regularly have vocalic l, n, r in the pret.
generally have -ede, especially in the combination long syllable
+l, n, r, as hyngran, *to hunger*, dīeglan, *to hide*, pret. hyngrede,
dīeglede (§ 97); but in the combination short syllable+l, n, r
they generally had -de in the oldest period of the language, and
then later -ede, as eglan, *to trouble*, pret. eglde beside later
eglede; the verbs of this type often went over into class II.

The uninflected form of the past participle generally ended
in -ed from older -id just as in sub-division (*a*). In those
cases where the e was regularly syncopated (§ 98), the same
consonantal changes took place as in the preterite, as gen. sing.
gefyldes, gedrenctes, gesendes, gegrēttes, gefæstes, &c. beside

nom. sing. gefylled, gedrenced, gesend(ed), gegrēt(ed), gefæst(ed). See § 290.

On the loss or retention of the final -e (older -i) from prim. Germanic -ī in the imperative singular, see § 85. 3.

§ 374. The full conjugation of dēman (Goth. dōmjan), *to judge*, drencan (Goth. dragkjan), *to submerge*, hyngran (Goth. huggrjan), *to hunger*, and gierwan from *ʒearwjan, *to prepare*, will serve as models for verbs belonging to sub-division (*b*).

Present.

Indicative.

Sing.	1. dēme	drence	hyngre	gierwe
	2. dēm(e)st	drenc(e)st	hyngrest	gierest
	3. dēm(e)þ	drenc(e)þ	hyngreþ	giereþ
Plur.	dēmaþ	drencaþ	hyngraþ	gierwaþ

Subjunctive.

Sing.	dēme	drence	hyngre	gierwe
Plur.	dēmen	drencen	hyngren	gierwen

Imperative.

Sing. 2.	dēm	drenc	hyngre	giere
Plur. 2.	dēmaþ	drencaþ	hyngraþ	gierwaþ

Infinitive.

dēman	drencan	hyngran	gierwan

Participle.

dēmende	drencende	hyngrende	gierwende

Preterite.

Indicative.

Sing.	1. dēmde	drencte	hyngrede	gierede
	2. dēmdes(t)	drenctes(t)	hyngredes(t)	gieredes(t)
	3. dēmde	drencte	hyngrede	gierede
Plur.	dēmdon	drencton	hyngredon	gieredon

Subjunctive.

Sing.	dēmde	drencte	hyngrede	gierede
Plur.	dēmden	drencten	hyngreden	giereden

Participle.

gedēmed   gedrenced   gehyngred   gegier(w)ed

§ 375. Like dēman are conjugated a large number of verbs, as ǣlan, *to set on fire*; bærnan, *to burn up*; brǣdan, *to broaden*; byrgan, *to bury*; cēlan, *to cool*; cemban, *to comb*; dǣlan, *to share*; fēdan, *to feed*; fylgan, *to follow*; gīeman, *to heed*; giernan, *to desire, yearn for*; hǣlan, *to heal*; hīeran, *to hear*; hȳdan, *to hide*; lǣdan, *to lead*; lǣfan, *to leave*; lǣran, *to teach*; mǣnan, *to moan*; rǣran, *to raise*; sengan, *to singe*; stīeran, *to steer*; tǣsan, *to pull, tear*. The contracted verbs, as hēan (pret. hēade, pp. hēad), *to heighten, raise*; and similarly tȳn, *to teach*; þȳn (also in form þȳwan), *to press*. cȳþan (pret. cȳþde, later cȳdde), *to make known*; and similarly cwīþan, *to lament*; sēþan, *to testify*. fyllan (pret. fylde), *to fill*; and similarly āfierran, *to remove*; clyppan, *to embrace*; cyssan (pret. cyste), *to kiss*; fiellan, *to fell*. ieldan (pret. ielde), *to delay*, sendan (pret. sende), *to send*, gyrdan (pret. gyrde), *to gird*; and similarly gyldan, *to gild*; wieldan, *to control, subdue*; bendan, *to bend*; wendan, *to turn*; andwyrdan, *to answer*; hierdan, *to harden*. fæstan (pret. fæste), *to make fast*; and similarly āfyrhtan, *to frighten*; hiertan, *to hearten, encourage*; līehtan, *to give light*; restan, *to rest*; þyrstan, *to thirst*.

§ 376. Like drencan are conjugated ācwencan, *to quench*; bētan, *to atone for*; cēpan, *to keep*; grētan, *to greet*; hǣtan, *to heat*; mētan, *to meet*; sencan, *to cause to sink*; wǣtan, *to wet*; wȳscan, *to wish*.

§ 377. Like hyngran are conjugated bīecnan, *to make a sign*; dīeglan, *to conceal*; timbran, *to build*; &c. efnan (pret. efnde, later efnede), *to level, perform*; and similarly bytlan, *to build*;

eglan, *to trouble, afflict*; seglan, *to sail*; þrysman, *to suffocate*. The verbs of this type often went over into class II (cp. § 100).

§ 378. gierest, giereþ, gierede from older *gierwis, *gierwiþ, *gierwide with regular loss of **w** (§ 144). At a later period the verbs of this type mostly generalized the forms with or without **w**, and often went over into class II. The verbs with a long vowel or long diphthong in the stem generally had **w** in all forms of the verb. Like gierwan are conjugated hierwan, *to despise, ill-treat*; nierwan, *to constrain*; smierwan, *to anoint, smear*. lǣwan (pret. lǣwde), *to betray*; and similarly forslǣwan, *to delay, be slow*; getrīewan, *to trust*; īewan, *to show, disclose*.

§ 379. A certain number of verbs belonging to class I formed their preterite and past participle already in prim. Germanic without the medial vowel -i-, as bycgan (Goth. bugjan), *to buy*, pret. bohte (Goth. baúhta), pp. geboht (Goth. baúhts), whence the absence of i-umlaut in the pret. and pp. of verbs of this type. In addition to a few verbs which had long stems originally, they embrace verbs whose present stems end in cc, ll from West Germanic kj and lj (§ 135). On the interchange between c, cc from kj, cg from ʒj, and h, see § 119. At a later period the pret. and pp. of verbs with -ecc- in the present were re-formed with e from the present, as cweccan, cwehte, gecweht; and similarly rǣcan, tǣcan, generally had pret. rǣhte, tǣhte with ǣ from the present, beside the regular forms rāhte, tāhte. The verbs with ll in the present often formed the pret. and pp. on analogy with the verbs of sub-division (*a*) especially in late OE., as dwelede, -ode, beside dwealde. Beside sellan (Goth. saljan) there also occurs siellan (later syllan) from *sealljan with ea borrowed from the pret. and pp. in prehistoric OE. bringan, *to bring*, is the strong form (cp. § 340); the regular weak form brengan is rare in OE.

bycgan, *to buy*	bohte	geboht
cweccan, *to shake*	cwehte	gecweaht
dreccan, *to afflict*	dreahte	gedreaht

leccan, *to moisten*	leahte	geleaht
reccan, *to narrate*	reahte	gereaht
streccan, *to stretch*	streahte	gestreaht
þeccan, *to cover*	þeahte	geþeaht
weccan, *to awake*	weahte	geweaht
cwellan, *to kill*	cwealde	gecweald
dwellan, *to hinder*	dwealde	gedweald
sellan, *to sell*	sealde	geseald
stellan, *to place*	stealde	gesteald
tellan, *to count*	tealde	geteald
rǣcan, *to reach*	rǣhte, rāhte	gerǣht
tǣcan, *to teach*	tǣhte, tāhte	getǣht, getāht
sēcan, *to seek*	sōhte	gesōht
bringan, *to bring*	brōhte	gebrōht
þencan, *to think*	þōhte	geþōht
þyncan, *to seem*	þūhte	geþūht
wyrcan, *to work*	worhte	geworht

NOTE.—The presents reccan for *rēcan (pret. rōhte), *to care for, reck*; and lǣccan for *lǣcan (pret. lǣhte, pp. gelǣht), *to seize*, are difficult to account for.

2. Especially in late OE. verbs with medial c, cc often formed their pret. and pp. in -hte, -ht after the analogy of the above type of verbs, but with the retention of i-umlaut, as bepǣcan, *to deceive*, bepǣhte, bepǣht, beside older bepǣcte, bepǣct; and similarly gewǣcan, *to weaken*; īecan, *to increase*; nēalǣcan, *to approach*; ōleccan, *to flatter*; sȳcan, *to suckle*; þryccan, *to press, crush*; wleccan, *to warm*.

Class II.

§ 380. With the exception of a few primary verbs all the verbs belonging to this class are denominative. The primary verbs had originally no -j- in the forms of the present. The denominative verbs were originally all formed from nouns belonging to the Germanic ō-declension (§ 211), and had -j- in all forms of the present. The two types of conjugation became blended together in prehistoric OE. in such a manner that all forms of both denominative and primary verbs came to have -j- in the present except the second and third pers. sing. indicative and the imperative singular. The -ōj- regularly became -i- (§ 94. 3) which not being original did not cause i-umlaut of the stem-syllable, whence the forms: indic. **sealfie, sealfiaþ**; subj. **sealfie, sealfien**; inf. **sealfian**; participle **sealfiende**; but **sealfas(t), sealfaþ**; imperative sing. **sealfa**. The -i- was often written -ig-, also -ige- before guttural vowels, as **sealfigan, sealfigean** beside **sealfian**. The ending -a in the imperative singular was from **sealfas(t)**; a form corresponding to Goth. **salbō** would have become in OE. *sealf from older *sealbu (§ 85. 1). The medial -ō- in the pret. indic. and subjunctive was regularly shortened to -u- in prehistoric OE. (§ 99) and then later became -o-, -a-, the former of which is usual in WS. and the latter in Anglian and Ken. On -e- beside -o-, -a- in the indic. pret. plural, see § 100. And similarly in the pp. WS. -od, Anglian and Ken. -ad.

A large number of the verbs which originally belonged to class III went over into this class in prehistoric OE.

The full conjugation of **sealfian**, *to anoint*, will serve as a model for the verbs of this class.

Present.

	Indic.	Subj.	Imper.
Sing. 1.	sealfie	sealfie	
2.	sealfas(t)	,,	sealfa
3.	sealfaþ	,,	
Plur.	sealfiaþ	sealfien	sealfiaþ

Infinitive.

sealfian

Participle.

sealfiende

Preterite.

	Indic.	Subj.
Sing. 1.	sealfode	sealfode
2.	sealfodes(t)	,,
3.	sealfode	,,
Plur.	sealfodon	sealfoden

Participle.

gesealfod

§ 381. Like sealfian are conjugated a large number of verbs, as ācealdian, *to become cold*; āscian, *to ask*; behōfian, *to have need of*; bletsian, *to bless*; cēapian, *to buy*; clǣnsian, *to cleanse*; dysigian, *to be foolish*; earnian, *to earn*; endian, *to end*; fæstnian, *to fasten*; folgian, *to follow*; grāpian, *to grope*; hālgian, *to hallow*; hangian, *to hang*; hatian, *to hate*; hergian (cp. § 370), *to harry*; hopian, *to hope*; langian, *to long for*; lēasian, *to tell lies*; līcian, *to please*; lōcian, *to look*; losian, *to lose*; lufian, *to love*; macian, *to make*; offrian, *to offer*; scamian, *to be ashamed*; sorgian, *to sorrow*; sparian, *to spare*; þancian, *to thank*; wacian, *to be awake*; wandrian, *to wander*; wundian, *to wound*; wundrian, *to wonder*.

On the second and third pers. sing. pres. indic., imperative sing., and pret. indic. of verbs like bifian, *to tremble*; clifian, *to adhere, cleave*; stician, *to prick, stab*, see § 59.

twēogan, Anglian twīogan, from *twixōjan (§§ 53, 68), *to doubt*; pres. indic. twēoge, twēost, twēoþ; pres. part. twēonde (poetical) beside twēogende; pret. indic. twēode, Anglian twīode; pp. twēod. And similarly in WS. the following verbs which originally belonged to class III: fēog(e)an, *to hate*; frēog(e)an, *to love, make free*; smēag(e)an, *to ponder, consider*; and þrēag(e)an, *to reprove, rebuke*.

Class III.

§ 382. Nearly all the verbs of this class were originally primary verbs of which there were two types in prim. Germanic:

(1) Verbs which had -ǣj- throughout the present, and -ǣi- in the preterite and past participle. This type was best preserved in Goth. and OHG., but not at all in OE. (2) Verbs which had -j- in the present first pers. singular, and third pers. plural and in the infinitive, but no medial vowel in the preterite and past participle, which accounts for the absence of i-umlaut in these forms. This type was well preserved in OE. and OS. Of the many verbs which originally belonged to this class OE. only preserved **habban**, *to have*, **libban**, *to live*, **secgan**, *to say*, **hycgan**, *to think*, and traces of a few others, see note 2.

Present.

Indicative.

Sing. 1.	hæbbe	libbe	secge	hycge
2.	hafas(t) / hæfst	liofas(t)	sagas(t) / sægst	hogas(t) / hyg(e)st
3.	hafaþ / hæfþ	liofaþ	sagaþ / sægþ	hogaþ / hyg(e)þ
Plur.	habbaþ	libbaþ	secg(e)aþ	hycg(e)aþ

Subjunctive.

Sing.	hæbbe	libbe	secge	hycge
Plur.	hæbben	libben	secgen	hycgen

Imperative.

Sing. 2.	hafa	liofa	saga, sæge	hoga, hyge
Plur. 2.	habbaþ	libbaþ	secg(e)aþ	hycg(e)aþ

Infinitive.

habban	libban	secg(e)an	hycg(e)an

Participle.

hæbbende	libbende	secgende	hycgende

Preterite.

Indicative.

Sing. 1.	hæfde	lifde	sægde	hogde
2.	hæfdes(t)	lifdes(t)	sægdes(t)	hogdes(t)
3.	hæfde	lifde	sægde	hogde
Plur.	hæfdon	lifdon	sægdon	hogdon

Subjunctive.

Sing.	hæfde	lifde	sægde	hogde
Plur.	hæfden	lifden	sægden	hogden

Participle.

gehæfd   gelifd   gesægd   gehogod

NOTE. 1.—The endings -as(t), -aþ of the second and third pers. sing. pres. indicative, and -a of the imperative sing., were from verbs of class II. The regular form of hæbbe would be *hebbe (OS. hebbiu) from West Germanic *habbjō, but the a of the second and third pers. sing. was extended to the first and then a became æ by i-umlaut, cp. § 58 and notes. On the æ beside a in the second and third pers. singular, see §§ 29, 30. hafas(t), hafaþ are rare in pure WS., the usual forms are hæfst, hæfþ; and similarly with sægst, sægþ; hyg(e)st, hyg(e)þ. habbaþ, habban (West Germanic *habbjanþ, *habbjan, OS. hebbiad, hebbian, § 135) had the a in the stem-syllable from hafas(t), hafaþ.

libbe (OS. libbiu), libban (OS. libbian), from West Germanic *libbjō, *libbjanan. Beside libban there was also lifian, common in Anglian and Ken., which was inflected like sealfian (§ 380) in the present. On the io in liofas(t) and liofaþ, see § 59. 2.

secge (OS. seggiu), secg(e)an (OS. seggian), from West Germanic *saggjō, *saggjanan. In the present the e as in secge, secg(e)an was often extended to forms which regularly had æ, and vice versa. In late WS. the e was extended to all forms of the present. On forms like pret. sǣde beside sægde, see § 72.

On the y in hycg(e)an beside the o in hogde, see § 23. In the pret. this verb was also inflected like class II, hogode, &c; cp. also the past participle gehogod for *gehogd.

2. Traces of the old inflexion of verbs which originally belonged to class III are seen in such forms as bȳa (Nth.), *to dwell*, fylg(e)an, *to follow*, onscynian (Anglian), *to shun*, wæccende, *being awake*, beside būan, folgian, onscunian, waciende; hettend, *enemy*, beside hatian, *to hate*; pret. plægde, trūde, beside plagode, *he played*, trūwian, *to trust*.

C. Minor Groups.

A. Preterite-Presents.

§ 383. These verbs were originally unreduplicated strong perfects which acquired a present meaning like Gr. οἶδα = OE. wāt, *I know*. In prim. Germanic a new weak preterite, an infinitive, a present participle, and in some verbs a strong past participle, were formed. They are inflected in the present like the preterite of strong verbs, except that the second pers. singular has the same stem-vowel as the first and third persons, and has preserved the old ending -t (§ 324). It should be noted that the ending of the weak past participles of verbs belonging to the preterite-presents goes back to Indg. -tós, and not -itós as in the first class of weak verbs (§ 368). This is no doubt the reason why the preterites do not have the medial -i- which is found in the preterites and past participles of the first class of weak verbs, as **nerede** (Goth. **nasida**), *I saved*, **genered** (Goth. **nasiþs**); and similarly with the preterites like **bohte** (Goth. **baúhta**), *I bought*, **þōhte** (Goth. **þāhta**), *I thought*, and the past participles, see § 379.

The following verbs, many of which are defective, belong to this class:—

§ 384. I. Ablaut-Series.

wāt, *I know, he knows*, 2. sing. **wāst** (§ 119), pl. **witon** beside **wioton, wieton** (§ 59. 1), **wuton** (§ 63); subj. **wite**, pl. **witen**; imperative **wite**, pl. **witaþ** with -aþ from the pres. indic. 3. pers. pl. of other verbs (§ 319); inf. **witan** beside **wiotan, wietan** (§ 59. 2); pres. part. **witende** beside **weotende**; pret. **wisse** beside **wiste** (§ 119), pl. **wisson** beside **wiston**; pp. **gewiten**; participial adj. **gewiss**, *certain*. On forms like **nāt** beside **ne wāt**, see § 144.

§ 385.   II. Ablaut-Series.

dēag (Anglian dēg) beside dēah (§ 172), *I avail, he avails*; pl. dugon; subj. dyge beside the more common form duge (§ 325); inf. dugan; pres. part. dugende; pret. dohte (§ 23).

§ 386.   III. Ablaut-Series.

an(n), on(n), *I grant, he grants*; pl. unnon; subj. unne; imperative unne; inf. unnan; pres. part. unnende; pret. ūþe (§ 73), pl. ūþon; pp. geunnen.

can(n), con(n), *I know, can*, 2. sing. canst, const with -st from forms like dearst, pl. cunnon; subj. cunne, pl. cunnen; inf. cunnan; pret. cūþe (Goth. kunþa), pl. cūþon; pp. -cunnen; participial adj. cūþ (Goth. kunþs), *known*.

þearf, *I need, he needs*, 2. sing. þearft, pl. þurfon; subj. þyrfe beside the more common form þurfe (§ 325); inf. þurfan; pres. part. þurfende beside participial adj. þearfende (formed from þearf), *needy*; pret. þorfte, pl. þorfton.

dear(r) (Goth. ga-dars), *I dare, he dares*, with rr from the plural, 2. sing. dearst, pl. durron with rr from Germanic rz by Verner's law (§ 115); subj. dyrre beside the more common form durre (§ 325); pret. dorste, pl. dorston.

§ 387.   IV. Ablaut-Series.

sceal, *I shall, owe*, 2. sing. scealt, 3. sing. sceal, pl. sculon beside sceolon (cp. § 56, note 4); subj. scyle, later scule, sceole, pl. scylen, sculen, sceolen; inf. sculan, sceolan; pret. sc(e)olde, pl. sc(e)oldon.

man, mon, *I think, he thinks*, 2. sing. manst, monst with -st from forms like dearst, pl. munon; subj. myne beside the more common form mune (§ 325), pl. munen; imperative -mun beside -myne, -mune; inf. munan; pret. munde (Goth. munda); pp. gemunen.

§ 388.   V. Ablaut-Series.

mæg, *I, he can*, 2. sing. meaht later miht, pl. magon; subj. mæge, pl. mægen; inf. magan; pres. part. magende; pret.

meahte, mehte, later mihte ; participial adj. meaht later miht, *mighty, powerful.*

be-neah (Goth. bi-nah), ge-neah (Goth. ga-nah), *it suffices,* pl. -nugon ; subj. -nuge ; inf. -nugan ; pret. -nohte (§ 23).

§. 389. VI. Ablaut-Series.

mōt, *I, he may,* 2. sing. mōst (§ 119), pl. mōton ; subj. mōte, pl. mōten ; pret. mōste (§ 119), pl. mōston.

§ 390. The following verb probably belonged originally to the seventh class of strong verbs (§ 355) : āg beside āh (§ 172), *I have, he has,* 2. sing. āhst with -st from forms like dearst, pl. āgon ; subj. āge, pl. āgen ; imperative āge ; inf. āgan ; pret. āhte, pl. āhton ; pp. āgen, ǣgen (§ 290), *own.*

B. Verbs in -mi.

§ 391. The first pers. sing. pres. indicative of the Indg. verb ended either in -ō or -mi (cp. Gr. verbs in -ω and -μι, like φέρω, *I bear,* δίδωμι, *I give*). To the verbs in -ō belong all the regular Germanic verbs ; of the verbs in -mi only scanty remains have been preserved. Here belong the following OE. verbs :

§ 392. 1. The Substantive Verb.

The full conjugation of this verb is made up out of several distinct roots, viz. es- ; er- (perfect stem-form or-) ; bheu- (weak grade form bhw-) ; and wes-. From es- and or- were formed a pres. indicative and subjunctive ; from bhw- a pres. indicative (also with future meaning), pres. subjunctive, imperative, infinitive, and present participle ; and from wes- an infinitive, present participle, imperative, and a pret. indicative and subjunctive.

Present.

Indicative.

	WS.	Anglian.	WS.	Anglian.
Sing. 1.	eom	eam, am	bīo, bēo	bīom
2.	eart	earþ, arþ	bist	bis(t)
3.	is	is	biþ	biþ
Plur.	sint sindon, -un	sint, sind sindon, -un earon, aron, -un	bīoþ, bēoþ	bīoþ bi(o)þon, -un

Subjunctive.

| Sing. | sīe, sī | sīe | bīo, bēo |
| Plur. | sīen, sīn | sīen | bīon, bēon |

Imperative.

| Sing. | bīo, bēo | wes |
| Plur. | bīoþ, bēoþ | wesaþ |

Infinitive.

bīon, bēon   wesan

Participle.

bīonde,
bēonde   wesende

Preterite.

Indic.   wæs, wǣre, wæs, pl. wǣron (§ 349)
Subj.   wǣre, pl. wǣren

NOTE.—Pres. indicative: eom was the unaccented form of *ēom with ēo from bēo (cp. the opposite process in Anglian bīom); the regular form would have been *im = Goth. im; eart, earþ, arþ, and pl. earon, aron are old perfects from the root er-, perfect stem-form or-, prim. Germanic ar-, of which nothing further is known; on the -þ in earþ, arþ, see § 324; is with loss of -t from older *ist = Goth. ist, Lat. est; sind from prim. Germanic *sinđi = Indg. *sénti; sint was the unaccented form of sind; sindon, -un, with the ending of the pret. pl. added on (§ 324); beside sint, sindon there also occur in WS. sient, siendon. bīo later bēo (cp.

§ 69), from *biju, Indg. *bhwĭjō, Lat. fīō ; Anglian bīom with m from eom; bist from older bis, Indg. *bhwĭsi, Lat. fīs; biþ from older *biþi, Indg. *bhwĭti, Lat. fīt; Anglian bioþon with u-umlaut (cp. § 59. 1) was a new formation from biþ; bīoþ from *bijanþi.

Pres. subjunctive: sīe, sīen later sī (OS. OHG. sī), sīn (OS. OHG. sīn), beside sīo, sēo with īo, ēo from bīo, bēo.

§ 393.   2. THE VERB dōn, *to do*.

Present.

	Indic.	Subj.	Imper.
Sing. 1.	dō	dō	
2.	dēst	,,	dō
3.	dēþ	,,	
Plur.	dōþ	dōn	dōþ

Infinitive dōn

Participle dōnde

Preterite.

	Indic.	Subj.
Sing. 1.	dyde	dyde
2.	dydes(t)	,,
3.	dyde	,,
Plur.	dydon	dyden

Participle gedōn

NOTE.—Anglian has the older form dōm for the first pers. singular; dēst, Nth. dœ̄s(t); dēþ, Nth. dœ̄þ, dœ̄s, from *dō-is, *dō-iþ (§ 57); dōþ from *dō-anþi; Anglian often has longer forms in the present, as imper. dōa, dōaþ, inf. dōa(n). The y from older u in the pret. indic. and subj. is of obscure origin; in poetry there occurs the real old pret. pl. indic. dǣdon, corresponding to OS. dādun, OHG. tātun. Pret. subj. dyde, dyden from *dudī-, *dudīn (cf. § 325); beside dyde there also occurs in poetry dǣde, corresponding to OS. dādi, OHG. tāti. Beside the pp. -dōn there also occurs in poetry -dęn, Nth. -dœ̄n (§ 290).

§ 394. 3. The Verb gān, *to go.*

Present.

	Indic.	Subj.	Imper.
Sing. 1.	gā	gā	
2.	gǣst	,,	gā
3.	gǣþ	,,	
Plur.	gāþ	gān	gāþ

Infinitive **gān**. Past participle **gegān**.

NOTE.—gǣst, gǣþ, from older *ȝā-is, *ȝā-iþ (§ 57). The pret. indic. and subjunctive were supplied by ēode from older *īode which is a defective verb inflected like the pret. of **nerian** (§ 369).

§ 395. 4. The Verb willan, *will.*

The present tense of this verb was originally an optative (subjunctive) form of a verb in -mi, which already in prim. Germanic came to be used indicatively. To this was formed in OE. a new infinitive, present participle, and weak preterite.

Present.

	Indic.	Subj.	Infin.
Sing. 1.	wille	wille, wile	willan
2.	wilt	,,	
3.	wile, wille	,,	Participle
			willende
Plur.	willaþ	willen	

NOTE.—The pret. indic. and subjunctive **wolde** was inflected like the pret. of **nerian** (§ 369). **wilt** was a new formation with -t from the preterite-present verbs, cp. OHG. wili, Goth. wileis, Lat. velīs; wile, indic. and subj. = Goth. OHG. wili, Lat. velit; willaþ was a new formation with the ordinary ending of the pres. indic. (§ 319), the old form was preserved in Goth. wilein-a = Lat. velint. The various forms of this verb often underwent contraction with the negative particle ne, as nille, nylle, nelle (especially in late WS.), pret. nolde.

CHAPTER XIII

ADVERBS, PREPOSITIONS, AND CONJUNCTIONS

1. Adverbs.

§ 396. The -e, generally used to form adverbs from adjectives, is originally a locative ending and is identical with the -e (= prim. Germanic -ai, § 89) in the instrumental case of adjectives (§ 271). Examples are: dēope, *deeply*: dēop; nearwe, *narrowly*: nearu, -o (cp. § 282); yf(e)le, *wickedly*: yfel; and similarly bit(e)re, *bitterly*; gearwe, *completely*; georne, *eagerly*; rihte, *rightly*; sōþe, *truly*; ungemete, *excessively*; &c.

When the adjective ends in -e (§ 280) the adverb and adjective are alike in form, as blīþe, *joyfully*: blīþe, *joyful*. A few adverbs, the corresponding adjective of which did not originally belong to the ja- or i-declension, do not have umlaut in the stem-syllable, as ange, *anxiously*, smōþe, *smoothly*, sōfte, *gently*, *softly*, swōte, *sweetly*, beside the adjectives enge, smēþe, sēfte, swēte.

In adverbs like frēondlīce, *kindly*; loflīce, *gloriously*, which were regularly formed from adjectives ending in -lic, the -līce came to be regarded as an adverbial ending, and was then used in forming adverbs from adjectives which did not end in -lic, as eornostlīce, *earnestly*; stearclīce, *vigorously*; &c.

§ 397. The adverbial ending in the other Germanic languages, as Goth. -ō, OS. OHG. -o, goes back to an original ablative ending -ōd which regularly became -a in OE. (§ 85). This -a was only preserved in a few isolated forms, as sōna, *soon*; twiwa, *twice*; and in a few adverbs ending in -inga, -unga, -linga, -lunga, as eallunga, -inga, *entirely*; unwēnunga (Goth. unwēniggō), *unexpectedly*; stierninga, *sternly*; grundlunga, -linga, *to the ground, completely*.

§ **398.** The comparative and superlative degrees of the adverbs in -e generally ended in -or and -ost, as earme, *wretchedly*, earmor, earmost ; strange, *violently*, strangor, strangost.

§ **399.** A certain number of adverbs had originally -iz (Goth. -is, -s, cp. the -is in Lat. magis, *more*) in the comparative and -ist (Goth. -ist, -st), rarely -ōst, in the superlative (cp. § 291), as ēaþe, *easily*, īeþ from *auþiz, ēaþost; feorr, *far*, fierr from *ferriz, fierrest; lange, *long*, leng from *langiz, lengest; sōfte, *softly*, sēft from *samftiz; tulge, *strongly, firmly*, tylg from *tulȝiz, tylgest; ǣr from *airiz (Goth. áiris), *earlier, formerly* ; sīþ from *sīþiz (Goth. þana-seiþs, *further, more*), *later*. The following form their comparative and superlative from a different word than the positive:—lȳt, lȳtle, *little*, lǣs from *laisiz, lǣst; micle, *much*, mā (Goth. máis, Anglian mǣ), mǣst; wel, *well*, comp. bet from *batiz, with loss of -e after the analogy of comparatives with long stems, beside sēl from *sōliz, superl. betst, sēlest ; yf(e)le, *badly, wretchedly*, wiers, wyrs, from *wirsiz (Goth. waírs, OHG. wirs), wierrest, wyrrest, wyrst.

§ **400.** A large number of adverbs consist of the various cases of nouns and adjectives used adverbially :—

Acc. sing.: ealne weg, ealneg, *always*; eall tela, *quite well*; fela, feola, *very much* ; ungefyrn, *not long ago*.

Gen. sing.: dæges, *daily, by day*; hū gēares, *at what time of year* ; orþances, *heedlessly*; willes, *willingly*. The -es was sometimes extended to fem. nouns, as nīedes, *of necessity, needs* ; nihtes, *at night, by night*. ealles, *entirely, wholly* ; sōþes, *truly, verily*; hāmweardes, *homewards*. A preposition was sometimes prefixed to the gen., as tō-ǣfenes, *till evening*; in-stæpes, *instantly, at once*.

Gen. pl.: gēara, *of yore, formerly* ; ungēara, *not long ago, recently*.

Dat. and instrumental sing.: bearhtme, *instantly*; nīede, *of need, necessarily*; recene, *instantly, at once*. dæg-hwām, *daily*; wrāþum, *fiercely*.

Dat. pl.: dæg-tīdum, *by day*; hwīlum, *sometimes*; spēdum,

speedily; **wundrum**, *wonderfully*; **dǣlmǣlum**, *piecemeal*; **stundmǣlum**, *gradually*.

By nouns, &c., in conjunction with prepositions, as **ætgædere**, *together*; **be ungewyrhtum**, *undeservedly*; **in-stede**, *at once*; **on scipwīsan**, *like a ship*; **onweg**, *away*; **tō-morgen**, *to-morrow*; **underbæc**, *backwards*; **wiþinnan**, *within*.

§ 401. The following are the chief adverbs of place:

Rest.	*Motion towards.*	*Motion from.*
feorr(an), *far, afar*	feorr	feorran
foran, fore, *before*	forþ	foran
hēr, *here*	hider	hionan
hindan, *behind*	hinder	hindan
hwǣr, *where*	hwider	hwanon
inne, innan, *within*	in(n)	innan
nēah, *near*	nēar	nēan
nioþan, *beneath*	niþer	nioþan
þǣr, *there*	þider	þanan, þonan
uppe, *up, above*	up(p)	uppan
ūte, ūtan, *outside*	ūt	ūtan

sūþ, *southwards*; **sūþan**, *from the south*; and similarly **ēast, ēastan**; **norþ, norþan**; **west, westan**; **æftan**, *from behind*; **ufan**, *from above*; **ūtane**, *from without*; **wīdan**, *from far*. **ǣghwǣr, ǣghwider, gehwǣr**, *everywhere, in all directions*; **ǣghwanon**, *from all parts*; **āhwǣr, āwer, ōwer**, *anywhere*; **āhwanon**, *from anywhere*; **nāhwǣr, nāwer, nōwer**, *nowhere*; **welhwǣr, welgehwǣr, gewelhwǣr**, *nearly everywhere*; **hidergeond**, *thither*; **hidres þidres**, *hither and thither*.

§ 402.   2. PREPOSITIONS.

(1) With the accusative: **geond**, *throughout, during*; **geondan**, *beyond*; **underneoþan**, *underneath, below*; **wiþgeondan**, *beyond*; **ymb**, *around, about, at*; **ymbūtan**, *around, about*; **oþ** (more rarely dat.), *to, up to, as far as, until*; **þurh** (more rarely dat. or gen.), *through, during*.

(2) With the genitive: andlang, andlanges, *alongside*.

(3) With the dative: æfter, *behind, after, along, during, through, according to, in consequence of*; ǣr, *before*; ætforan, *before, in the presence of*; bī (be), also with instr., *by, along, in*; bæftan, *behind*; beheonan, *on this side of*; beneoþan, *beneath, below*; binnan, *within, in, into*; ēac, *in addition to, besides*; fram (from), also with instr., *from, by*; gehende, *near*; mid, also with instr., *together with, among*; nēah (also comp. nēar, superl. nīehst), *near*; of, *from, away from, out of*; ongemang, onmang, *among*; oninnan, *in, within, into, among*; onufan, *upon*; samod, *together with, at (of time)*; til (NE. dial. tul), *to*; tō-emnes, *alongside, on a level with*; tōforan, *before, in front of*; tōmiddes, *in the midst of*; wiþæftan, *behind*; wiþforan, *before*; wiþūtan, *outside, without, except*. The following also sometimes govern the acc.: æt, *at, by, in, on, upon*; beforan, *before, in the presence of*; būtan, *outside, without, free from*; fore, *before, in the sight of*; tō (also occasionally gen. and instr.), *to, into, at, by*; wiþinnan, *within*.

(4) With the accusative and dative: ābūtan, onbūtan, *around, about (of time)*; begeondan, *beyond*; behindan, *behind*; betwēonan, betwēonum, *between, among*; betweox, betweoh, bet(w)uh, betwih, betwix, *between, among*; bufan, *above, away from*; for (also instr.), *before, in the sight of, during, for, on account of, instead of*; gemang, *among, in the midst of*; in, *in, into, on, among, during*; ofer, *over, above, beyond, contrary to*; on (also instr.), *on, in, into, on to, to, among*; ongēan, ongeagn, ongegn, ongēn, *opposite, in front of, against*; onuppan, *on, upon*; tōgēanes, tōgegnes, tōgēnes, *towards, against*; under, *under, beneath, among*; uppan, *on, above*.

(5) With the genitive and dative: tōweard, tōweardes, *towards*.

(6) With the accusative, genitive, and dative: innan, *within, in, into*; wiþ, *against, towards, to, opposite, near*.

§ 403. 3. CONJUNCTIONS.

(1) Co-ordinate: ac, *but*; and, *and*; ǣgþer ... and, ǣgþer ... ge, *both ... and*; ēac, *also*; ēac swelc (swylc), swelc ēac, *as also*; for þǣm (þām), for þon, for þȳ, þonne, *therefore*; ge, *and*; ge ... ge, *both ... and*; hwæþ(e)re, þēah, swā þēah, swā þēah hwæþ(e)re, *however*; ne ... ne, ne ... ne ēac, nāhwæþer ne ... ne, *neither ... nor*; oþþe, *or*; oþþe ... oþþe, *either ... or*; samod ... and, *both ... and*.

(2) Subordinate: æfter þǣm (þām) þe, *after*; ǣr þām þe, *before*; būtan, *unless, unless that*; for þǣm (þām) þe, for þon þe, for þȳ þe, *because*; gelīc and, *as if*; gif, *if, whether*; hwæþer, *whether*; hwæþer þe ... þe, *whether ... or*; mid þȳ þe, mid þām þe, *when, although*; nemne, nefne, nymþe, *unless, except*; nū þe, *now that*; oþ, oþ þæt, oþ þe, *until, until that*; swā ... swā, *so ... as*; swā swā ... ealswā, *just ... as*; swā sōna swā, *as soon as*; swā þæt, tō þon þæt, *so that*; tō þon þe, *in order that*; þæs þe, siþþan þe, *after, since*; þæt, þætte, *that, in order that*; þā, þā þe, *when*; þā hwīle þe, *whilst, so long as*; þēah, *although*; þēah þe ... swā þēah, hwæþ(e)re, *although ... yet*; þenden, *while*; þonne, *when*; þȳ, *because*; þȳ þe, *so that*.

INDEX

The numbers after a word refer to the paragraphs in the Grammar.

ā (ō) 65.
ābūtan 402.
ac 403.
āc 41, 166. 1, 258.
ācealdian 381.
ācol 278.
ācwencan 376.
ād 18.
ādl 217.
ǣ (ǣw) 237 n.
æcer 18, 29, 96, 110, 166. 1, 184.
æces (æx) 58, 166 n.
æf 81.
æfen 36.
æfnung 85. 1, 220.
æftan 401.
æfter 57 n. 2, 158, 293, 402.
æfterra 294.
ǣg 267.
ǣghwā 315.
ǣghwǣr 401.
ǣghwæþer 315.
ǣghwanon 401.
ǣghwelc (-hwilc) 315.
ǣghwider 401.
ǣgþer 403.
ǣht 237.
ǣl 181.
ǣlan 123, 375.
ǣlc 315.
ǣne 299.
ǣnig, 57, 141, 315.
æppel (æpl) 136, 244.
æps (æsp) 143.
ǣr 292 n., 399, 402.
ǣrende 204.

ǣrendra 248.
ǣrest(a) 294.
ærn 51 n. 2, 143.
ærnan 57.
ǣs 119.
æsc 234.
ǣsce 251.
æsp 143, 214.
æt 80. 2, 142.
ætforan 402.
ætgædere 400.
æthwā 315.
ætwītan 332.
æþelcund 272.
æþele 58, 97. 1, 281.
æx 166 n., 223.
āfierran 375.
āfyrhtan 375.
āgan 390.
āgen (ǣgen) 278, 290.
āgend 265.
āhnēapan 362.
āht 315.
āhwā 315.
āhwǣr 401.
āhwæþer 315.
āhwanon 401.
alan 352.
alter 51 n. 5.
ān 17, 57, 294, 315.
anclēow 210.
and 403.
andgietful(l) 272.
andlang (-es) 402.
andswerian 370.
andweard 272.
andwyrdan 375.
ānfeald 272, 298.
ange 396.

angel 185.
angsum 273.
ānlic 273.
ānlīepige 301.
apa 248.
ār 212.
ārfæst 272.
ārīsan 117, 333.
arn 51 n. 2.
asce 251.
āscian 381.
āseolcan 52.
assa 30, 165, 248.
asse 251.
atollic (atelic) 145.
ātor (attor) 146, 194.
āþ 139, 161, 181.
āwer 401.
āwierdan 117.
āwiht (āwuht) 315.
āwþer 65, 315.
axe 143.
āxian 143.

bā 295.
bacan 166. 1, 352.
bæc 166 1, 191.
bæcere 201.
bæftan 402.
bǣr 273.
bǣr 214.
bærnan 57, 375.
bæþ 29, 30, 191.
bān 41, 189.
bana 248.
bānlēas 272.
bannan 359.
bār 181.
bāt 181.
be 402.

bēacen 42, 67 n. 1, 194.
beadu 59. 2 n. 1, 102, 226.
bēag (bēah) 67 n. 1, 140.
beald 162, 272.
bealdor 185.
bealu 141, 149, 208.
bēam 181.
beard 181.
bearhtme 400.
bearn 51, 189.
bearu 206.
bēatan 362.
bēaw 207.
bebod 190.
bēce 251.
bedd 57, 203.
beforan 402.
bēgen 295.
begeondan 402.
behāt 189.
beheonan 402.
behindan 402.
behionan 59. 2 n. 2.
behōfian 381.
belgan 172, 341.
bellan 341.
bēn 237.
benc 154, 237.
bend 85. 3, 91.
bendan 375.
beneah 388.
beneoþan 402.
bēo 250.
bēodan 17, 23, 104, 335.
bēon 316.
bēor 189.

Index

beorc 214.
beorcan 52, 342.
beorg (beorh) 172.
beorgan 342.
bēorscipe 233.
bēot 144.
bēow 210.
bepǣcan 379 n. 2.
bera 248.
beran 18, 21. 2, 23, 29, 31, 32, 45, 59. 2 n. 2, 80. 2, 81, 85. 1, 89. 1, 91, 93. 1, 3, 4, 94. 2, 104, 112, 116, 152, 156, 277, 318, 319, 321–4, 327, 329, 344.
bere 233.
berian 370.
berstan 52 n. 1, 319, 343.
beswīcend 265.
bet 399.
bētan 376.
bēte 25, 37 n.
beteldan 341.
bet(e)ra (bettra) 57, 101 n. 2, 152, 292.
bet(e)st 292.
betweoh 402.
betwēonan (-um) 402.
betweox 402.
betwih 402.
betwix 402.
bet(w)uh 402.
betwux (betux) 63.
bī 402.
bīdan 17, 332, 351.
biddan 135, 140, 144, 160, 164, 318, 319, 327.
bīecnan 377.
bīegan 170. 2.
bieldu 230.
bierce 67 n. 1.
bierhtu 230.
biernan 143, 340 n.

bifian 381.
bile 233.
bindan 21. 1, 23, 32, 34, 93. 2, 95, 101, 104, 112, 140, 160, 278, 318, 319, 324, 329, 340.
binnan 402.
bīo (bēo) 69.
bīon (bēon) 392.
birce 166. 2.
biren 225.
bis(e)n 216.
bītan 32, 38, 41, 59. 1, 104, 164, 332.
bite 233.
bit(e)re 396.
bitter (biter) 136, 278.
blæc 166. 1, 273.
blǣdre (blæddre) 36, 77, 146, 251.
blandan 357.
blāwan 64, 148, 361.
bledsian (bletsian) 77, 381.
bliccettan (bliccetan) 145.
blind 32, 85. 1, 88. 2, 89. 1, 93. 1, 156, 270, 271, 288.
bliss 77, 142, 223.
blīþe 281, 285, 396.
blīþs 142, 223.
blōd, 39, 152, 189.
blōd(es)lǣs 228.
blōstm 185.
blōtan 363.
blōwan 363.
bōc 84, 166. 1, 2, 257.
bodig 33.
boga 137, 170. 1, 248.
bolt 181.
bord 33.
bōsm 139, 185.

bōt 85. 1.
botm 186.
box 34 n.
brād 291.
brǣdan 375.
brǣdu 229.
brægen 195.
brǣs 29, 191.
brastlian 30.
brēadru 268.
brecan 166, 346.
brēdan 72.
bregdan 72, 343.
bregu 59. 2 n. 2, 243.
brēm(b)el 77, 185.
brēost 189.
brēowan 335.
bridd 199.
brīdel 72, 144.
brīdels 143.
brigdel 72, 144.
bringan 35, 119, 140, 154, 169. 1, 174, 379.
brōc 258.
brōd 214.
brōden 72.
brogden 72.
broþ 190.
brōþor 17, 39, 57, 109, 112, 139, 262.
brūcan 57, 338.
brūn 40, 272.
bryce 166, 285.
brȳce 285.
brycg 145, 222.
brȳd 237.
bū 295.
būan 382 n. 2.
bucc 66, 124, 145, 166. 1.
bucca 66, 166, 248.
bufan 402.
būgan 338.
bulluc 187.
burg (burh) 91, 102, 140, 172, 258.
burne 251.
būtan 402, 403.

bȳa 382 n. 2.
bycgan 23, 57, 119, 174, 379, 383.
bydel 187.
byden 85. 1, 216.
byre 233.
byrgan 375.
byrgels 143.
byrþen(n) 224.
bysig 277.
bytlan 377.

calan 352.
calu 283.
camb 112, 166. 1, 181.
caru 30, 213.
cēace 56, 67, 251.
ceaf 56, 158, 166. 2, 190.
cēafl 139.
cealc 166. 2.
ceald 51, 56 n. 2, 110, 166. 2.
cealf 56 n. 2, 67, 166. 2, 267.
cēap 67, 181.
cēapian 166. 2, 381.
ceaster 56, 56 n. 5, 67 n. 1, 217.
cēlan 166. 1, 375.
cemban 166. 1, 375.
cēn 25, 37.
cēne 281.
çēo 252.
ceorfan 56 n. 2, 166. 2, 342.
cēosan 18, 24, 33, 42–4, 57, 104, 116, 133, 164, 166. 2, 277, 317–18, 327, 329, 336.
cēowan 166. 2, 335.
cēpan 166. 1, 376.
cīcen 67 n. 1.
cīegan 79.
ciele (cile, cyle) 57 n. 3, 67, 233.

Index

cieres (cires) 56.
cierran 57 n. 2.
cīese 166. 2.
cietel 57.
cild 32, 166 2, 268.
cildhād 184.
cildisc 278.
cīnan 25.
cine 251.
cinn 121, 166. 2, 245.
cinu 251.
cīpe 37 n.
cirice 251.
clǣne 281, 285, 291.
clǣnsian 381.
clāþ 161, 181.
clawu 144, 226.
clēa 30, 69, 144, 226.
clēofan 335.
clīewen (clīwen) 196.
clif 59. 1, 190.
clifian 381.
climban 153, 156, 166. 1, 340.
cliopian (cleopian) 59. 1.
cliopung 59. 1.
clipian 59. 1.
clūt 181.
clynnan (clynian) 371.
clyppan 375.
cnapa 248.
cnāwan 64, 79, 148, 361.
cnedan 346.
cnēo(w) 60, 69, 79, 110, 148, 149, 166. 1, 208.
cneoht 67.
cnieht (cniht) 52, 67, 174.
cnocian 66.
cnotta 124.
cnucian 66.
cnyll 199.

cnyttan 372.
cocc 181.
col, 33, 190.
cōl 152, 166. 1.
cōlnes(s) 225.
copor 34 n.
corn 189.
coss, 23, 166. 1.
cradol 187.
cræft 166. 1, 181.
crāwan 361.
crāwe 251.
crēda 37 n.
crēopan 43, 335.
cribb 222.
cropp 124.
cruma 248.
crycc 222.
cū 142. 2, 258.
cuman 48, 49, 110, 114. 2, 153, 166. 1, 317, 345.
cunnan 386.
cuppe 251.
cūþ 50, 73, 144, 386.
cweccan 379.
cwelan 344.
cwellan 379.
cwēn 57, 147, 166. 1, 236.
cwene, 110, 251.
cweorn 245.
cweþan 63 n. 3, 104, 116, 119, 144, 160, 319, 327, 349.
cwic(u) 22, 63, 110, 114.2, 286.
cwide 233.
cwiorn (cweorn) 63.
cwīþan 375.
c(w)ucu 63, 286.
c(w)udu 209.
cycene 57.
cȳf 237.
cylen 57.
cyme 233.
cymen 290.
cynedōm 184.
cynig 144.

cyning 57, 57 n. 2, 97. 2, 144, 166. 1, 169. 1, 183, 197.
cyn(n) 57, 135, 166. 1, 202.
cyre 233.
cyssan 23, 145, 164, 319, 373, 375.
cyst 237.
cȳþan 42, 57, 166. 1, 373, 375.
cȳþþ(u) 219.

dǣd 36, 36 n. 1, 237.
dæg 29 n. 2, 30, 59. 2 n. 1, 80. 1, 3, 81, 86, 89. 1, 91, 93. 1, 133, 141, 153, 166, 170. 1, 2, 180.
dæges 400.
dæg-hwām 400.
dæg-tīdum 400.
dæl 191.
dǣl 234.
dǣlan 98, 375.
dǣlmǣlum 400.
dāg (dāh) 140, 172.
dagian 170. 1.
daru 213.
dēad 118, 160, 272.
dēadlic 78.
dēaf 42, 42 n.
dear(r) 51, 386.
dēaþ 42, 118.
dēaw 62, 79, 207.
delfan 341.
dēman 57, 144, 374.
dene 233.
Dene 232.
dēofol (dīofol) 101 n. 1, 185.
dēop 43, 77, 110, 155, 272.
dēope 396.

dēopra (deoppra) 146.
dēor 43, 43 n. 2, 133, 189.
derian 370.
dīeglan 97. 3, 373, 377.
dīere (dīore, dēore) 44, 57 n. 5, 281.
dogga 33, 168, 248.
dohtor 23, 57, 83, 112, 160, 174, 262.
dol 273.
dōm 181.
dōn 39, 68, 393.
dor 190.
draca 59. 2 n. 1.
dragan 170. 1, 352.
dreccan 379.
drenc 234.
drencan 374.
drēogan 335.
drēopan 335.
drēosan 116, 336.
drepan 346.
drīfan 38, 59. 1, 332.
drincan 46, 154, 166. 1, 340.
drohtaþ 184.
dropa 137.
drȳ 68, 235.
dryhten 185.
dūfan 338.
dugan 385.
duguþ 94. 4.
dumb 153, 156.
dung 258.
*durran 17, 386.
duru 18, 34, 112, 152, 212, 245.
dwellan 379.
dweorg 67 n. 1.
dyne 233.
dyn(n) 197, 199.
dynnan 371.
dysig 57 n. 2.
dysigian 381.

Index

ēa 68, 144.
ēac 402, 403.
ēacian 18.
ēadig 278.
eafora 59. **2** n. 3.
ēage 42, 67 n. 1, 88. 3, 91,170. 1, 253.
eahta 17, 51, 67, 91, 109. 2, 174, 294.
eahtatēoþa 294.
eahtatīene 294.
eahtoþa 294.
eald 162, 291.
ealdor 185.
ealh 182.
eall 51, 145, 269.
ealles 400.
eall tela 400.
eallunga (-inga) 397.
ealneg 400.
ealswā 403.
ealu 59. 2 n. 1, 3, 152, 261.
ēar 68.
earc 67 n. 1.
ēare 18, 42, 42 n., 118, 254.
earm 51 n. 4, 181.
earm (*adj.*) 291.
earme 398.
earnian 381.
ēast 293, 401.
ēastan 401.
ēaþe 399.
ebba 137, 156.
ecg 222.
ednīwunga 85. 4.
ef(e)n 96, 142, 277.
efes 57.
efnan 377.
ege 170. 2, 233.
eglan 170. 2, 373, 377.
egle 286.
ēhtan 57.
elboga (elnboga) 144.
emn 142.

ende 57, 197, 198.
endian 381.
en(d)le(o)fan 294.
en(d)le(o)fta 294.
enge 112.
engel 98, 183.
Engle 232.
englisc 93. 3, 169. 1.
engu 230.
enlefan 77.
ent 234.
ēode (īode) 394.
eofor 59, 187.
eoh 182.
eolh 52, 182.
eorl 181.
eornostlīce 396.
ēorod 78, 144.
eorþe 52, 139.
ēow (īow) 304.
ēower (īower) 304, 308.
eowestre 61.
ēowic 304, 306.
erian 370.
esne 201.
esol 59. 2 n. 2.
ēst 57, 87, 90, 91, 237.
etan 18, 29 n. 2, 31, 32, 36, 45, 59. 2 n. 2, 119, 159, 164, 317, 319, 348.
eþþa 89. 2, 161.

fæder 17, 21. 3, 29, 29 n. 2, 80. 4, 118, 134, 152, 158, 160, 262.
fæge 281.
fægen 170. 2, 277.
sæg(e)nian 101 n. 2.
fæger 277.
fæhþ(u) 219.
færunga 85. 4.
fæstan 373, 375.
fæsten(n) 205.

fæstnian (fæsnian) 144, 381.
fæt 59. 2 n. 1, 188.
fætels 84, 97. 2.
fæþm 29, 139, 186.
fāh 275.
fals 51 n. 5.
fām 111, 189.
faran 29 n. 1, 39, 58 n. 1, 2, 104, 318, 319, 327, 352.
faru 213.
fēa 69, 144.
fealdan 162, 360.
feallan 57, 67 n. 3, 111, 145, 152, 318, 319, 327, 360.
fealu 283.
fearh 67 n. 1, 76, 182.
fēawe (fēa) 269, 284.
fēdan 131, 375.
fela (feola) 286, 400.
feld 21. 2, 31, 162, 242.
fēog(e)an 151, 381.
feoh 68, 109, 176, 192.
feohtan 52, 58, 67, 67 n. 1, 342.
fēol 20.
fēolan 76, 144, 342 n.
fēond (fīond) 69, 264.
feorh 67 n. 1, 76.
feorr 291, 399, 401.
feorran 152, 401.
fēorþling 184.
fēower 114 n.,249 n. 2.
fēowerfeald 298.
fēowertēoþa 294.
fēowertīene 294.
fēowertig 294.
fēowertigoþa 294.
fēo(we)rþa 294.

fersc 52 n. 1.
feter 216.
feþer 31, 158, 216.
fiellan 57, 375.
fierd 237.
fierst 234.
fīf 50, 73, 81, 114 n., 144, 158, 294.
fīfel 50.
fīfta 294.
fīftēoþa 294.
fīftīene 294.
fīftig 294.
fīftigoþa 294.
findan 46, 140, 153, 340.
finger 169. 1, 185.
firen 215.
fisc 18, 32, 109, 143, 167, 181.
fiscoþ 184.
fiþele 251.
flā 252.
flǣsc 240.
flāh 192.
flasce 30.
flēa 249.
flēan 353.
fleax 51, 189.
flēogan 34, 67 n.1, 172, 319, 335.
flēon 116, 337.
flēos 43.
flicce 166. 2, 204.
flīes 240.
flōcan 363.
flocc 166. 1.
flōd 18.
flōr 245.
flōwan 79, 363.
flyge 233.
flyht 234.
fōdor (foddor) 146, 194.
fola 248.
folc 33, 189.
folgian 381, 382 n. 2.
fōn 20, 35, 57, 68, 116, 318, 358.
for 402.

foran 401.
ford 244.
fore 292 n., 401, 402.
forgiefennes 145.
forgietan 56, 347.
forlēosan 116, 366.
forma 293, 294.
formest(a) 294.
forsc 143.
forslǣwan 378.
forþ 292 n., 401.
fōstor 131.
fōt 18, 21.3, 39, 57, 83, 84, 109, 110, 158, 159, 255.
fox 181.
fracuþ (-oþ) 94.4.
frǣtwa, -e 102, 227.
fram (from) 402.
frēa 247.
frēfran 97 3.
fremian 371.
fremman 368, 369.
frēo (frīo) 281.
frēog(e)an 381.
frēols 144.
frēond (frīond) 69, 263.
frēondlīce 396.
frēosan 42, 336.
fretan 348.
fricgan 351.
frīegea (frīgea) 151.
frignan 72, 343.
frīnan 72.
frōfor 217.
frogga 33, 137, 168, 248.
fugol 66, 96, 170.1, 183.
fūl 18.
full 17, 23, 66, 122, 152.
fulluht 238.
fulwiht 238
furh 17, 74, 176, 258.
furþor 66.

furþra 292 n.
furþum 66.
fūs 73.
fylgan 102, 375.
fylg(e)an 382 n. 2.
fyllan 145, 373, 375.
fyllu 230.
fȳr 152.
fyrest(a) 292 n., 294.
fyrmest(a) 293, 294.
fȳst 144, 237.
fyþer-fēte 114 n.
fyxen 23, 225.

gād 214.
gaderian 100, 101 n. 2.
gaderung 101.
gǣdeling 58.
gærs (græs) 51 n.2, 143, 165, 191.
galan 352.
gamen 195.
gān 68, 394.
gangan 359.
gār 244.
gāst 165, 181.
gāt 41, 258.
ge (cj.) 403.
gē 304.
gealga 248.
gēar 56, 67, 150, 189.
gēara 400.
geard 56 n. 2, 181.
gearu 102, 141, 148, 189, 282.
gearwe 396.
geat 56, 56 n. 5, 67 n. 1, 168, 190.
geatwa, -e 227.
gebierhtan 67 n. 1.
gebod 190.
gebrōþor (gebrōþru) 262.
gebyrd 238.
gecynd 238.
gedēaw 284.

gedryhtu 238.
gefa 249.
(ge)fēa 249.
gefēg 240.
gefeoht 67.
gefēon 350.
gefīend 264.
gefilde 21.2, 204.
gefōh 274.
gefrīend 264.
gegrynd 240.
gehende 402.
gehlēow 284.
gehlōw 210.
gehlȳd 240.
gehrēow 210.
gehwā 315.
gehwǣr 401.
gehwæþer 315.
gehwilc 315.
gehygd 238.
gelīc 94.2.
gelīefan 57, 57 n. 4, 67 n. 1.
gelīehtan 57.
gelimpan 340.
gemǣne 285.
gemang 402.
gemynd 17, 238.
gemyne 285.
geneah 388.
genesan 117, 349.
genōg (genōh) 172, 269, 272, 274.
genyht 240.
geoc (gioc, iuc) 23, 56 n. 4, 85.1, 110, 150, 166, 190.
geolu 102, 168.2, 283.
geōmor 56 n. 4, 278.
geond 402.
geondan 402.
geong (giong, giung, iung) 56 n. 4, 150, 154, 291.
georn 56 n. 2.
georne 396.

gēotan 67, 113, 168.2, 335.
geresp 240.
gerīsan 333.
gesceaft 119, 158, 238.
gesēaw 284.
gesibb 279.
gesīene 281.
gesweostor (·tru, -tra) 262.
geswinc 240.
gesyntu (-o) 140, 164
getimbre 204.
getiohhian 67 n.1.
getrīewan 378.
getrīewe 62, 281.
geþeaht 238.
geþīedan (geþīodan, geþēodan) 44.
geþungen 20.
geþyld 238.
gewǣcan 379 n. 2.
gewēd 240.
gewelhwǣr 401.
gewieldan 145.
gewihte (gewyhte) 67.
gewiss 384.
gewītan 332.
gewyrht 238.
giefan 56, 67, 140, 157, 168.2, 347.
giefu 80.1, 85.1, 86, 88.1, 2, 89.1, 94.3, 133, 212.
gieldan 168.2, 341.
giellan 341.
gielpan 341.
gīeman 375.
gierd 221.
giernan 375.
gierwan 144, 374, 378.
giest (guest) 17, 57, 57 n. 3, 83, 84, 91, 109.1, 113, 168.2, 232.

Index

giest (*yeast*) 56, 150.
gift 119, 168. 2.
giftu 238.
gimm 21. 1, 47 n.
git 304.
gladian 59. 2 n. 1.
glæd 29, 29 n. 1, 101 n. 1, 270, 271, 291.
glæs 191.
glēaw 62, 284, 286.
glēd 237.
glīdan 332.
glioda 59. 2 n. 2.
glōf 214.
gnagan 352.
god 23, 190.
gōd 39, 168. 1, 272, 292.
gōddōnd 264.
gōdlic 94. 2.
gōdscipe 233.
gold 23, 162, 189.
gōs 50, 73, 113, 165, 168. 1, 258.
græg 79.
græs 168. 1.
grafan 352.
grāpian 381.
grēat 272, 291.
grēne 153, 281, 285.
grētan 373, 376.
grim(m) 291.
grīn 238.
grindan 340.
grīpan 59. 1.
grōwan 363.
grund 168. 1.
grundlunga (-linga) 397.
grūt 258.
guma 82, 91, 133, 168. 1, 246, 247.
gyden 23, 57, 225.
gylden 23, 94. 2, 168. 1, 278, 375.
gyrdan 145, 375.

habban 30, 144, 156, 157, 164, 173, 316, 382.
haca 248.
hād 244.
hæg(e)l 186.
hægtes(s) 225.
hæl 240.
hǣlan 57, 375.
hǣle 233.
hǣlend 265.
hǣleþ 261.
hǣlu 230.
hærfest 58, 184.
hǣring 184.
hǣs 237.
hǣtan 376.
hǣtu 230.
hǣþ 57.
hafola (hafela) 100.
hafuc, -oc (heafuc, -oc) 30, 59. 2 n. 1, 2, 3, 187.
hagol 186.
hāl, 41, 272.
hālbǣre 281.
hālgian 381.
hālig 85. 1, 98, 101, 101 n. 1, 276, 291.
hām 153, 178, 181.
hamor 187.
hāmweardes 400.
hana 84, 88. 3, 109.
hand 83, 84, 91, 173, 212, 245.
hangian 381.
hara 30, 118, 248.
hāt 159.
hātan 25, 37, 316, 355, 356.
hatian 159, 381, 382 n. 2.
hē 71, 305, 306.
hēafod 42, 42 n., 85. 1, 98, 173, 193.
hēah 67 n. 1, 68, 176, 274, 291.

healdan 51, 360.
healf 140, 302.
healh 182.
heals, 113. 1.
hēan 375.
hēap 124.
heard 51, 51 n. 4, 94. 3, 286.
hearg 244.
hēawan 62, 362.
hebban 57, 158, 354.
hefig 141.
hege 233.
hēla 144.
helan 344.
helian 371.
hell 57, 135, 144, 222.
helpan 21. 1, 2, 23, 31, 32, 33, 85. 1, 104, 278, 317, 318, 319, 327, 329, 341.
helpend 265.
helustr 59.
hengest 184.
hen(n) 221.
heofun (-on) 59, 97. 1, 100, 183.
heol(o)stor 59.
heord 21. 2, 214.
heorte 52 n. 3, 109, 251.
heoru 242.
heorut (-ot) 59, 187.
hēr 25, 37, 401.
here 57, 141, 151, 152, 197, 200.
hergian 381.
herian (herigan) 133, 135, 151, 370.
hete 233.
hettend 265.
hider 25, 401.
hider-geond 401.
hidres 401.
hīe (hī) 305, 306.
hīeg 151.
hīehra 142.

hīehst(a) 57.
hiera (hira) 305.
hīeran 57 n. 4, 67 n. 1, 3, 98, 375.
hierdan 375.
hierde 21. 2, 57, 57 n. 5, 67, 201.
hiere (hire) 305.
hiertan 375.
hierwan 378.
hīew (hīw) 79.
hild 144, 223.
hilt 240.
him 305.
hind 223.
hindan 293, 401.
hindema 293.
hinder 401.
hine (hiene) 305.
hīo (hēo) 69, 305, 306.
hionan 401.
hiora (heora) 59. 2, 305, 306.
his 305.
hit 305.
hladan 173, 352.
hlædel 29.
hlǣfdige 251.
hlāf 140, 173, 181.
hlāford 41, 144, 152.
hlāfweard 144.
hlammæsse 77.
hleahtor 51, 185.
hlēapan 42, 362.
hlēapestre 251.
hlēo(w) 210.
hlid 173.
hliehhan 57, 57 n.1, 67, 135, 174, 327, 354.
hlīep 234.
hlōwan 363.
hlūd 40.
hlūtor (hlŭttor) 96, 136.
hnæpp 124.
hnīgan 114. 4, 173, 332.
hnitu 259.

186 Index

hnutu 91, 173, 257.
hōcede 281.
hof 188.
hol 190.
holh 74, 114. 5, 176, 192.
hōn 35, 37, 116, 358.
hopian 381.
hoppian 124.
horh 114. 5.
hors 143, 189.
hrēa(w) 284.
hreddan 372.
hrēosan 336.
hrēow 226.
hrēowan 335.
hring 32, 173, 181.
hrōpan 363.
hrycg 199.
hū 313.
hū gēares 400.
hund (*dog*) 18, 34, 109, 181.
hund (*hundred*) 17, 120, 130, 294, 297.
hundeahtatig 294.
hundeahtatigoþa 294.
hundendleofantig 294.
hundendleofantigoþa 294.
hundendlufontig 294.
hundendlufontigoþa 294.
hundnigontig 294.
hundnigontigoþa 294.
hundred 294, 297.
hundseofontig 294.
hundseofontigoþa 294.
hundtēontig 294.
hundtēontigoþa 294.
hundtwelftig 294.
hundtwelftigoþa 294.

hungor 34, 173.
hunig (-eg) 23, 48, 93. 1.
hunta 248.
hūs 40, 119, 139, 189.
hūsrǣden(n) 225.
hwā 71, 91, 109, 114.1, 173, 313.
hwæl 111, 173, 182.
hwǣr 63 n. 3, 401.
hwæt 17, 29, 80. 2, 313.
hwǣte 57, 173, 201.
hwæthwugu 315.
hwæþer 21. 3, 93, 2, 314, 315.
hwæþ(e)re 63.
hwanon 401.
hwelc 166. 2, 314.
hwelchwugu 315.
hweogol 59.
hwēol 114. 5.
hweowol 114. 5.
hwettan 372.
hwider 401.
hwīl 114. 1, 173, 214.
hwilc (hwylc) 314.
hwīlum 400.
hwīt 38, 124, 146, 173.
hwone 46 n.
hwonne 46 n.
hwōpan 363.
hwȳ (hwī) 313.
hwyrft 234.
hycgan 382.
hȳd 237.
hȳdan 119, 375.
hȳf 237.
hyge 170. 2.
hyht 234.
hyll 122, 199.
hyngran 97. 3, 373, 374.
hype 233.
hyse 233.

ic 110, 166. 2, 303.
īecan 140, 379 n. 2.
īeg 151.
ieldan 375.
ielde 232.
ieldest(a) 97. 2.
ieldra 57, 57 n. 1, 67 n. 3, 98, 291.
ieldu (ildu) 67.
ielfe 232.
ierfe 57, 57 n. 1, 67 n. 3, 204.
iernan 143, 340 n.
ierre 57, 57 n. 5, 204, 281.
īeþe 291.
īewan 378.
igil 171.
īl 171.
ilca 269, 311.
ile 233.
in 402.
inc 304, 306.
incer 304, 308.
incit 304.
in(n) 401.
innan 401, 402.
inne 293, 401.
in-stæpes 400.
in-stede 400.
is 21. 2.
īs 189.

lācan 355, 356.
lǣce 201.
lǣdan 117, 152, 375.
lǣfan 375.
lǣn 240.
lǣran 375.
lǣrestre 251.
lǣs (*sb.*) 228.
lǣs (*adv.*) 399.
lǣssa 57 n. 2, 142, 292.
lǣst 292, 399.
lǣt 293.
lǣtan 25, 37, 355, 356, 357.
lǣwan 378.
lagu 170. 1, 243.

lamb 156, 267.
land 152, 189.
lang 46, 112, 272, 291.
lange 399.
langian 381.
lappa 137.
lār 214.
lārēow 207.
lāttēow 207.
laþu 212, 213.
lēac 67 n. 1.
lēaf 42, 189.
lēan 353.
lēasian 381.
lēasung 220.
leccan 379.
lecgan 135, 135. n 152, 372.
lengra 57, 154, 169. 2.
lengþ(u) 57.
lēo 249.
lēof 113, 291.
lēogan 67 n. 1, 335.
lēoht (*sb.*) 24, 67 n. 1, 2.
lēoht (*adj.*) 67 n. 2.
leornung (liornung) 85. 1, 218.
lesan 349.
lettan 372.
libban 22, 59. 2, 382.
liccian 124, 166. 1.
licgan 21. 2, 45, 171, 277, 327, 351.
līchama 144.
līcian 381.
līcuma 144.
līeg 234.
līehtan (*to give light*) 24, 44, 57, 67, 67 n. 1, 174, 375.
līehtan (*to make easier*) 67 n. 1.
līf 38.

Index

lim 32, 59. 2 n. 2, 3.
līn 189.
līode (lēode) 24, 44, 57 n. 5, 232.
līoht (lēoht) *adj.* 55.
līon (lēon) 55, 57, 67 n. 1, 68, 109, 114. 5, 334.
liornian (leornian) 53.
liss 142.
līþan 104, 116, 117, 333.
līþe 281.
līþs 142.
loc 190.
locc 124.
lōcian 101 n. 3, 124, 166.1, 381.
loflīce 396.
losian 381.
lūcan 317, 338.
lufian 66, 381.
lufu 66, 213.
lufwende 281.
lūs 258.
lyft 234.
lȳt (lȳtle) 399.
lȳtel 278, 292.

mā 399.
macian 30, 166. 1, 381.
mǣd 227.
mǣden 71, 144, 196.
mǣg 45, 182.
mǣgden 58, 72, 79, 144.
mǣgen 195.
mǣg(e)þ 261.
mǣgþ(u) 57 n. 2, 219.
mǣl 36.
mǣnan 375.
mǣst 292, 399.
mǣw 79, 234.
magan 59. 2 n. 1, 119, 388.
magu 114. 4, 243.

man 315.
manig 93. 1, 269, 276.
manigfeald 298.
man(n) 46, 57, 145, 153, 256.
manna 256.
māra 133, 152, 292.
martyr 51 n. 5.
masc 129.
mattuc (-oc) 30, 187.
māþum 185.
māwan 361.
mē 71, 303, 306.
meaht (miht) *sb.* 51, 237, 324.
meahta (*pret.*) 119.
mearc 214.
mearg 67 n. 1, 129, 172.
mearh 76, 144, 180.
mearu 283.
mec 303, 306.
mēce 201.
mēd 25, 37.
medu (meodu) 59. 2 n. 2, 243.
meduma (medema) 293.
melcan 342.
meltan 31, 341.
menigu (mengu) 230.
meolcan 52, 342.
meolu (melu) 59, 209.
meol(u)c 258.
meord 25, 129.
meowle 61, 79, 148, 251.
mere 83, 233.
mergen 57.
mēse 25.
metan 104, 346.
mētan 376.
mete 233.
metod 59. 2 n. 2, 187.

micel 101 n. 1, 146, 277, 292.
micle 399.
mid 402.
midd 21. 2, 113, 279, 293.
mieht (miht) 51, 57 n. 1, 67.
Mierce 232.
mihtig 94. 2.
milde 281.
mīn 303, 308.
minte 21. 1, 47 n.
mioluc (miolc, milc) 59. 1, 67 n. 1.
miox (meox) 53.
mioxen (meoxen) 67 n. 1.
mittȳ 164.
mīþan 333.
mōdor 17, 39, 118, 153, 262.
molde 251.
mōna 18, 49, 153, 248.
mōnaþ 49, 94. 3, 98, 101 n. 3, 261.
mōr 181.
morgen 33, 57, 185.
morþ 189.
morþor 96, 194.
mōt 119, 289.
moþþe 161, 251.
munan 387.
munuc 48.
murcnian 66.
murnan 66, 317, 343.
mūs 18, 40, 57, 258.
mūþ 50, 161, 181.
mycg 145, 199.
mynster 57.

nacod 166. 1, 277.
nǣdl 36, 163, 217.
nǣg(e)l 29, 170. 2, 186.
nǣnig 315.

nǣp 36 n. 2.
nāht 315.
nāhwǣr 401.
nāhwæþer 315.
nama 46, 153, 248.
nān 315.
nānþing 315.
nāuht 144.
nāwer 401.
nāwiht (nāwuht) 144, 315.
nāwþer 315.
ne 403.
nēah 54, 275, 291, 401, 402.
nēahra 142.
neaht (niht) 51, 109. 2, 159, 258.
nēalǣcean 379 n. 2.
nēan 401.
nēar 54, 68, 401.
nearu 149, 283.
nearwe 396.
nebb 203.
nefa 31, 109, 137, 153, 248.
neowol 79.
nerien 85. 2, 88. 1, 91, 93. 3, 94. 1, 97. 1, 101, 117, 135, 368, 369, 370.
ner(i)gend 265.
nest 22, 129, 189.
netel 216.
nett 203.
nīed 57, 57 n. 4, 67, 67 n. 1.
nīede 400.
nīedes 400.
nieht (niht) 67.
nīehst(a) 67 n. 2, 69.
nierwan 378.
nīeten 196.
nīewe (nīwe) 62, 281.
nifol 113.
nift 109. 2, 223.
nigon 294.
nigontēoþa 294.

Index

nigontīene 294.
nigoþa 294.
niht 51.
nihtes 400.
niman 23, 47, 48, 49, 59. 2 n. 2, 97. 2, 153, 345.
nioþan 293, 401.
nioþor 59. 2 n. 3.
niþer 401.
nōht 315.
nōhwæþer 315.
norþ 293, 401.
norþan 401.
Norþhymbre 232.
nosu 33, 139, 245.
nōwer 401.
nōwiht (nōwuht) 65, 315.
nōwþer 65, 315.
nyrþra 293.
nytt 279.

ō (ā) 65.
of 402.
ofdæle 240.
ofen 139, 186.
ofer 402.
oferhygd 238.
oferslege 240.
oferspræce 281.
offrian 381.
ōht 315.
ōhwæþer 315.
ōleccan 379 n. 2.
on 46 n., 402.
onbūtan 402.
ondrædan 355, 357.
ongēan (-geagn, -gegn, -gēn) 402.
on(ge)mang 402.
onginnan 340.
oninnan 402.
onscynian (onscunian) 382 n. 2.
onufan 402.
onuppan 402.
onweg 402.
open 33, 277.
orlege 240.

orsorg 34 n.
orþances 400.
orwēne 34 n.
ōsle 144.
oþ 402, 403.
ōþer 50, 73, 101, 144, 145, 269, 278, 294, 302.
oþþe 161, 403.
ōwer 401.
ōwiht (ōwuht) 65, 315.
ōwþer 65, 315.
oxa 57, 175, 248.

pād 110, 155.
pæþ 29, 29 n. 1, 182.
palm 51 n. 5.
pearroc 187.
pening (penig) 144, 155.
peru (pere) 32 n., 155.
pic 155, 166. 2.
Pihtisc 67.
pīn 37 n.
pinsian 50 n., 155.
pīpe 251.
pisan 59. 2 n. 2.
plega 248.
plēon 350.
plōg (plōh) 172.
pohha 174.
pott 181.
pund 48, 155.

rā 68, 249.
racu 212, 213.
rǣcan 379.
rǣdan 355, 357.
rǣdels 143.
rǣden(n) 225.
rǣran 117, 375.
rāp 181.
rēad 17, 113, 152.
reccan 379.
reced 85. 1, 195.
recene 400.
reg(e)n 72, 186.
regol (reogol) 59. 2 n. 2.

rēn 72.
rēocan 67 n. 1, 335.
reoht (rieht, ryht) 67, 67 n. 4.
rest 223.
restan 145, 375.
ribb 203.
rīce 204.
rīcsian 166 n.
rīdan 38, 41, 152, 318, 329, 332.
rignian 144.
rieht (riht, ryht) 67.
riehtan 67 n. 1.
rihte 396.
rihtlīce (rihlīce) 144.
rima 47.
rīnan 144.
rinnan 121, 340.
rīpe 281.
rīxian 166 n.
rōd 214.
rodor 187.
rōwan 68, 148, 363.
rūh 275.
rūm 152, 153, 181.
rūst 40.
ryge 233.
rȳman 57.
ryne 233.

sacan 29 n. 1, 352.
sacu 29 n. 1, 166, 213.
sadol 187.
sǣ 57, 68, 144, 235.
sǣd 165.
sǣdere 201.
sǣl 45, 234.
sǣp 191.
sæter(n)dæg 144.
sǣwet(t) 205.
salu (sealu) 283.
samcucu 77.
samhwilc 315.
samod 402, 403.

sangestre 251.
sār 189, 272.
sāwan 64, 361.
sāwol 41, 79, 98, 148, 215.
scādan (sceādan) 18, 56 n. 3, 356.
scafan 352.
scamian 120, 381.
scand 120, 167.
sc(e)acan 56 n. 3, 167.
sc(e)adu 144, 227.
sceal 56 n. 5, 67 n. 1, 152.
scealt 56 n. 2, 67, 324.
scēap 56, 67, 167, 189.
scearp 167.
sceatt 56, 159.
scēawian 109. 1.
sc(e)olde 56 n. 3.
sceolh 275.
sceorpan 342.
sc(e)ort 291.
scēotan 43, 67, 335.
sceþþan 111, 354, 371.
scield 56.
sciell 222.
scieppan 57, 57 n. 3, 67, 119, 354.
scieran 56, 167, 344.
scīnan 109. 1, 332.
scinn 167.
scip 32, 59. 1, 155, 167.
scofl 214.
scōh (scēoh) 56 n. 3, 68, 176, 182.
scōl 167.
screpan 346.
scrīþan 333.
scrūd 167, 260.
sculan 316, 387.
scūr 167.
scurf 66.

Index

scyld 237.
scyldig 57 n. 2, 167.
sē 309.
sealfian 94. 3, 99, 100, 157, 380.
sealh 76, 182.
sealt 18, 51.
searu 209.
sēaþ 244.
Seaxe 232.
sēcan 57, 85. 3, 165, 166, 379.
secg (*man*) 168, 197, 198.
secg (*sword*) 222.
secg(e)an 29, 72, 382.
seglan 377.
segn 32 n.
sēl 399.
seldlic (sellic) 144.
sele 233.
sēlest 292.
self (seolf, sylf, silf) 307, 311.
sellan 379.
sēlra (sēlla) 292.
sencan 376.
sendan 57, 145, 373, 375.
seng(e)an 169. 2, 375.
sēo 252.
sēoc 43, 67 n. 1, 166. 1, 272.
seofon 118, 157, 294.
seofontēoþa 294.
seofontīene 294.
seofoþa 294.
seolh 52, 67 n. 1, 76, 182.
sēon 51, 52, 57, 64, 67, 67 n. 1, 68, 75, 114. 1, 5, 116, 144, 174, 176, 350.
sēoþan 336.
seox 52, 67 n. 1.
sess 119.

setl 31, 195.
settan 57, 135, 368, 369.
sēþan 375.
sibb 135, 156, 222.
sicol 59. 2 n. 2.
sicor 277.
sidu 59. 2 n. 2, 243.
sīen 114. 5.
siex (six) 52, 67, 175, 294.
si(e)xta 294.
si(e)xtēoþa 294.
si(e)xtīene 294.
si(e)xtig 294.
si(e)xtigoþa 294.
sife 240.
sīgan 332.
sige 233.
sigþe 72.
sīn 308.
sincan 34, 114. 2, 340.
singan 32, 46, 169. 1, 340.
sinu (sionu) 59. 2 n. 2, 227.
sīo (sēo) 309.
sioluc 59. 1.
siolufr (siolfor) 59. 1.
sīon (sēon) 20, 114. 5, 334.
sittan 21. 2, 29, 36, 119, 159, 165, 351.
sīþ 50, 293, 299, 300, 399.
sīþe 72, 171.
siþþan (sioþþan) 78.
slā (slāh) 252.
slǣpan 45, 110, 152, 155, 165, 357.
slǣwþ 79.
slaga 248.
slāpan 45.
slāpol 45.
slāw 284.

slēan 51, 57, 67 n. 3, 68, 75, 116, 130, 144, 176, 318, 319, 353.
slegen 290.
slīdan 332.
slieht 234.
slincan 340.
slītan 332.
slōh 182.
slūpan 338.
smæl 165, 273.
smēag(e)an 381.
smēocan 335.
smeoru 209.
smēþe 281.
smīec 234.
smierwan 57, 378.
smītan 38.
smiþþe 161.
smōþe 396.
smūgan 338.
snā(w) 79, 148, 149, 206.
snegl 31.
snīþan 116, 333.
snīwan 114. 4.
snottor (snotor) 136, 278.
sōfte 50, 73, 144, 396, 399.
sōna 49, 397.
sorg (sorh) 172, 214.
sorgian 381.
sōþe 396.
sōþes 400.
spade, -u 251.
spannan 352, 359.
sparian 381.
spātl 194.
spearwa 148, 248.
spec 22.
spēd 237.
spēdum 400.
speld 268.
spere 59, 239.
spic 22.
spinel 216.
spinnan 153, 319, 340.

spitu 243.
spīwan 109. 1, 148.
spornan 66, 343.
spōwan 363.
sprǣc 223.
sprecan 45, 59. 2 n. 2, 166. 1, 346.
spryttan 372.
spura (spora) 66.
spurnan 66, 343.
spyrian 370.
stæf 182.
stæppan (steppan) 155, 354.
stān 41, 80. 1, 153, 180.
standan 46, 352.
staþol 123.
stealdan 360.
steall 123.
stearclīce 396.
steaþul 59. 2 n. 1.
stede 17, 84, 85. 3, 87, 91, 232.
stef(e)n 142, 157, 216.
stelan 29, 31, 33, 45, 104, 152, 344.
stellan 379.
stemn 142.
stenc 166. 2.
steng 169. 2.
stēopfæder 18.
steorfan 342.
steorra 52, 52 n.3.
sticca 166. 1.
stician 59. 2 n. 2, 381.
stīele 204.
stīeran 44, 375.
stierninga 397.
stīgan 17, 109. 1, 113, 140, 170. 1, 172, 319, 332.
stige 233.
stigol 59. 2 n. 2.
stiht(i)an 67.
stingan 340.

Index

stōl 39.
stōw 79, 226.
strǣt 36 n. 2.
strang 291.
strange 398.
strēam 131, 165, 181.
strēa(w) 69, 79, 149, 210.
streccan 379.
stregdan 343.
streng 169. 2, 234.
strenge 281.
strengþu (-o) 218.
strengu (-o) 229.
streowan 61.
strīdan 332.
studu (stuþu) 259.
stundmǣlum 400.
stycce 204.
styrc 102.
sūcan 40, 338.
sūgan 338.
sulh 74, 258.
sum 296, 315.
sumor 244.
sund 120, 128.
sunne 251.
sunu 34, 84 n., 89. 2, 90, 91, 93. 4, 153, 165, 242.
sūpan 338.
sūþ 50, 293, 401.
sūþan 401.
swā 71, 403.
swǣr 45.
swāpan 114 n., 361.
swaþu 29 n. 1.
swealwe 251.
swefan 346.
sweger 118.
swelc (swilc, swylc) 166. 2, 315, 403.
swelgan 319, 341.
swellan 128, 341.
sweltan 341.
sweng 240.
Swēon 249.
swēor 68, 118.

sweord (swurd) 63, 189.
sweostor (swustor) 9, 63, 131, 147, 165, 262.
sweotol 59.
swerian 39, 354.
swēte 285.
sweþian 371.
sweþþan 371.
swice 285.
swimman 120, 128, 145, 340.
swīn 18.
swingan 128, 340.
swiþ 73.
swōgan 363.
swōte 396.
sȳcan 379 n. 2.
syll 222.
synn 153, 222.
sȳþerra 293.

tā 68, 252.
tāc(e)n 194.
tǣcan 379.
tǣl 45.
tǣsan 375.
talu 213.
tēar 136.
tellan 152, 159, 379.
temman 371.
temp(e)l 47 n.
tēon 18, 57, 67 n. 1, 68, 109, 116, 318, 319, 327, 337.
tēond 264.
teoru 59, 209.
tēoþa 294.
teran 31, 344.
tīd 38, 159, 237.
tīen (tȳn, tēn) 110, 118, 294.
til 273, 402.
tilian 59. 1.
tīma 38, 159.
timbram 97. 3, 377.
tiohhian (teohhian) 53, 174.

tiolian (teolian) 59. 1.
tīon (tēon) 334.
tīr 25.
tō 402.
tō-ǣfenes 400.
tō-emnes 402.
tōforan 402.
tōgēanes (-gegnes, -gēnes) 402.
tōh 35. 275.
tōmiddes 402.
tō-morgen 400.
topp 124.
tōþ 50, 57, 159, 161, 256.
tōweard(es) 402.
tredan 346.
trēo(w) (tree) 60, 69, 149, 210, 226.
trēow (trust) 62.
trog (troh) 172.
trūwian 382 n. 2.
trymman 371.
tū 295.
tulge 399.
tunge 34, 88. 3, 91, 94. 3, 250.
tungol 96, 193.
turf 66, 258.
tuwa 299.
twā 41, 147, 294, 295.
twēgen 295.
twelf 63 n. 3, 294.
twelfta 294.
twelfwintre 286.
twēntig 294, 297.
twēntigoþa 294.
twēo 249.
twēogan 381.
twi(e)feald 298.
twig 32.
twiwa (twywa) 299, 397.
tygen 290.
tȳn 375.

þā 403.
þæc 191.
þǣr 36, 401.

þæt 309, 403.
þan (þon) 80. 1.
þanan 401.
þanc 166. 1.
þancian 161, 166. 1, 381.
þawian 30.
þē (pers. pr.) 304.
þĕ (rel. pr.) 312.
þe (cj.) 403.
þēah 403.
þearft 324.
þēaw 207.
þec 304, 306.
þeccan 166, 379.
þeg(e)n 79, 186.
þegnian 144.
þencan 20, 35, 154, 161, 162. 2, 166, 174, 379, 383.
þenden 403.
þēnian 144.
þēo 60.
þēof 43, 161, 181.
þēoh 67 n. 1, 192.
þēo(w) 79, 206.
þēow (adj.) 284.
þerscan 52 n. 1, 343.
þĕs 310.
þicgan 45, 351, 371.
þider 401.
þidres 401.
þīefþ(u) 219.
þīestru 230.
þīn 304, 308.
þing 169. 1, 189.
þīon (þēon) 20, 334.
þīos (þēos) 142, 310.
þis 310.
þō 252.
þon 309.
þonan 401.
þone 46 n.
þonne 46 n., 403.
þrāwan 361.
þrawu 226.
þrēa 226.

Index

þrēag(e)an 381.
þrēotēoþa 294.
þrēotīene 294.
þrī (þrīe) 109, 294, 295.
þridda 294, 302.
þri(e)feald 298.
þrīnes(s) 225.
þrīo (þrēo) 69.
þrītig 294.
þrītigoþa 294.
þriwa (þrywa) 299.
þriwintre 281.
þrūh 68, 258.
þryccan 379 n. 2.
þrysman 377.
þū 304.
þullic 315.
þūma 248.
þunor 161, 187.
þurfan 386.
þurh 176, 402.
þūsend 40, 294, 297.
þuslic 315.
þwēan 69, 353.
þweorh 275.
þweran 344.
þȳ 309, 403.
þyllic 315.
þȳmel 185.
þȳn 375.
þyncan 20, 40, 119, 166. 2, 379.
þynne 121, 281.
þyrre 286.
þyrs 234.
þyrstan 375.
þyslic 315.

ūder 113.
ufan 66, 293, 401.
ufor 66.
ūhta 20.
unc 303, 306.
uncer 308.
uncit 303.
underbæc 400.
underneoþan 402.
ungēara 400.
ungefyrn 400.
unnan 386.
unwēnunga 85. 4, 91, 397.
up(p) 401.
uppan 401, 402.
uppe 401.
ūre 308.
ūs 50, 144, 303.
ūser 303, 308.
ūsic 93.3,303,306.
ūt 401.
ūtan 401.
ūtane 401.
ūte 293, 401.

wāc 272.
wacan 352.
wacian 381.
wadan 352.
wæc(c)er 136.
wæd 237.
wædl 163.
wægn 29, 72.
wæl 191.
wēn 72.
wǣpen 63 n. 3, 96, 194.
wæps (wæfs) 143.
wæsma 144.
wæsp 143.
wæstm 144.
wǣt 272.
wǣtan 376.
wæter 97. 1, 147, 193.
wan 273.
wandrian 381.
wange 254.
wascan 167, 352.
wāwan 361.
wē 71, 303, 306.
wēa 249.
wealcan 360.
weald 244.
wealdan 360.
wealdend 265.
wealh 76, 182.
weall 51, 181.
weallan 360.
wearm 51.
weaxan 51, 67, 67 n. 1, 144, 175, 319, 360.
weccan 379.
weder 31, 195.
wefan 31, 59. 2 n. 2, 346.
weg 59. 2 n. 2, 63 n. 3, 79, 141, 181.
wegan 45, 113, 346.
wel 399.
wel(ge)hwǣr 401.
wēn 237.
wendan 375.
wēnung 220.
weorc 52, 63, 67 n. 1, 189.
weorold 63.
weorpan 63,114 n., 318, 327, 342.
weorþan 17, 52, 63, 104, 109, 116, 117, 134, 144, 316, 319, 342.
weorud, -od (werod) 195.
wēpan 363.
wer 22.
werian 370.
wesan 29, 29 n. 2, 45, 63 n. 1, 165, 316, 349, 392.
west 293, 401.
westan 401.
wēsten(n) 202.
wicce 251.
wice (wuce) 251.
wicu (wucu) 251.
wīdan 401.
wieldan 375.
Wieht (Wiht) 67.
wierman 57.
wierrest 142, 292, 399.
wiers (wyrs) 399.
wiersa (wyrsa) 63, 292.
wierst 292.
wierþe 281.
wīf 157, 189.
wīfman 142, 256.
wīgend 263.
wiht 238.
wilde 147, 162, 280.
wile 80. 2, 85. 3, 91.
willan 316, 395.
willes 400.
wimman 77, 142.
wind 21. 1.
windan 340.
wine 232.
winnan 145.
winster (winester) 50 n.
winter 147, 244.
wīoh (wēoh) 55.
Wioht 67 n. 4.
wīs 119, 272.
wist 237.
wit 303.
wita 248.
witan 17, 18, 59. 2 n. 2, 81, 91, 110, 119, 147, 384.
wīte 202.
witt 203.
wiþ 402.
wiþæftan 402.
wiþforan 402.
wiþgeondan 402.
wiþinnan 400, 402.
wiþūtan 402.
wlacu 286.
wlanc 147.
wleccan 379 n. 2.
wlōh 258.
wōcor 217.
word 33, 85. 1, 91, 134, 188.
wracu 213.
wrāþ 272.
wrāþum 400.
wreþþan 371.
wrīon (wrēon) 334.
wrītan 147, 332.
wrīþan 333.
wrōtan 363.
wucu (wiocu) 63.
wudu 243.
wuduwe 63, 251.

wuht 63, 238.
wuldor 162, 194.
wulf 17, 66, 80. 1, 81, 114 n., 139.
wull(e) 23, 66, 122.
wund 214.
wundian 381.
wundor 17, 194.

wundrian 381.
wundrum 400.
wylf 223.
wynn 222.
wyrcan 23, 102, 119, 379.
wyrd 237.
wyrhta 248.
wyrm 63, 234.

wyrt 237.
wȳscan 376.

yfel 57, 85. 1, 101 n. 1, 277, 292.
yf(e)le 396, 399.
yfemest 293.
yferra 293.
yfes 57.

ymb 402.
ymbe 112.
ymbūtan 402.
ȳmest 144.
yppan 145.
ȳst 237.
ȳt(e)mest 293.
ȳterra 293.

Printed in England at the Oxford University Press

6 (b.) raggi *P.C* regi- Indg. relk ook
 reggjo racks Halic. g. rag
 recg reap ragu secare

(New English Dictionary).
'indicate Indg. root —
(Skeat's etymological
         dictionary
(Kluge, Lutz - English etymolog
(Wheatley

(German —
    Grimm's
         any large german dictionary
    Bosworth - Toller.